Who Will Build the Ark?

Who Will Build the Ark?

Debates on Climate Strategy
from *New Left Review*

Edited by
Benjamin Kunkel and Lola Seaton

VERSO
London • New York

First published by Verso 2023
Collection © Verso 2023
Contributions © *New Left Review* 2023

1 3 5 7 9 10 8 6 4 2

Verso
UK: 6 Meard Street, London W1F 0EG
US: 388 Atlantic Avenue, Brooklyn, NY 11217
versobooks.com

Verso is the imprint of New Left Books

ISBN-13: 978-1-83976-747-0
ISBN-13: 978-1-83976-748-7 (UK EBK)
ISBN-13: 978-1-83976-749-4 (US EBK)

British Library Cataloguing in Publication Data
A catalogue record for this book is available from the British Library

Library of Congress Cataloging-in-Publication Data

Names: Kunkel, Benjamin, editor. | Seaton, Lola, editor.
Title: Who will build the ark? : debates on climate strategy from new left
  review / edited by Benjamin Kunkel and Lola Seaton.
Other titles: New Left review.
Description: London ; New York : Verso, 2023. | Includes bibliographical
  references and index.
Identifiers: LCCN 2023003608 (print) | LCCN 2023003609 (ebook) | ISBN
  9781839767470 (trade paperback) | ISBN 9781839767494 (ebook)
Subjects: LCSH: Ecosocialism.
Classification: LCC HX550.E25 W56 2023 (print) | LCC HX550.E25 (ebook) |
  DDC 304.2—dc23/eng/20230309
LC record available at https://lccn.loc.gov/2023003608
LC ebook record available at https://lccn.loc.gov/2023003609

Typeset in Sabon by Biblichor Ltd, Scotland
Printed and bound by CPI Group (UK) Ltd, Croydon CR0 4YY

Contents

Introduction

BENJAMIN KUNKEL

If it is true that the few books worth introducing are exactly those which it is impertinent to introduce, such hesitation to speak up on behalf of work that speaks for itself is especially justified when it comes to an anthology of essays on left ecological politics published in the year 2023. Who that has glanced at a newspaper in the first decades of the twenty-first century, or even ventured outdoors, could need persuading of the necessity of a politics that answers at one and the same time to the imperatives of socioeconomic remedy and ecological rescue? The plain want, in a world that delivers neither the remedy nor the rescue, is to approximate to both conditions with all deliberate haste. And just this problem – the conjoint ecological and economic problem, with the root of both words in the Greek word *oikos*, for household – is the shared context of the pieces within this volume, in spite of their divergences from and disputes with one another. Here is the planetary household we dwell in and must remake, and pointing out as much comes very close to a statement of the obvious.

But the self-evidence of a world-historical crisis has by no means resulted in a superfluous volume, in spite of the hundreds of books on left ecopolitics that have appeared in recent years. Not only is it a rare thing to find the combination of passion and cool thinking characteristic of the fourteen articles (plus an afterword from Lola Seaton) below, all of which first appeared in *New Left Review*; the collection also stands out in another way. For the vast ruck of left titles on ecological matters are essentially partisan or one-sided, with degrowthers, on the one hand, clustered together, as are so-called ecomodernists or advocates of green growth, on the other. Meanwhile various eminent left thinkers propound their individual, isolate visions. Soapboxes and soliloquies are commonplace, real debate far less so. By contrast, the writers assembled here are genuinely attentive to one another – a striking break with the partyless but sectarian social-media discourse that surrounds and divides left ecological thought. For example, Robert Pollin frames his single-minded campaign for a rapid transition to renewable energy as a response to degrowthism, pointing out what such opposing positions have in common; while Sharachchandra Lele, for his part, responds to Herman Daly – an early proponent of a steady-state or non-growing economy – and Pollin alike by emphasizing a criterion of well-being distinct from either economic growth or its absence. Naturally, the articles herein often represent intellectual conflicts – but, just as fundamentally and even more frequently, they complement one another. Mary Mellor and Nancy Fraser equip with feminist insights and principles a discussion otherwise at risk of dwelling excessively on economic statistics; Zion Lights, at the time a spokesperson for Extinction Rebellion, raises questions of activist tactics that are elsewhere either muted or silent; and Troy Vettese ventures a proposition of a rewilded earth that answers, among other things, to the more generic but no less ardent utopianism of Mike Davis. Degrowth is a persistent theme, but not an unvaried one: Mark Burton and Peter Somerville are stout advocates, Kenta Tsuda a sympathetic sceptic. And if the older contributions to the collection provoke the objection that they pay little attention to current events, the same can't be said of recent interventions from Cédric Durand (on the vexed economics of the transition away from fossil fuels), Alyssa Battistoni (on the dispiriting COP26 conference in Glasgow), and Thomas Meaney (on Biden's Inflation Reduction Act as a species of 'Green New Deal'). Together, these pieces show left thinking on the climate crisis becoming topical without any loss of theoretical intelligence. Finally, Lola Seaton, co-editor of this volume, makes explicit and newly lucid, in both of her essays, the dialogue among contributors that was at once our starting-point and our end.

Within the covers of this book, as in the world at large, serious discussion of ecological politics derives much of its urgency from being overdue. Readers will notice that the earliest of the present texts, 'Who Will Build the Ark?' by Mike Davis, from 2010, already appears belated from the point of view of a global crisis that announced itself at least as long ago as the 1980s. It was in 1988, after all, that Dr James Hansen of NASA testified before a committee of the US Congress that he could be 99 per cent certain that the buildup of carbon dioxide emitted by human activity was already heating the planet. As the *New York Times* quoted his testimony in a page-one story: 'Global warming has reached a level such that we can ascribe with a high degree of confidence a cause and effect relationship between the greenhouse effect and observed warming. It is already happening now.' Also in 1988, James O'Connor, a founding editor of *Capital Nature Socialism*, outlined, in an essay in the first issue of the eco-Marxist journal, his idea of a second contradiction of capitalism — that of the capital–nature relation — accompanying the more familiar contradiction of the capital–labour relation. For O'Connor, a properly ecological Marxism would take heed of both contradictions, with an 'account of capitalism as a crisis-ridden system' focusing 'on the way that the combined power of capitalist production relations and productive forces self-destruct by impairing or destroying rather than reproducing their own conditions ("conditions" defined in terms of both their social and material dimensions).' As O'Connor went on to say:

> Examples of capitalist accumulation impairing or destroying capital's own conditions hence threatening its own profits and capacity to produce and accumulate more capital are well-known. The warming of the atmosphere will inevitably destroy people, places and profits, not to speak of other species life. Acid rain destroys forests and lakes and buildings and profits alike. Salinization of water tables, toxic wastes, soil erosion, etc. impair nature and profitability. The pesticide treadmill destroys profits as well as nature.

(Nancy Fraser's analysis of an ecologically self-undermining capitalism herein bears some resemblance to O'Connor's thesis, and also advances beyond it.)

The late 1980s were a long time ago. Why did *New Left Review* tarry across several decades in bringing ecological questions front and centre? Environmental alarums were not absent, it's true, from the work of NLR writers between the end of the Cold War and the so-called Global Financial Crisis of 2008 and after. During the 1990s, the journal published important articles on the ecological critique of Marxism; on 'political ecology'; on the global food crisis; on the strategy of the German Green Party; and so on. And, in the first decade of this century, NLR, in a special issue on 'globalization and biopolitics', hosted a debate between Clive Hamilton and George Monbiot on the latter's international scheme for a 90 per cent cut in carbon emissions. Even so, eco-socialist concerns didn't receive sustained and systemic treatment until the later 2010s.

Why was this so? A few hypotheses suggest themselves. First, *New Left Review* was for many decades, as its name suggests, a journal with a marked generational character, and ecological issues were simply of less moment to most of the New Left than they are today to younger generations of radicals. Second, during the 1990s and the first decade of the 2000s, the eco-Marxism enunciated in such (American) publications as *Capitalism Nature Socialism* and *Monthly Review* tended to be of a highly abstracted kind, more devoted, in other words, to demonstrating the theoretical compatibility of ecological thought with historical materialism than truly capable of seeing the contemporary world, in all its particulars, through lenses simultaneously green and red. This made for a contrast with the more hard-headed mood and empirical approach of (the London-based) *New Left Review* during the same period, as laid out by Perry Anderson in the editorial that announced a new series of the journal in 2000: 'Its general approach, I believe, should be an uncompromising realism. Uncompromising in both senses: refusing any accommodation with the ruling system, and rejecting every piety and euphemism that would understate its power. No sterile maximalism follows.' From this point of view, the axioms of a nascent eco-Marxism may well have seemed both insufficiently attentive to the real world of neoliberalism and wildly unrealistic in their implied political maximalism: namely, the demand for a revolutionary eco-socialism nowhere seriously on offer around the turn of the millennium.

Finally, the presence on NLR's Editorial Committee of a global-warming sceptic such as Alexander Cockburn, until his untimely death in 2012, suggests something of the resistance to the possibility of a left climate politics that was felt by many radicals until the last half dozen years or so, when the onrushing disaster of an increasingly disordered climate has become plain to see. For Cockburn, environmental complaints against excessive carbon emissions represented a theological holdover from the Christian doctrine of the sinfulness of humankind: socialists should, by contrast, insist on the happiness available to an emancipated humanity (in large part – on this view – through fossil fuels) rather than on the immemorial depravity of the species whenever it groped for pleasure. In 2007, Cockburn could write, in the *Nation*:

> There is still zero empirical evidence that anthropogenic production of carbon dioxide is making any measurable contribution to the world's present warming trend. The greenhouse fearmongers rely on unverified, crudely oversimplified models to finger mankind's sinful contribution – and carbon trafficking [i.e., a market in carbon credits], just like the old indulgences, is powered by guilt, credulity, cynicism and greed.

In fairness, Cockburn was not only a fine writer, with a wicked eloquence about left-liberal pieties in particular, but also an environmentalist after his fashion, notably in his dedication to the ragged splendour of his adopted Humboldt County, California. But the notion that universal emancipation lies in the increased combustion of fossil fuels has today been overtaken by weather events.

None of this institutional history would be worth mentioning if *New Left Review* were alone in having paid only scattered attention, until recent years, to the ecological underpinnings of social and political life. In this, the journal simply belonged to the tradition of classical social thought of which it has been a distinguished modern heir. Marx of course wrote in *Capital* that capitalism 'only develops the technique and the degree of combination of the social process of production by simultaneously undermining the original sources of all wealth – the soil and the worker'. And Max Weber, in *The Protestant Ethic and the Spirit of Capitalism*, wondered whether the iron cage of modernity would endure 'until the last hundredweight of fossil fuel is burned up'. More recently, but now already long ago, in 1960, Sartre, in his *Critique of Dialectical Reason*, described hydrocarbons as 'capital bequeathed to mankind by other living beings'. But these stray glimpses of the lacerated geological body that sustains capitalist humanity were never integrated into a comprehensive vision that could at once explain social – that is, eco-social – conditions and seek to upend them for the better.

What changed for NLR, around the middle of the last decade, is what changed for everyone: the emergence of new left forces in a slew of advanced capitalist countries, enabling and requiring the development of new left programmes. As small and weak as a left that takes climate change seriously may be today, it remains vastly larger and more concentrated than before the 2010s. With luck – and assistance – it will go on gathering strength.

The articles below arrive very late in the history of fossil capitalism, and quite early as yet in the emergence of a powerful international eco-left; they therefore represent both an overdue and a preliminary confrontation with the task of articulating a thoroughgoing eco-socialist politics. Such an eco-socialist politics – to call it that: other names might also do – should, first, be capable of advancing a programme of ecological triage and socioeconomic amelioration on this side of capitalism, as well as of discovering a strategy to enlist decisive masses of people, both in wealthy countries and in what's called the Global South, to this end. Either success or failure along these lines should then prompt the once and future question of the seizure and elimination of capitalist states, so that what might provisionally be called eco-socialist movements may eventuate in what might be accurately called eco-socialist societies. In these terms, the present book has more to do with (pre-revolutionary) eco-socialist strategies than with any (post-revolutionary) utopia, and more still to do with intermediate programmes than with the strategies that might realize them. But each of these necessary objects – programme, strategy, utopia – will appear in sharpest definition the more that the other objects are kept in view.

Forming the background to their tableau is a common circumstance: no socialism of the foreseeable future can inherit the comparatively unspoiled planet that lay before the revolutionary left in, say, 1919, or before a triumphant capitalism in 1991. If eco-socialism gains power at all, this can only be on the menaced and despoiled earth left behind by global capital. Such a fact is undeniably tragic. It may also seem discouraging. The truth, however, is that it makes the project of an ecological socialism more compelling and timely, not less – since the world which is to be won will only be a greener and more thriving planet the sooner that it's gained. In this sense, a small collective of editors and an incipient global movement might converge on a motto: *Better late than never.*

Delayed victories meanwhile entail a degraded prize. They also deprive many of those who struggled for a new society of the chance of setting foot in one. Arguably the two most eloquent contributors to this book, Mike Davis and Herman Daly, both died, just days apart, in late October of 2022.

Who Will Build the Ark?

MIKE DAVIS

2010

What follows is rather like the famous courtroom scene in Orson Welles's *The Lady from Shanghai* (1947).[1] In that noir allegory of proletarian virtue in the embrace of ruling-class decadence, Welles plays a left-wing sailor named Michael O'Hara who rolls in the hay with *femme fatale* Rita Hayworth, and then gets framed for murder. Her husband, Arthur Bannister, the most celebrated criminal lawyer in America, played by Everett Sloane, convinces O'Hara to appoint him as his defence, all the better to ensure his rival's conviction and execution. At the turning point in the trial, decried by the prosecution as 'yet another of the great Bannister's famous tricks', Bannister the attorney calls Bannister the aggrieved husband to the witness stand and interrogates himself in rapid schizoid volleys, to the mirth of the jury. In the spirit of *Lady from Shanghai*, this chapter is organized as a debate with myself, a mental tournament between analytic despair and utopian possibility that is personally, and probably objectively, irresolvable.

In the first section, 'Pessimism of the Intellect', I adduce arguments for believing that we have already lost the first, epochal stage of the battle against global warming. The Kyoto Protocol, in the smug but sadly accurate words of one of its chief opponents, has done 'nothing measurable' about climate change. Global carbon dioxide emissions rose by the same amount they were supposed to fall because of it.[2] It is highly unlikely that greenhouse gas accumulation can be stabilized this side of the famous 'red line' of 450 ppm by 2020. If this is the case, the most heroic efforts of our children's generation will be

---

1 This paper was given as a talk at the UCLA Center for Social Theory and Comparative History in January 2009.

2 The Cato Institute's execrable Patrick Michaels, in the *Washington Times*, 12 February 2005.

unable to forestall a radical reshaping of ecologies, water resources and agricultural systems. In a warmer world, moreover, socioeconomic inequality will have a meteorological mandate, and there will be little incentive for the rich northern-hemisphere countries, whose carbon emissions have destroyed the climate equilibrium of the Holocene, to share resources for adaptation with those poor subtropical countries most vulnerable to droughts and floods.

The second part of the chapter, 'Optimism of the Imagination', is my self-rebuttal. I appeal to the paradox that the single most important cause of global warming – the urbanization of humanity – is also potentially the principal solution to the problem of human survival in the later twenty-first century. Left to the dismal politics of the present, of course, cities of poverty will almost certainly become the coffins of hope; all the more reason that we must start thinking like Noah. Since most of history's giant trees have already been cut down, a new Ark will have to be constructed out of the materials that a desperate humanity finds at hand in insurgent communities, pirate technologies, bootlegged media, rebel science and forgotten utopias.

I. PESSIMISM OF THE INTELLECT

Our old world, the one that we have inhabited for the last 12,000 years, has ended, even if no newspaper has yet printed its scientific obituary. The verdict is that of the Stratigraphy Commission of the Geological Society of London. Founded in 1807, the Society is the world's oldest association of earth scientists, and its Stratigraphy Commission acts as a college of cardinals in the adjudication of the geological time-scale. Stratigraphers slice up Earth's history as preserved in sedimentary strata into a hierarchy of eons, eras, periods and epochs, marked by the 'golden spikes' of mass extinctions, speciation events, or abrupt changes in atmospheric chemistry. In geology, as in biology and history, periodization is a complex, controversial art; the most bitter feud in nineteenth-century British science – still known as the 'Great Devonian Controversy' – was fought over competing interpretations of homely Welsh greywackes and English Old Red Sandstone. As a result, Earth science sets extraordinarily rigorous standards for the beatification of any new geological division. Although the idea of an 'Anthropocene' epoch – defined by the emergence of urban–industrial society as a geological force – has long circulated in the literature, stratigraphers have never acknowledged its warrant.

At least for the London Society, that position has now been revised. To the question 'Are we now living in the Anthropocene?' the twenty-one members of the Commission have unanimously answered, 'Yes.' In a 2008 report, they marshalled robust evidence to support the hypothesis that the Holocene epoch – the interglacial span of unusually stable climate that allowed the rapid evolution of agriculture and urban civilization – has ended, and that the Earth has now entered 'a stratigraphic interval without close parallel' in the last several million years.[3] In addition to the build-up of greenhouse gases, the stratigraphers cited human landscape transformation, which 'now exceeds [annual] natural sediment production by an order of magnitude', the ominous acidification of the oceans, and the relentless destruction of biota.

This new age, they explained, is defined both by the heating trend – whose closest analogue may be the catastrophe known as the Paleocene Eocene Thermal Maximum, 56 million years ago – and by the radical instability expected of future environments. In sombre prose, they warned:

> The combination of extinctions, global species migrations and the wide-spread replacement of natural vegetation with agricultural monocultures is producing a distinctive contemporary biostratigraphic signal. These effects are permanent, as future evolution will take place from surviving (and frequently anthropogenically relocated) stocks.[4]

Evolution itself, in other words, has been forced onto a new trajectory.

Spontaneous decarbonization?

The Commission's recognition of the Anthropocene coincided with growing scientific controversy over the Fourth Assessment Report issued by the Intergovernmental Panel on Climate Change in 2007. The IPCC, of course, is mandated to assess the possible range of climate change and establish appropriate targets for the mitigation of emissions. The most critical baselines include estimates of 'climate sensitivity' to increasing accumulations of greenhouse gas, as well as socioeconomic tableaux that configure different futures of energy use, and thus of emissions. But an impressive number of senior researchers, including key participants in the IPCC's own working groups, have recently expressed unease or disagreement with the methodology

---

3   Jan Zalasiewicz et al., 'Are We Now Living in the Anthropocene?', *GSA Today*, vol. 18, no. 2, February 2008.
4   Ibid.

of the four-volume Fourth Assessment, which they charge is unwar-rantedly optimistic in its geophysics and social science.[5]

The most celebrated dissenter is James Hansen, from NASA's Goddard Institute. The Paul Revere of global warming, who first warned Congress of the greenhouse peril in a famous 1988 hearing, he returned to Washington with the troubling message that the IPCC, through its failure to parameterize crucial Earth-system feedbacks, has given far too much leeway to further carbon emissions. Instead of the IPCC's proposed red line of 450 ppm carbon dioxide, Hansen's research team found compelling paleoclimatic evidence that the threshold of safety was only 350 ppm, or even less. The 'stunning corollary' of this recalibration of climate sensitivity, he testified, is that 'the oft-stated goal of keeping global warming below two degrees Celsius is a recipe for global disaster, not salvation'.[6] Indeed, since the current level is about 385 ppm, we may already be past the noto-rious 'tipping point'. Hansen has mobilized a Quixotic army of scientists and environmental activists to save the world via an emer-gency carbon tax, which would reverse greenhouse concentrations to pre-2000 levels by 2015.

I do not have the scientific qualifications to express an opinion on the Hansen controversy, or the proper setting on the planetary ther-mostat. Anyone, however, who is engaged with the social sciences, or simply pays regular attention to macro-trends, should feel less shy about joining the debate over the other controversial cornerstone of the Fourth Assessment: its socioeconomic projections, and what we might term their 'political unconscious'. The current scenarios were adopted by the IPCC in 2000 to model future global emissions based on different 'storylines' about population growth, as well as techno-logical and economic development. The Panel's major scenarios – the A1 family, the B2, and so on – are well known to policymakers and greenhouse activists, but few outside the research community have actually read the fine print, particularly the IPCC's heroic confidence that greater energy efficiency will be an 'automatic' by-product of future economic growth. Indeed, all the scenarios, even the 'business as usual' variants, assume that almost 60 per cent of future carbon

---

5   Indeed, three leading contributors to Working Group 1 charged that the Report deliberately understated the risks of sea-level rise and ignored new research on insta-bility in the Greenland and West Antarctic ice sheets. See the debate in 'Letters', *Science* 319, 25 January 2008, pp. 409–10.

6   James Hansen, 'Global Warming Twenty Years Later: Tipping Point Near', testimony before Congress, 23 June 2008.

reduction will occur independently of explicit greenhouse-mitigation measures.[7]

The IPCC, in effect, has bet the ranch, or rather the planet, on a market-driven evolution towards a post-carbon world economy: a transition that requires not only international emissions caps and carbon trading, but also voluntary corporate commitments to technologies that hardly exist even in prototype, such as carbon capture, clean coal, hydrogen and advanced transit systems, and cellulosic biofuels. As critics have long pointed out, in many of its 'scenarios' the deployment of non-carbon-emitting energy-supply systems 'exceeds the size of the global energy system in 1990'.[8]

Kyoto-type accords and carbon markets are designed – almost as analogues to Keynesian 'pump-priming' – to bridge the shortfall between spontaneous decarbonization and the emissions targets required by each scenario. Although the IPCC never spells it out, its mitigation targets necessarily presume that windfall profits from higher fossil-fuel prices over the next generation will be efficiently recycled into renewable-energy technology and not wasted on mile-high skyscrapers, asset bubbles and mega-payouts to shareholders.

Overall, the International Energy Agency estimates that it will cost about $45 trillion to halve greenhouse gas output by 2050.[9] But without the large quotient of 'automatic' progress in energy efficiency, the bridge will never be built, and IPCC goals will be unachievable; in the worst case – the straightforward extrapolation of current energy use – carbon emissions could easily triple by mid-century.

Critics have cited the dismal carbon record of the last – lost – decade to demonstrate that the IPCC baseline assumptions about markets and technology are little more than leaps of faith. Despite the EU's much-praised adoption of a cap-and-trade system, European carbon emissions continued to rise, dramatically in some sectors. Likewise, there has been scant evidence in recent years of the automatic progress in energy efficiency that is the *sine qua non* of IPCC scenarios. Much of what the storylines depict as the efficiency of new technology has in fact been the result of the closing down of heavy

---

7   Scientific Committee on Problems of the Environment (SCOPE), *The Global Carbon Cycle*, Washington, DC, 2004, pp. 77–82; and IPCC, *Climate Change 2007: Mitigation of Climate Change: Contribution of Working Group III to the Fourth Assessment Report*, Cambridge, 2007, pp. 172, 218–24.

8   SCOPE, *Global Carbon Cycle*, p. 82.

9   International Energy Agency, *Energy Technology Perspectives: In Support of the G8 Plan of Action – Executive Summary*, Paris, 2008, p. 3.

industries in the United States, Europe and the ex-Soviet bloc. The relocation of energy-intensive production to East Asia burnishes the carbon balance-sheets of some OECD countries, but deindustrialization should not be confused with spontaneous decarbonization. Most researchers believe that energy intensity has actually risen since 2000 – that is, global carbon dioxide emissions have kept pace with, or even grown marginally faster than, energy use.[10]

Return of King Coal

Moreover, the IPCC carbon budget has already been broken. According to the Global Carbon Project, which keeps the accounts, emissions have been rising faster than projected even in the IPCC's worst-case scenario. From 2000 to 2007, carbon dioxide rose by 3.5 per cent annually, compared with the 2.7 per cent in IPCC projections, or the 0.9 per cent recorded during the 1990s.[11] We are already outside the IPCC envelope, in other words, and coal may be largely to blame for this unforeseen acceleration of greenhouse emissions. Coal production has undergone a dramatic renaissance over the last decade, as nightmares of the nineteenth century return to haunt the twenty-first. In China 5 million miners toil under dangerous conditions to extract the dirty mineral that reportedly allows Beijing to open a new coal-fuelled power station each week. Coal consumption is also booming in Europe, where fifty new coal-fuelled plants are scheduled to open over the next few years, and North America, where 200 plants are planned.[12] A giant plant under construction in West Virginia will generate carbon equivalent to the exhaust of 1 million cars.

In a commanding study titled *The Future of Coal*, MIT engineers concluded that usage would increase under any foreseeable scenario, even in the face of high carbon taxes. Investment in CCS technology – carbon-capture and sequestration – is, moreover, 'completely inadequate'; even assuming it is actually practical, CCS would not become a utility-scale alternative until 2030 or later. In the United States, 'green energy' legislation has only created a 'perverse incentive' for utilities to build more coal-fired plants in the 'expectation

---

10   Josep Canadell et al., 'Contributions to Accelerating Atmospheric CO_2 Growth', *Proceedings of the National Academy of Sciences*, vol. 104, no. 47, 20 November 2007, pp. 18, 866–70.

11   Global Carbon Project, *Carbon Budget 2007*, p. 10.

12   Elisabeth Rosenthal, 'Europe Turns Back to Coal, Raising Climate Fears', *New York Times*, 23 April 2008.

that emissions from these plants would potentially be "grandfathered" by the grant of free CO2 allowances as part of future carbon emission regulations'.[13] Meanwhile, a consortium of coal producers, coal-burning utilities and coal-hauling railroads – calling themselves the American Coalition for Clean Coal Electricity – spent $40 million over the 2008 election cycle to ensure that both presidential candidates sang in unison about the virtues of the dirtiest but cheapest fuel.

Largely because of the popularity of coal, a fossil fuel with a proven 200-year supply, the carbon content per unit of energy may actually rise.[14] Before the American economy collapsed, the US Energy Department was projecting an increase of national energy production by at least 20 per cent over the next generation. Globally, the total consumption of fossil fuels is predicted to rise by 55 per cent, with international oil exports doubling in volume. The UN Development Programme, which has made its own study of sustainable energy goals, warns that it will require a 50 per cent cut in greenhouse gas emissions worldwide by 2050, against 1990 levels, to keep humanity outside the red zone of runaway warming.[15] Yet the International Energy Agency predicts that, in all likelihood, such emissions will actually increase over the next half-century by nearly 100 per cent – enough greenhouse gas to propel us past several critical tipping points. The IEA also projects that renewable energy, apart from hydropower, will provide only 4 per cent of electricity generation in 2030 – up from 1 per cent today.[16]

A green recession?

The current world recession – a non-linear event of the kind that IPCC scenarists ignore in their storylines – may provide a temporary respite, particularly if depressed oil prices delay the opening of the Pandora's box of new mega-carbon reservoirs such as tar sands and oil shales. But the slump is unlikely to slow the destruction of the Amazon rainforest, because Brazilian farmers will rationally seek to defend their gross incomes by expanding production. And because electricity demand is less elastic than automobile use, the share of

---

13   Stephen Ansolabehere et al., *The Future of Coal*, Cambridge, MA, 2007, p. xiv.

14   Pew Center on Global Climate Change, quoted in Matthew Wald, 'Coal, a Tough Habit to Kick', *New York Times*, 25 September 2008.

15   *UN Human Development Report 2007/2008: Fighting Climate Change: Human Solidarity in a Divided World*, p. 7.

16   IEA report quoted in *Wall Street Journal*, 7 November 2008.

coal in carbon emissions will continue to increase. In the United States, in fact, coal production is one of the few civilian industries that is currently hiring rather than laying off workers. More importantly, falling fossil-fuel prices and tight credit markets are eroding entrepreneurial incentives to develop capital-intensive wind and solar alternatives. On Wall Street, eco-energy stocks have slumped faster than the market as a whole, and investment capital has virtually disappeared, leaving some of the most celebrated clean-energy start-ups, like Tesla Motors and Clear Skies Solar, in danger of sudden crib death. Tax credits, as advocated by Obama, are unlikely to reverse this green depression. As one venture capital manager told the *New York Times*, 'natural gas at $6 makes wind look like a questionable idea and solar power unfathomably expensive'.[17]

Thus the economic crisis provides a compelling pretext for the groom once again to leave the bride at the altar, as major companies default on their public commitments to renewable energy. In the United States, Texas billionaire T. Boone Pickens has downscaled a scheme to build the world's largest wind farm, while Royal Dutch Shell has dropped its plan to invest in the London Array. Governments and ruling parties have been equally avid to escape their carbon debts. The Canadian Conservative Party, supported by Western oil and coal interests, defeated the Liberals' 'Green Shift' agenda based on a national carbon tax in 2007, just as Washington scrapped its major carbon-capture technology initiative.

On the supposedly greener side of the Atlantic, the Berlusconi regime – which is in the process of converting Italy's grid from oil to coal – denounced the EU goal of cutting emissions by 20 per cent by 2020 as an 'unaffordable sacrifice'; while the German government, in the words of the *Financial Times*, 'dealt a severe blow to the proposal to force companies to pay for the carbon dioxide they emit' by backing an almost total exemption for industry. 'This crisis changes priorities', explained a sheepish German foreign minister.[18] Pessimism now abounds. Even Yvo de Boer, director of the UN Framework Convention on Climate Change, concedes that, as long as the economic crisis persists, 'most sensible governments will be reluctant to impose new costs on [industry] in the form of carbon-emissions caps.' So even if invisible hands and interventionist leaders can restart the engines of

---

17   Clifford Krauss, 'Alternative Energy Suddenly Faces Headwinds', *New York Times*, 21 October 2008.

18   Peggy Hollinger, 'EU Needs Stable Energy Policy, EDF Warns', *Financial Times*, 5 October 2008.

economic growth, they are unlikely to be able to turn down the global thermostat in time to prevent runaway climate change. Nor should we expect that the G7 or the G20 will be eager to clean up the mess they have made.[19]

Ecological inequalities

Climate diplomacy based on the Kyoto–Copenhagen template assumes that, once the major actors have accepted the consensus science in the IPCC reports, they will recognize an overriding common interest in gaining control over the greenhouse effect. But global warming is not H. G. Wells's *War of the Worlds*, where invading Martians democratically annihilate humanity without class or ethnic distinction. Climate change, instead, will produce dramatically unequal impacts across regions and social classes, inflicting the greatest damage upon poor countries with the fewest resources for meaningful adaptation. This geographical separation of emission source from environmental consequence undermines proactive solidarity. As the UN Development Programme has emphasized, global warming is above all a threat to the poor and the unborn, the 'two constituencies with little or no political voice.'[20] Coordinated global action on their behalf thus presupposes either their revolutionary empowerment – a scenario not considered by the IPCC – or the transmutation of the self-interest of rich countries and classes into an enlightened 'solidarity' with little precedent in history.

From a rational-actor perspective, the latter outcome only seems realistic if it can be shown that privileged groups possess no preferential 'exit' option, that internationalist public opinion drives policymaking in key countries, and that greenhouse gas mitigation can be achieved without major sacrifices in northern-hemispheric standards of living – none of which seem likely. Moreover, there is no

---

19 The shameful charade in Copenhagen, crowned by Obama's desperate deceit of an agreement, exposed less the political gulf between nations than the moral abyss between governments and humanity. In the meantime, the famous 2°C of additional warming, which president and premier have vowed to prevent, is already working its way through the world ocean: a future that will happen even if all carbon emissions ceased tomorrow. On 'committed' warming and the underlying illusion of Copenhagen, see the harrowing if awkwardly titled article by Scripps Institution researchers V. Ramanathan and Y. Feng, 'On Avoiding Dangerous Anthropogenic Interference with the Climate System: Formidable Challenges Ahead', *Proceedings of the National Academy of Science*, vol. 105, no. 38, 23 September 2008, pp. 14, 245–50.

20 *UN Human Development Report 2007/2008*, p. 6.

shortage of eminent apologists, like Yale economists William Nord-
haus and Robert Mendelsohn, ready to explain that it makes more
sense to defer abatement until poorer countries become richer and
thus more capable of bearing the costs themselves. In other words,
instead of galvanizing heroic innovation and international cooperation, growing environmental and socioeconomic turbulence may
simply drive elite publics into more frenzied attempts to wall themselves off from the rest of humanity. Global mitigation, in this
unexplored but not improbable scenario, would be tacitly abandoned – as, to some extent, it already has been – in favour of
accelerated investment in selective adaptation for Earth's first-class
passengers. The goal would be the creation of green and gated oases
of permanent affluence on an otherwise stricken planet.

Of course, there would still be treaties, carbon credits, famine
relief, humanitarian acrobatics, and perhaps the full-scale conversion
of some European cities and small countries to alternative energy.
But worldwide adaptation to climate change, which presupposes trillions of dollars of investment in the urban and rural infrastructures
of poor and medium-income countries, as well as the assisted migration of tens of millions of people from Africa and Asia, would
necessarily command a revolution of almost mythic magnitude in the
redistribution of income and power. Meanwhile, we are speeding
towards a fateful rendezvous around 2030, or even earlier, when the
convergent impacts of climate change, peak oil, peak water and an
additional 1.5 billion people on the planet will produce negative
synergies probably beyond our imagination.

The fundamental question is whether rich countries will ever actually mobilize the political will and economic resources to achieve
IPCC targets, or help poorer countries adapt to the inevitable, already
'committed' quotient of global warming. More vividly: Will the electorates of the wealthy nations shed their current bigotry and walled
borders to admit refugees from predicted epicentres of drought and
desertification – the Maghreb, Mexico, Ethiopia and Pakistan? Will
Americans, the most miserly people when measured by per capita
foreign aid, be willing to tax themselves to help relocate the millions
likely to be flooded out of densely settled mega-delta regions like
Bangladesh? And will North American agribusiness, the likely bene-
ficiary of global warming, voluntarily make world food security, not
profit-taking in a seller's market, its highest priority?

Market-oriented optimists, of course, will point to demonstration-
scale carbon-offset programmes like the Clean Development Mechanism,
which, they claim, will ensure green investment in the Third World.

But the impact of CDM is thus far negligible; it subsidizes small-scale reforestation and the scrubbing of industrial emissions rather than fundamental investment in domestic and urban use of fossil fuels. Moreover, the standpoint of the developing world is that the North should acknowledge the environmental disaster it has created and take responsibility for cleaning it up. Poor countries rightly rail against the notion that the greatest burden of adjustment to the Anthropocene epoch should fall on those who have contributed least to carbon emissions and drawn the slightest benefits from two centuries of industrial revolution. A recent assessment of the environmental costs of economic globalization since 1961 – in deforestation, climate change, overfishing, ozone depletion, mangrove conversion and agricultural expansion – found that the richest countries had generated 42 per cent of environmental degradation across the world, while shouldering only 3 per cent of the resulting costs.[21]

The radicals of the South will rightly point to another debt as well. For thirty years, cities in the developing world have grown at breakneck speed without counterpart public investments in infrastructure, housing, or public health. In part this has been the result of foreign debts contracted by dictators, with payments enforced by the IMF, and public spending downsized or redistributed by the World Bank's 'structural adjustment' agreements. This planetary deficit of opportunity and social justice is summarized by the fact that more than 1 billion people, according to UN Habitat, currently live in slums, and that their number is expected to double by 2030. An equal number, or more, forage in the so-called informal sector – a first-world euphemism for mass unemployment. Sheer demographic momentum, meanwhile, will increase the world's urban population by 3 billion people over the next forty years, 90 per cent of whom will be in poor cities. No one – not the UN, the World Bank, the G20: no one – has a clue how a planet of slums with growing food and energy crises will accommodate their biological survival, much less their aspirations to basic happiness and dignity.

The most sophisticated research to date into the likely impacts of global warming on tropical and semi-tropical agriculture is summarized in William Cline's country-by-country study, which couples climate projections to crop process and neo-Ricardian farm-output models, allowing for various levels of carbon-dioxide fertilization, to

---

21   U. Srinivasan et al., 'The Debt of Nations and the Distribution of Impacts from Human Activities', *Proceedings of the National Academy of Science*, vol. 105, no. 5, 5 February 2008, pp. 1, 768–73.

look at possible futures for human nutrition. The view is grim. Even in Cline's most optimistic simulations, the agricultural systems of Pakistan (minus 20 per cent of current farm output) and Northwestern India (minus 30 per cent) are likely devastated, along with much of the Middle East, the Maghreb, the Sahel belt, parts of Southern Africa, the Caribbean and Mexico. Twenty-nine developing countries, according to Cline, stand to lose 20 per cent or more of their current farm output to global warming, while agriculture in the already rich North is likely to receive, on average, an 8 per cent boost.[22]

This potential loss of agricultural capacity in the developing world is even more ominous in the context of the UN warning that a doubling of food production will be necessary to sustain the earth's mid-century population. The 2008 food affordability crisis, aggravated by the biofuel boom, is only a modest portent of the chaos that could soon grow from the convergence of resource depletion, intractable inequality and climate change. In face of these dangers, human solidarity itself may fracture like a West Antarctic ice shelf, and shatter into a thousand shards.

2. OPTIMISM OF THE IMAGINATION

Scholarly research has come late in the day to confront the synergistic possibilities of peak population growth, agricultural collapse, abrupt climate change, peak oil and, in some regions, peak water, and the accumulated penalties of urban neglect. If investigations by the German government, Pentagon and CIA into the national-security implications of a multiply determined world crisis in the coming decades have had a Hollywoodish ring, it is hardly surprising. As a 2007/2008 UN Human Development Report observed, 'There are no obvious historical analogies for the urgency of the climate change problem.'[23] While paleoclimatology can help scientists anticipate the non-linear physics of a warming Earth, there is no historical precedent or vantage point for understanding what will happen in the 2050s, when a peak species population of 9 to 11 billion struggles to adapt to climate chaos and depleted fossil energy. Almost any scenario, from the collapse of civilization to a new golden age of fusion power, can be projected onto the strange screen of our grandchildren's future.

---

22 William Cline, *Global Warming and Agriculture: Impact Estimates by Country*, Washington, DC, 2007, pp. 67–71, 77–8.
23 *UN Human Development Report 2007/2008*, p. 6.

We can be sure, however, that cities will remain the ground zero of convergence. Although forest clearance and export monocultures have played fundamental roles in the transition to a new geological epoch, the prime mover has been the almost exponential increase in the carbon footprints of urban regions in the northern hemisphere. Heating and cooling the urban built environment alone is responsible for an estimated 35–45 per cent of current carbon emissions, while urban industries and transportation contribute another 35–40 per cent. In a sense, city life is rapidly destroying the ecological niche – Holocene climate stability – which made its evolution into complexity possible.

Yet there is a striking paradox here. What makes urban areas so environmentally unsustainable are precisely those features, even in the largest megacities, that are most anti-urban or sub-urban. First among these is massive horizontal expansion, which combines the degradation of vital natural services – aquifers, watersheds, truck farms, forests, coastal ecosystems – with the high costs of providing infrastructure to sprawl. The result is grotesquely oversized environmental footprints, with a concomitant growth of traffic and air pollution and, most often, the downstream dumping of waste. Where urban forms are dictated by speculators and developers, bypassing democratic controls over planning and resources, the predictable social outcomes are extreme spatial segregation by income or ethnicity, as well as unsafe environments for children, the elderly and those with special needs; inner-city development is conceived as gentrification through eviction, destroying working-class urban culture in the process. To these we may add the socio-political features of the megalopolis under conditions of capitalist globalization: the growth of peripheral slums and informal employment, the privatization of public space, low-intensity warfare between police and subsistence criminals, and bunkering of the wealthy in sterilized historical centres or walled suburbs.

By contrast, those qualities that are most 'classically' urban, even on the scale of small cities and towns, combine to generate a more virtuous circle. Where there are well-defined boundaries between city and countryside, urban growth can preserve open space and vital natural systems, while creating environmental economies of scale in transportation and residential construction. Access to city centres from the periphery becomes affordable, and traffic can be regulated more effectively. Waste is more easily recycled, not exported downstream. In classic urban visions, public luxury replaces privatized consumption through the socialization of desire and identity within collective urban space. Large domains of public or non-profit housing reproduce ethnic and income heterogeneity at fractal scales throughout the city. Egalitarian public services and cityscapes are designed with children, the elderly and those with special needs in mind. Democratic controls offer powerful capacities for progressive taxation and planning, with high levels of political mobilization and civic participation, the priority of civic memory over proprietary icons, and the spatial integration of work, recreation and home life.

The city as its own solution

Such sharp demarcations between 'good' and 'bad' features of city life are redolent of famous twentieth-century attempts to distil a canonical urbanism or anti-urbanism: Lewis Mumford and Jane Jacobs, Frank Lloyd Wright and Walt Disney, Corbusier and the CIAM manifesto, the 'New Urbanism' of Andrés Duany and Peter Calthorpe, and so on. But no one needs urban theorists to have eloquent opinions about the virtues and vices of built environments and the kinds of social interactions they foster or discourage. What often goes unnoticed in such moral inventories, however, is the consistent affinity between social and environmental justice, between the communal ethos and a greener urbanism. Their mutual attraction is magnetic, if not inevitable. The conservation of urban green spaces and waterscapes, for example, serves simultaneously to preserve vital natural elements of the urban metabolism while providing leisure and cultural resources for the popular classes. Reducing suburban gridlock with better planning and more public transit turns traffic sewers back into neighbourhood streets while reducing greenhouse emissions.

There are innumerable examples like these, and they all point towards a single unifying principle: namely, that the cornerstone of the low-carbon city, far more than any particular green design or technology, is the priority given to public affluence over private wealth. As we all know, several additional Earths would be required to allow all of humanity to live in a suburban house with two cars and a lawn, and this obvious constraint is sometimes evoked to justify the impossibility of reconciling finite resources with rising standards of living. Most contemporary cities, in rich countries or poor, repress the potential environmental efficiencies inherent in human-settlement density. The ecological genius of the city remains a vast, largely hidden power. But there is no planetary shortage of 'carrying capacity' if we are willing to make democratic public space, rather than modular, private consumption, the engine of sustainable equality. Public affluence – represented by great urban parks, free museums, libraries and infinite possibilities for human interaction – represents an alternative route to a rich standard of life based on Earth-friendly sociality. Although seldom noticed by academic urban theorists, university campuses are often little quasi-socialist paradises around rich public spaces for learning, research, performance and human reproduction.

The utopian ecological critique of the modern city was pioneered by socialists and anarchists, beginning with Guild Socialism's dream – influenced by the bio-regionalist ideas of Kropotkin and later Geddes – of garden cities for re-artisanized English workers, and ending with the bombardment of the Karl Marx-Hof, Red Vienna's great experiment in communal living, during the Austrian Civil War in 1934. In between are the invention of the kibbutz by Russian and Polish socialists, the modernist social housing projects of the Bauhaus, and the extraordinary debate over urbanism conducted in the Soviet Union during the 1920s. This radical urban imagination was a victim of the tragedies of the 1930s and 1940s. Stalinism, on the one hand, veered towards a monumentalism in architecture and art, inhumane in scale and texture, that was little different from the Wagnerian hyperboles of Albert Speer in the Third Reich. Postwar social democracy, on the other hand, abandoned alternative urbanism for a Keynesian mass-housing policy that emphasized economies of scale in high-rise projects on cheap suburban estates, and thereby uprooted traditional working-class urban identities.

Yet the late-nineteenth and early-twentieth-century conversations about the 'socialist city' provide invaluable starting points for thinking about the current crisis. Consider, for example, the Constructivists. El Lissitzky, Melnikov, Leonidov, Golosov, the Vesnin brothers and other brilliant socialist designers – constrained as they were by early Soviet urban misery and a drastic shortage of public investment – proposed to relieve congested apartment life with splendidly designed workers' clubs, people's theatres and sports complexes. They gave urgent priority to the emancipation of proletarian women through the organization of communal kitchens, day nurseries, public baths and cooperatives of all kinds. Although they envisioned workers' clubs and social centres, linked to vast Fordist factories and eventual high-rise housing, as the 'social condensers' of a new proletarian civilization, they were also elaborating a practical strategy for leveraging poor urban workers' standard of living in otherwise austere circumstances.

In the context of global environmental emergency, this Constructivist project could be translated into the proposition that the

egalitarian aspects of city life consistently provide the best sociological and physical supports for resource conservation and carbon
mitigation. Indeed, there is little hope of mitigating greenhouse emissions or adapting human habitats to the Anthropocene unless the
movement to control global warming converges with the struggle to
raise living standards and abolish world poverty. And in real life,
beyond the IPCC's simplistic scenarios, this means participating in
the struggle for democratic control over urban space, capital flows,
resource-sheds and large-scale means of production.

The inner crisis in environmental politics today is precisely the lack
of bold concepts that address the challenges of poverty, energy, biodiversity and climate change within an integrated vision of human
progress. At a micro-level, of course, there have been enormous strides
in developing alternative technologies and passive-energy housing,
but demonstration projects in wealthy communities and rich countries will not save the world. The more affluent, to be sure, can now
choose from an abundance of designs for eco-living, but what is the
ultimate goal: to allow well-meaning celebrities to brag about their
zero-carbon lifestyles or to bring solar energy, toilets, paediatric
clinics and mass transit to poor urban communities?

Beyond the green zone

Tackling the challenge of sustainable urban design for the whole
planet, and not just for a few privileged countries or social groups,
requires a vast stage for the imagination, such as the arts and sciences
inhabited in the May Days of Vkhutemas and the Bauhaus. It presupposes a radical willingness to think beyond the horizon of neoliberal
capitalism towards a global revolution that reintegrates the labour of
the informal working classes, as well as the rural poor, in the sustainable reconstruction of their built environments and livelihoods. Of
course, this is an utterly unrealistic scenario, but one either embarks
on a journey of hope, believing that collaborations between architects, engineers, ecologists and activists can play small but essential
roles in making an *alter-monde* more possible, or one submits to a
future in which designers are just the hireling imagineers of elite,
alternative existences. Planetary 'green zones' may offer pharaonic
opportunities for the monumentalization of individual visions, but
the moral questions of architecture and planning can only be resolved
in the tenements and sprawl of the 'red zones'.

From this perspective, only a return to explicitly utopian thinking
can clarify the minimal conditions for the preservation of human

solidarity in the face of convergent planetary crises. I think I understand what the Italian Marxist architects Tafuri and Dal Co meant
when they cautioned against 'a regression to the utopian'; but to raise
our imaginations to the challenge of the Anthropocene, we must be
able to envision alternative configurations of agents, practices and
social relations, and this requires, in turn, that we suspend the politico-
economic assumptions that chain us to the present. But utopianism is
not necessarily millenarianism, nor is it confined just to the soapbox
or pulpit. One of the most encouraging developments in that emergent intellectual space where researchers and activists discuss the
impacts of global warming on development has been a new willingness to advocate the Necessary rather than the merely Practical. A
growing chorus of expert voices warn that either we fight for 'impossible' solutions to the increasingly entangled crises of urban poverty
and climate change, or become ourselves complicit in a de facto triage
of humanity.

Thus I think we can be cheered by a 2008 editorial in *Nature*.
Explaining that the 'challenges of rampant urbanization demand integrated, multidisciplinary approaches and new thinking', the editors
urge the rich countries to finance a zero-carbon revolution in the cities
of the developing world. 'It may seem utopian,' they write,

> to promote these innovations in emerging and developing-world mega-
> cities, many of whose inhabitants can barely afford a roof over their heads.
> But those countries have already shown a gift for technological fast-
> forwarding, for example, by leapfrogging the need for landline infra-
> structure to embrace mobile phones. And many poorer countries have a
> rich tradition of adapting buildings to local practices, environments and
> climates – a home-grown approach to integrated design that has been all
> but lost in the West. They now have an opportunity to combine these
> traditional approaches with modern technologies.[24]

Similarly, the UN Human Development Report warns that the 'future
of human solidarity' depends upon a massive aid programme to help
developing countries adapt to climate shocks. The Report calls for
removing the 'obstacles to the rapid disbursement of the low-carbon
technologies needed to avoid dangerous climate change' – 'the world's
poor cannot be left to sink or swim with their own resources while
rich countries protect their citizens behind climate-defence fortifi-
cations.' 'Put bluntly,' it continues, 'the world's poor and future

---

24 'Turning Blight into Bloom', *Nature*, vol. 455, 11 September 2008, p. 137.

generations cannot afford the complacency and prevarication that continue to characterize international negotiations on climate change.' The refusal to act decisively on behalf of all humanity would be 'a moral failure on a scale unparalleled in history'.[25] If this sounds like a sentimental call to the barricades, an echo from the classrooms, streets and studios of forty years ago, then so be it; on the basis of the evidence before us, taking a 'realist' view of the human prospect, like seeing Medusa's head, would simply turn us into stone.

_____

25   UN *Human Development Report 2007/2008*, pp. 6, 2.

2

Ecologies of Scale

HERMAN DALY

Interview by Benjamin Kunkel

2018

If fidelity to GDP growth amounts to the religion of the modern world, then Herman Daly surely counts as a leading heretic. Arguably the preeminent figure in ecological economics, a field he did much to establish, and the author in his many works of perhaps the most fundamental and eloquently logical case against endless economic growth yet produced, Daly was born in 1938, in Houston, Texas. Then and now the headquarters of the US oil industry and epitome, after World War II, of unplanned urban sprawl, Houston fell victim in summer 2017 to Hurricane Harvey. The lumbering storm, bred on the climate-changed waters of the Gulf of Mexico, doused the city's built-over wetlands and tangle of freeways in fifty inches of rain, at a cost of scores of lives and tens of billions of dollars. Prophets can't expect hometown honours, but Houston in particular, among American cities, has flouted Daly's warnings against what he calls 'growthmania' or, more neutrally, 'growthism'. The irony – the heretic hailing from the citadel – took some time to ripen, as Daly explains below. Once he perceived that economic growth could not long continue without forfeiting its ecological basis and moral justification, he achieved a series of breakthroughs. Steady-State Economics (1977) rivals Keynes's programme of full employment or Hayek's free-market catallaxy in its visionary force, while exceeding either of these in the scale of its implications. But this was only so much abstract reasoning. Recognizing that GDP could not be displaced as a measure of social well-being and progress without some equally empirical alternative, Daly in 1989 proposed, in collaboration with the Whiteheadean philosopher John Cobb, an Index of Sustainable Human Welfare to assess the wealth of nations. More recently, he has insisted on the theoretical possibility and historical actuality of 'uneconomic growth', which 'occurs when increases in production come at an expense in resources and well-being that is worth more than the items made'. The world today is faced with a pair of contradictory terrors: the economic fear that growth will soon come to an end, and the ecological fear that it will not. Daly has conceived a form of society removed from this perplex, though not any historical dynamic that would clear the path to it.

~

May I start by asking about your background – your upbringing and general formation. Did your parents care much about politics? Were there any influences that contributed to your ideas on ecology and economics?

I was born and raised in Houston, Texas. My father had a little hardware store – he'd had to quit school around the eighth grade, at the start of the Great Depression. My mother had worked as a secretary, but the boss insisted she leave when she was pregnant with me; this was 1938. It was hard to make a profit from running a hardware store, so my parents were mostly concerned with making a living; larger questions weren't really on their mind. I worked in the store through high school and college – I took my first degree at Rice University, in Houston. Most of the people who came in were carpenters, plumbers and so on. In a general way I supported the Democrats, because they seemed more in tune with the working class – the people I identified with from my family background and from working in the hardware store. My high school was on the edge of the richest part of town, and there were kids from all sorts of backgrounds, so I got a picture of the whole spectrum – the rich, the middle class and the poor. I didn't really like the upper-class way of life. From my parents, there was the general influence of the church, of course, on moral issues.

What particular church was it?

Evangelical and Reformed – the denomination of Reinhold Niebuhr – subsequently merged with the Congregationalists to become the United Church of Christ. It was the church that German immigrants to Texas brought with them, and that was my mother's family background. Even as a five-year-old, singing songs like, 'Jesus loves the little children, red and yellow, black and white, they are precious in His sight' – you could look out at the world and see that this was not the way things were being done: 'Why can't I play with the black kids, then?' So the realization that the way things are in the world wasn't necessarily the way they should be came rather early. But it wasn't from formal education – it was more from a Sunday School song.

Houston is an oil town, a boom town, where the population has exploded – it's now the fourth biggest urban area in the United States. Do you think that had an influence on your thinking about growth and ecology?

The home of Enron, too. I got a solid dose of the new rich and the boom mentality, and felt a certain revulsion against that excess. But what influenced me more was travelling down through Mexico with a friend, after I graduated from high school – this was in the mid-fifties – and seeing the poverty there. A lot of the customers at the hardware store were Mexican and Central American, so I kept on practicing the Spanish I'd picked up when I got home. The experience of the poverty in Mexico, as well as in Texas, was what turned me on to economics. I thought it would be a useful thing to study – development as the cure for poverty.

Was it at Rice that you first encountered the classical political econo-mists' writings on the stationary state – Smith, Ricardo, Malthus, Mill? These would have been part of the curriculum at the time, though I don't think they would be now.

You are absolutely right – they would not be now, but they were then. The first course I took as an undergraduate was the history of economic thought, which is scarcely offered anymore. That was my introduction to the idea of limits to growth. I thought it was great: the history of economic thought included people talking about important things. That was what convinced me to major in economics.

Was the notion of the stationary state or an ultimate end to growth something you particularly concentrated on?

At the time, no, it was not. I thought it was interesting, but I bought the line that these were old ideas, and that technology and growth were the new thing. This was when Keynesian economics was really coming into its own in the universities. Investment meant growth, which was the solution to unemployment. I remember asking my professors at the time, 'Well, that's great, but how long can we keep growing?' They weren't interested – 'Oh, the multiplier will take care of that.' Which, looking back, was a really strange answer. But I wasn't really confident enough at the time to raise more questions. So I put that aside and got down to studying development economics. Then I went on to Vanderbilt for graduate work, in Nashville, Tennessee.

This was going into the sixties. Did you have any personal concerns about being called up for Vietnam?

Well, no – but I was the right age. I could have been. The reason I wasn't called up was that I was ineligible, because of the amputation of my left arm as a consequence of polio. I had polio at age eight and then, the summer I turned fifteen, I had it amputated.

Well, you clearly do very well without it – I didn't notice!

The amputation wasn't absolutely necessary, but the arm was atrophied, nothing but skin and bone, just a dead weight hanging off me. I had already spent far too much of my energy trying to recover the use of it. I decided I'd do better to devote my energy to things I *could* do, and stop wasting time on things I couldn't. Fortunately, my parents were very understanding, because the operation needed their consent.

This is very interesting – if you don't mind discussing it? Having had polio as a child often seems an important experience for an intellectual or an artist, imposing a kind of isolation for a spell. People report that they spent a lot of time reading and thinking. Do you think something like that happened for you?

For sure. From the age of eight, I couldn't really play sports, because the arm would always get hurt. This was in Texas, a sports-mad place, where football was the big thing. As you suggest, I spent my time reading, and I enjoyed it. That was definitely important. And if you're thinking of a lesson that might carry over into economics, the other thing I learned was that some things really are impossible. At the time, the popular idea was that if you had polio, you were supposed to get over it – if you just try harder, nothing's impossible. At a certain point I realized I was being fed a bunch of well-intentioned lies – some things really are impossible – so I said to myself, the best adaptation when you come up against an impossibility is to recognize it and switch your energy to good things that are still possible. I suppose that's what I did. Now, you could make a big leap from that to my later economic theories: unlimited growth is impossible, so let's adapt to a steady-state economy. That was never consciously on my mind, but looking back, if you were to put me on a psychiatrist's couch, that might occur to the analyst.

You studied at Vanderbilt under Nicholas Georgescu-Roegen, author of The Entropy Law and the Economic Process, *protégé of Schumpeter and Leontief – a seminal thinker for ecological economics and the de-growth movement. Was his presence on the faculty one of the things that drew you to Vanderbilt?*

No, it was fortuitous, really. I took his courses because they were required. The big attraction for me was that Vanderbilt had a programme in Latin American development economics – I started off looking to growth as a solution to poverty.

Have you reflected on how your life might have been quite different if you hadn't studied with Georgescu? Or do you think that you would have come to these ideas anyway?

That's a good question. Who knows? Curiously enough, they were holding a *homenagem* for Georgescu not long ago, on the twentieth anniversary of his death, at the University of São Paulo. I don't know what would have been different without him. My life would have been easier, but I would not have learned as much. He was surely a genius and a brilliant teacher, but also, perhaps because of that, a difficult personality.

When did your intellectual reorientation take place? Was there anything punctual about it, or was it a gradual process?

I would say it was gradual. It happened in different stages. From a theoretical point of view, Georgescu's idea of the entropy law as a fundamental basis for a physical root of value in economics was very important. The grounding of economics in physical science – in physics and the laws of thermodynamics – gave me a deeper understanding of the origin of scarcity, and of the fact that the problem of scarcity is not so easy to overcome. It certainly requires more than just appeals to technology. Then, in 1967, I went to north-eastern Brazil, the poorest region in the western hemisphere – a sort of southern Appalachia. The visible population explosion there made a real impression on me; the growth rate was very high, with a very strong class differential. The upper class used contraception, so they had maybe four kids, while the lower classes had eight or ten. I held what was almost a Marxist interpretation of population – though not one that Marx would have liked. There was a class monopoly on the means of production at that time in north-east Brazil and also a class monopoly on the means for controlling reproduction, via access to contraception – categorically denied to working people. The upshot was the permanent replenishment of the reserve army, as wages are never going to keep up with that scale of population increase. That was another dimension of exploitation. I went back to the meaning of the word 'proletariat', *prole* meaning children – in Portuguese and Spanish, that sense of the word comes right through, and in English, with 'proliferation', we still have a connection – and *proletarius*, in Roman society, those with no property except their children. Marx, however, completely shifted the meaning of the word – defining the proletariat as the non-owners of the means of production.

Why Brazil?

My wife Marcia is Brazilian, though I met her in Nashville, where she was studying. I had a job through the Ford Foundation, teaching at the University of Ceará State. My task was to prepare students from the north-east to go abroad and study economics, then come back to practice in Brazil. Students from the north-east were disadvantaged and lost out in national competitions, so this was a special preparatory course for them. That was my day job, as it were. Then the students went on strike against the military dictatorship and the university closed down, so I had an unexpected two-month vacation. I used it to undertake a study of population in the area and read, or re-read, everything I could find – John Stuart Mill on the stationary state in particular made a big impression the second time around. I'd also read Rachel Carson's *Silent Spring*, and that was a major influence on me: the question of inter-relations, feedback loops, within an ecosystem. In my mind, these three things – Georgescu's understanding of entropy and economics, Brazilian society and Carson's ecology – started to cohere. I was working on a paper that tried to generalize Leontief's input–output model of the interdependencies between economic sectors to include ecological sectors and the relations between them, so the economy became a subset of a larger ecosystem. Surprisingly enough, it was published in the University of Chicago's *Journal of Political Economy*, so that was a good thing for me.[1]

Would you say, then, that the first aspect of the steady state you thought about was a steady stock of people?

Yes, I studied the demographers' model of a stationary population, which seemed to me very generalizable to populations of things other than human bodies – artifacts, all 'dissipative structures' that have birth-production rates, death-depreciation rates, life expectancies, age structures. The two seemed to fit together.

For someone of your generation, the shift from a focus on growth to a scepticism about growth's ultimate wisdom must have involved a mental revolution. The synthetic measure of GDP dates from the thirties, I believe, not before. Of the PhD theses submitted at Harvard, very few in 1944 mention economic growth at all, and then ten years later, they all do. Of course, prosperity had been very important, if conceptually ill-defined, to capitalist economies for a very long time, not to mention profit. But growth itself, as a totem concept for governments and economists, was a relatively new thing, after the war?

Yes, the growthmania really took over after World War II.

'On Economics as a Life Science' and your work on population were your first publications in what we'd now call ecological economics. There were a few others already working in the field – Kenneth Boulding, for example. Did you think of yourself as belonging under a certain rubric, with Boulding and Georgescu? How about Schumacher – was he important to you?

Boulding and Georgescu I considered my best teachers – Georgescu literally so. Though I never took courses formally from Boulding, I read everything he wrote, got to know him over the years and learned a lot from him. Later on, Schumacher, too. I thought *Small Is Beautiful* was very important, and I included him in a book I

---

1   Herman Daly, 'On Economics as a Life Science', *Journal of Political Economy*, vol. 76, no. 3, May–June 1968; and 'The Population Question in Northeast Brazil: Its Economic and Ideological Dimensions', *Economic Development and Cultural Change*, vol. 18, no. 4, July 1970.

edited, *Towards a Steady-State Economy* (1973). That collection brought together work by Boulding, Georgescu, Schumacher, Garrett Hardin on population and the commons issue, and the geologist Preston Cloud on mineral resources. All this work seemed to fit together, and gave a biophysical foundation to the idea of a steady-state economy.

Your first fully authored book on the subject was Steady-State Economics, *which appeared in 1977?*

Yes. It's gone through several revisions and expansions. I guess the latest was 1992. The original subtitle was *The Economics of Biophysical Equilibrium and Moral Growth.*

Some readers of your work detect a certain religious orientation, without your laying any special emphasis on it. I don't really see that, beyond your sense that life, or a society, ought to have some purpose beyond economic growth.

I think that's well put. American universities, in spite of their overwhelmingly religious origins, are very secular places these days, understandably given that the main religious alternative now on offer in our culture is right-wing evangelical Trumpism. My students and colleagues are mostly faithful believers in neo-Darwinist materialism, which I think puts them in a rather difficult position when it comes to policy, which is what I've been teaching at the Maryland School of Public Policy for the last decade. I would ask them: 'What philosophical presuppositions are necessary if you're going to seriously be a student of public policy? What do you have to believe, to make it a reasonable undertaking?' My answer is that you can't be a determinist, and you can't be a nihilist – you have to believe that there are real alternatives, and you must have a criterion for saying one future is better than another. That's the minimum sort of philosophical-religious position, I think, that would be coherent with the idea of public policy, and it conflicts with 'scientific' materialism as a worldview, though not with science itself. I co-authored a book with John Cobb that looked at the connections of economics with ecology, ethics and religion.[2]

---

2 *For the Common Good: Redirecting the Economy Toward Community, the Environment and a Sustainable Future*, 2nd edn, Boston, 1994.

Steady-State Economics *must have taken some years of sustained work. It's a fundamental, philosophical book. Where were you working, after you came back from Brazil?*

I taught at Louisiana State University, Baton Rouge until 1988, though I had a year out at Yale in 1970, working on population, the entropy law and the environment. The first piece I wrote specifically on the idea of the steady-state economy came out of that.[3]

Can you tell us what a steady-state economy is and what institutional parameters it would need?

Steady state comes from the realization that the economy is a subsystem of a larger system, the ecosphere, which is finite, non-expanding, materially closed. It's open to a flow of solar energy, but the Sun itself is non-growing. So those are the overall conditions of the parent system. If the subsystem keeps growing, it eventually coincides with the whole parent system, at which point it'll have to behave as a steady state. Purists would force me to say quasi-steady, because there is of course development, continuous evolution and qualitative change. But the Earth itself is not getting quantitatively any bigger, and there comes a point in the expansion of a subsystem where it encroaches too much on the operation of the system as a whole. We convert too much of nature into ourselves and our stuff, and there's not enough left to provide the biophysical life-support services that we need. Standard economics does not have any mechanism to register the cost of the economy's scale, relative to the biosphere. Prices don't do that. They just measure the scarcity of one resource in relation to another, not the scarcity of all resources relative to the economy's total demand.

You make a basic distinction between growth and development. Could you elaborate on that?

Growth is a physical concept. When something grows, it gets bigger, either by assimilation or accretion. Development is a qualitative concept: something gets better, it doesn't necessarily get bigger. It evolves, it changes, it improves. As analogies: a snowball rolling down a mountain is pure growth, by accretion – it's getting bigger and bigger. An embryo is growing and developing at the same time,

---

3 'Towards a Stationary-State Economy', in John Harte and Robert Socolow, eds, *Patient Earth*, New York, 1971.

changing qualitatively as it gets bigger. Planet Earth as a whole is not growing, but it is evolving, either in a positive or a negative way. One problem with GDP as a measure is that it conflates these two very different processes.

What might be a measure of development, once biophysical growth had stopped? A way of measuring development in terms of increased complexity, or something like that?

That's a hard thing to do, but it's an important issue. Almost by definition, quality is fundamentally unmeasurable, but we do know that some things are better than others. Complexity could be a part of it. On the other hand, simplicity could be a qualitative improvement. I don't really have a good answer to that problem yet. For now, to my mind, the important thing is to force our attention onto the qualitative dimension by limiting quantitative expansion.

If we imagine a steady-state economy that's constant in terms of its physical inputs and outputs, we could envisage that some economic growth might take place in terms of increased efficiency – the same amount of steel could be used to produce more cars, homes could be heated to the same temperature using less electricity, and so forth. But once you've reached the point of maximum biophysical efficiency, would GDP then be capable of measuring an improvement in the quality of services?

It's a good question, but for me, the important thing is to limit the physical throughput. If you do that, then what happens to GDP doesn't matter very much from an environmental perspective. Whatever people do with it is fine. A consumer-sovereignty argument makes sense in that context, because there would no longer be huge external costs of ecological degradation. An economist might argue there would be technological solutions to resource use, so we can set limitations on throughput aside. Technology is something we love, limiting throughput is something we hate, so let's just focus on the former. My reply would be: if we're so good at increasing resource productivity, why would you object to throughput limits? That would force progress onto the path of better rather than more, raising the price of resources and increasing the incentive to use them more productively. Today this is discussed as 'decoupling' of GDP from throughput. Neoclassical economists argue that there is a very loose coupling between throughput and GDP but a tight coupling between

GDP and welfare. Ecological economists think the coupling of through-put with GDP is fairly tight while the coupling of GDP and welfare is loose, or even non-existent beyond some sufficiency threshold.

Limiting biophysical throughput implies one of your basic para-meters for the steady-state economy: depletion quotas. Can you explain how these would work?

The idea is to limit the rate of depletion – of fossil fuels, for example. We have something a bit like this with cap-and-trade. Governments can step in and say, fossil fuels are still privately owned – we haven't nationalized them – but we are nationalizing one thing out of your property bundle: your right to decide upon the rate of depletion. We're putting an aggregate limit on the right to deplete what you own. You have to purchase that right by auction from the government, because the total volume of depletion imposes social costs that are not reflected in your private decisions. The money that the government raises from the quota auction then becomes public revenue. You could use that revenue to reduce or eliminate some of the most regressive taxes for the poorest part of the population. So on the one hand the auction will drive up the price of petroleum, or whatever resource it is, but the scarcity rents reflected in that increased price are being redistributed back to the public. Or it could be used to finance a minimum income.

You're also in favour of a maximum income?

Yes. There's a wide acceptance of the idea of a minimum income; even Milton Friedman argued in favour of it. Why the maximum income to accompany that? If you have a limited total, and you also have a minimum income, then that implies a maximum somewhere. The question then becomes: should that maximum be such that a lot of people can receive it, or just a few? So it's a question of dis-tribution. I don't want to argue for absolute equality, because that creates a whole set of problems of its own, but I do want to argue for limits to *inequality*. What should those limits be? In Japan, the top CEO makes something like ten times what the average worker earns; here in the US, it's more like four or five hundred times that amount.

There was a referendum in Switzerland a few years ago, that didn't quite succeed, but it was intended to cap corporate compensation as a multiple of the lowest wage.

That's an approximation of what could happen. A lot of people, including some environmentalists, criticize the idea of a steady-state economy on the grounds that it would be too market-oriented, based on the commodification of nature. I say in response, yes, but that's more or less inevitable: we pay money for food, we pay money for all the materials we need for life – to some extent we're stuck with that. But if we're obliged to commodify vital services of nature, it's even more important that there should be limits to the distribution of income. Allocation by the price mechanism is much more acceptable within a system where inequality is limited.

What sort of depletion quotas would we establish besides those for fossil fuels? The pollution of groundwater or topsoil would be harder to measure. You speak in terms of biophysical throughput, with output as a type of waste. But of course there are no undifferentiated types of energy or waste. So how do you go about doing this?

A very good and difficult question – I've struggled with that. You can go a long way with energy alone, because energy is needed to mine all the materials that go into the throughput. If you start with energy, and perhaps water and fundamental minerals like phosphorus, that would impose limits. I emphasize depletion quotas rather than pollution quotas because depletion is more concentrated, spatially and entropically, at the beginning of the throughput. Furthermore, if you limit the input, then ultimately you always limit the output, in a quantitative sense, although not qualitatively – you still have the problem of extremely toxic pollutants that are generated from remaining inputs.

One could also imagine a steady-state population where people began to eat more and more meat, causing a major environmental problem.

This is one of the things I learnt from Robert Goodland, my former boss at the World Bank: he did some studies – on his own initiative, not for the Bank – which found that agriculture, and stock-rearing in particular, is even more disastrous for the environment than industrialization. He was a vegetarian, and I've always felt guilty about not being one myself. Having grown up in Texas, it was rather difficult. This is an area where individual actions really can have a cumulative effect if people reduce their intake of meat.

The third rail, so to speak, of your three institutional parameters for the steady state – the other two being the depletion quotas and the minimum/maximum incomes – is a cap on population. How has your thinking on that developed over the years?

The idea originated with Kenneth Boulding. He argued that the right to reproduce is treated as if it were a free good, but in reality it imposes costs on society. Even John Stuart Mill was adamant on this point: in his essay 'On Liberty', one of the few restrictions on personal freedom that he supported was on the ability to reproduce. He saw it as a legitimate area of social concern for the state. Boulding proposed a democratic way to do this: give everyone the right to reproduce once. That's going to give you a steady-state population, roughly speaking. But not everyone is able to reproduce, and not everyone wants to. They can then redistribute their rights, by sale or by gift, so that there is still macro control over the aggregate, without imposing a cast-iron rule on each and every person at the micro level.

In presenting your ideas to people, I've found that this is one of the proposals they find most difficult to contemplate.

Boulding must have had the same experience, because when he first presented the idea, he said it in all seriousness, and then a few years later he re-framed it as 'I somewhat jokingly suggested . . .' He backed off the idea in terms of its political feasibility. I have similar instincts, because people just don't want it. I'm not a dictator. I just present this as an idea. If one day people come to the realization that it's necessary to limit total population, but still want to have the maximum degree of individual freedom, then show me a better way – that's my challenge. Look at China: at one billion people, they panicked and adopted the one-child policy, a very drastic step – no brothers and sisters, aunts and uncles, a completely different family structure for the whole country. Is there a way of achieving the same goal that's less costly in terms of individual freedom? Perhaps a whole lot more women's rights and education will be enough. If we can achieve the same goal by other means that are less onerous, great.

If you've already compressed incomes quite radically, it becomes less offensive that you'd have to purchase the right to have a second child.

Yes, that's true. People might look at this and say, this is horrible because the rich would have an advantage and could always buy more licences. But the rich always have an advantage, in everything – that's the whole point of being rich. The effect of the Boulding plan on the distribution of income would be equalizing, if the rich have more children and the poor have fewer. It's the same logic as the cap-auction-trade system, in terms of combining macro control with micro freedom and variability.

It's clear that part of the antipathy to population policy is a concern for women's autonomy over their bodies. There is also the response frequently heard from progressive people: 'It's not population that's the problem, it's consumption.'

Environmental impact is the product of the number of people times per capita resource use. In other words, you have two numbers multiplied by each other – which one is more important? If you hold one constant and let the other vary, you are still multiplying. It makes no sense to me to say that only one number matters. Yet it is still very commonly said. It would, I suppose, make some sense if we were able to differentiate historically and geographically – to determine at what point in history, or in what country, which factor deserved most attention. In that sense, I would say that surely for the United States, per capita consumption is the crucial factor – but we are still multiplying it by population, so we cannot forget population. In north-east Brazil, on the other hand, population was – at the time I was there, at least – growing extremely fast, so maybe that is where the emphasis should be.

To what extent do you think about the right to have a child as fundamentally a woman's right? Given the societal shifts in attitudes towards gay marriage and parenthood that have taken place since Boulding's time, would you modify the way in which reproductive rights could be allocated?

That is an interesting question. I just have not thought in terms of gay marriage, about how that would work – because, ultimately, there has got to be a female involved somewhere. Now, I think with Boulding, you could do it various ways: you could, say, give one reproductive right to each male and female, or whatever number, and then those numbers join to get the total. The other way of doing it relies on the notion that the female is the limitative factor in reproduction, because a woman can't be a mother nearly as often as a man could be a father. In that case, all reproductive rights would be allocated to women. When I was at Yale, writing on this, I learned that there were some feminist Marxists who were quite sympathetic to the whole idea of neo-Malthusianism – whether you do it in terms of licences, or just by making contraception more available.

What's appealing about these basic administrative proposals is that they're very simple but they would bring about radical change. You don't specify the level at which they would be implemented, but you do speak of 'the government', which implies a nation-state framework. Yet the commons of reproduction is international or universal, as are many resources, like the earth's atmosphere. On the other hand, some resources are specific to individual countries: Chile has copper deposits, and one can imagine a depletion quota being paid out for Chilean copper mines to the Chileans, rather than the world at large. How do you envisage these depletion quotas and birth quotas functioning – would there be national or international markets? This is connected to the question of uneven development: how can growth and rising consumption take place in the poorest parts of the world, while de-growth takes place in the over-developed regions?

To take that last point first: if you want growth to continue in the poorer regions but not in the richer ones, then some borders will be required, because if it's all one big system, you're not going to be able to have different policies for each. I have tended to think in national terms, because that's where we have boundaries and the capacity to enforce laws, so I would put all this in a national context. What do you do about international relations and international trade? You could put depletion quotas on your own extraction of petroleum, but then that's going to make it more expensive in relation to imported petroleum, so you're going to start importing more. There are several ways of thinking about this question. One approach would be to have an equalizing tariff.

The difficulty is that the world – and economists in particular – have really bought into the idea of free trade. I must confess that I was a free-trader for much of my career; I used to enjoy teaching international economics to students and demonstrating the virtues of comparative advantage. But I found there were some objections that I couldn't answer, so I went back and re-read Ricardo. In his exposition of comparative advantage, he explicitly assumes capital immobility between nations. The whole logic of each nation specializing in its own good, and freely trading with mutual advantage guaranteed, only works if capital and labour do not cross national boundaries. If capital is free to move internationally, then it will follow *absolute* advantage, going wherever it is cheapest to produce, and selling anywhere else in the world. But if capital can't cross national boundaries, then it will go to whichever national use is most productive *relatively*, in comparison with other countries, and then trade that. Clearly that's not the situation today. So the fundamental assumption of comparative advantage doesn't work. Either we have a policy of limiting capital mobility, in order to keep the world safe for comparative-advantage trading, or we have to accept the consequences of absolute advantage, namely that gains from trade need not be mutual. It is logically absurd to defend capital mobility itself, off-shoring of production, as 'free trade', as is often done.

Can you imagine a global cap-and-trade system operating over the heads, as it were, of nation-states? A system in which an American born into an overconsuming society is immediately in hock to some-body in, say, the Central African Republic, and money is transferred from the former to the latter? Or would the revenues from depletion quotas end up in national accounts? That is, if Europe, North America and Japan are charged for having an excessive biophysical throughput, how is that revenue then disbursed on an international scale?

Yes, it ultimately implies something like a world government to administer such a thing. It might be best approached by first having national systems, and you might then be able to make transfers between them. My thought is that we ought first to make transfers *within* the nation, because there are poor people within the United States – I know something about them, I feel a kinship with them. After we've all started taking care of our own to some degree, then, as a second step, let's worry about inequalities between countries. The idea of collapsing everything into a single global system used to have some sort of appeal to me, but I just don't have much confidence in global institutions. That may be a result of having spent six years at the World Bank. The UN is a better model, as a federation of inter-dependent national communities. What I object to is the WTO vision of a single *integrated* global economy – that, I think, is beyond our capacity right now.

Do you think that a steady-state economy is compatible, in the long run, with capitalism – in the sense that capital would still need to accumulate, which implies that it at least is growing, and yet the economy would no longer be doing so?

There are some real problems there. Insofar as capitalism has to grow, then it is incompatible with the steady state. If you recognize the need to limit throughput, then the thrust towards growth, which comes from competition in the market, faces a boundary. I wouldn't really take the view that we should just abandon capitalism and opt for eco-socialism. I would say, what we're stuck with right now is capitalism, so let's take away its power to do the most damage. That means environmental destruction and the unequal distribution of income. If you take away from the capitalist system the ability to damage the environment and to concentrate wealth beyond all reason, then I think you will have made a big step forward. Does that mean you've fundamentally abandoned capitalism? In some ways perhaps, although there would still be private ownership of the means of production. I would be in favour of breaking up monopolies, and putting limits on the concentration of wealth – it infuriates me when the 'tax reform' lobby want to do away with inheritance tax. Capitalism in the sense of financialized monopoly capitalism, geared towards continuous growth and concentration of income, is really bad. If you have a Jeffersonian-type, small-scale capitalism, operating within scale and distributive limits, and you want to call that eco-socialism, that's fine with me.

It seems that you have a lot of respect for markets, in a certain way – you don't want the ultimate size of the economy to be dictated by the market, but you're impressed by the ability of markets to create Pareto optimality – to register and optimize people's preferences.

I do, if we're talking about markets with a small 'm'. If you're going to do away with the market altogether, then you're also doing away with self-employment – people who live off making a little profit through a market, they sell and they buy, and in that process they exchange information. I always recommend to my socialist friends that they should read Oskar Lange's *On the Economic Theory of Socialism* (1938), in which he outlined a kind of market socialism, demonstrating the increased fairness that one can generate through markets. In the Soviet Union, war communism – direct allocation through central planning, no buying or selling, physical requisitioning – broke down. They had to revert to the New Economic Policy, which relied on markets. If you try to get rid of markets, you're really creating a problem. Markets can be good servants, as well as bad masters.

It seems that a steady-state economy could be described in basic Marxian terms as simple commodity exchange – rather than M–C–M', it's C–M–C. One commodity goes briefly into the form of money, to become another type of commodity of the same basic dimensions.

Exactly. And I think that takes away a lot of the problems, because you're focused on use value, not exchange value; and use value always has a limit, whereas exchange value just keeps expanding indefinitely. It fits the model of simple reproduction rather than expanded reproduction. Steady-state economics cannot be a system of accumulation. There has to be a levelling out, just as the classical economists said, in which population and wealth – in its physical dimensions – stop growing, though the art of living continues to improve. For a while at Louisiana State University, I taught comparative economic systems, and I included a large section on Marxist economics. I got quite far in reading through that field, and I liked a lot of it, and still do; but I am fairly allergic to some aspects – materialism, whether dialectical or otherwise, and historical determinism – also the labour theory of value runs into some big problems. What I take from Marx is that there really is such a thing as social class and exploitation at the class level. The classical economists did recognize the existence of class, of course, but they didn't emphasize the conflict nearly as much.

It strikes me that Marx is something of an outlier, if we consider him one of the classical political economists, in not having a theory, really, of the stationary state, or an end to growth. He seems to imagine that, first, capitalism collapses, whether because of the falling rate of profit, or some other factor, and only then would any kind of limits to growth come about.

Yes, Marx doesn't have much in the way of limits to growth in his picture, although some recent Marxists have come around quite a bit on that subject. One reason for this was the conflict between Marx and Malthus, which I got interested in early on with regards to population. Malthus had his apologetic side. But Marx just *hated* Malthus. I think the reason was that Marx wanted the entire grounds for poverty to be in social relations. He didn't want any of it to be in nature – if it is in nature, then the revolution is not going to cure it, and therefore Malthus was a big ideological threat. So he went after Malthus, and I think his arguments there were fairly weak. Malthus had his own problems – but so did Marx, and Malthus was one of them.

What do you think of the dystopian steady-state scenario? You could have an essentially zero-sum economy of accumulation, where certain people were getting larger sums and other people were getting smaller sums, but with no growth in terms of GDP?

You certainly don't want to have a steady-state economy coupled with increasing inequality, because growth has been our solution to poverty; and without growth, we need another solution, which has to be redistribution, in some form or another. If you are just making the distribution more concentrated, then that really is dystopian – I agree. In fact, it seems like that is what we are currently experiencing with growth.

Would there be an ultimate limit to growth in economic value, in a steady-state economy?

I really don't know. The clear limits are in the physical dimensions. As to whether there is any limit to the psychic satisfaction that one can experience, that gets into neurology and ethics. My initial thought is that the capacity of the stomach and nervous system to consume and to get pleasure out of consumption is probably limited, but I don't know what the limits would be.

André Gorz's book Critique of Economic Reason *is interesting on this topic. One argument of the book is that one of the great terrains of struggle has been over what should be commodified and what should be decommodified. Within a steady-state economy, there could be a pretty clear correspondence between dollar values and physical values – they may change quite a bit, but it's easy to work out the relationship between them. But what happens to the service economy? Will people be commodifying the increases in psychic satisfaction, so you end up with a minutely ramified service economy, or will that become a realm that's more or less decommodified?*

Unfortunately I don't know the work of André Gorz, but I learned late in my career about a fundamental economic distinction that I never paid enough attention to: the simple classification of goods as either rival or non-rival. What fits the market are rival and excludable goods. 'Rivalness' is a physical property – I can't wear your shirt at the same time as you are wearing it – and 'excludability' is a legal concept: you have a right to prevent me from wearing your shirt, or to allow me to if you wish. There are various combinations of these categories, such as the rival but non-excludable – an open-access commons, for example, in which the market is a disaster – and the category of pure public goods, which are both non-rival and non-excludable, and then the category of the non-rival and excludable. That last combination is most pressing right now in the area of information, specifically the internet. They are attempting to impose legal excludability on a physical system that is basically non-rival. I do not think that this is going to work. Much of the emphasis in ecological economics has been on the tragedy of the commons – of avoiding open access to rival resources. At the same time, there is the other side – avoiding the enclosure of truly non-rival goods. These are, in a sense, opposite problems. Particularly as the so-called information economy grows, the basic 'non-rivalness' of knowledge and information is presenting a massive problem for property-based capitalist systems.

To what extent does growthmania seem to you connected to the heavy exploitation of fossil fuels? There have been periodic concerns about 'peak oil', and perhaps people ought to be more concerned about this than they are.

Fossil fuels were an enormous subsidy to short-term growthism. As long as societies remained largely dependent on solar energy, as peasant agricultural systems and village economies were, then a steady state is almost built in, because the solar energy arrives at a certain rate. With fossil fuels, that rate can be speeded up – we can mine it faster and accumulate reserves, but we can't mine the sun. Without this enormous subsidy, economies could not have gone on this growth spurt at all. Now, as you indicate, we are caught between two different possible limits to this. Is it going to be the climate-pollution limit of burning too much fossil fuel? Or is it the peak-oil limit of depletion? And that seems to go back and forth. With fracking, we're going to burn a whole lot more, so it looks like the climate is the more effective limit.

But only if we choose to make it that?

Yes. I think that part of the reason behind climate-change denial is that if we impose limits on burning all the fossil-fuel reserves that have been discovered underground, many of the assets on the balance sheets of big oil companies would lose their value – would become what people have started to refer to as 'stranded assets'.

Some work is being done at the University of Vienna to measure the embodied energy of various commodities. In other words, not so much a labour theory of value, but an energy theory of value – which I know has been discussed theoretically before.

This has a long history in ecological economics. Robert Costanza, who was my partner in founding *Ecological Economics* (the journal and the society), was very active in this area. The energy theory of value was his big idea: using input–output analysis to get the embodied energy content. I have a lot of sympathy for that as a way of describing the physical interrelations of the economy: energy is a meaningful common denominator. However, I don't buy the energy theory of value.

Is this more of a technical problem, in terms of the heterogeneous types of energy? Or is it more of a philosophical matter, in the sense that value is ultimately psychic utility?

It is both. Value is hard to reduce to a physical quantity. Ultimately, on that point, I go along with the neoclassical economists: you have to look at the utility and the marginal-utility side to explain prices and value. There are definitely biophysical roots of value, but there are also ethical-social roots; in that sense, I see it as the economist's old scissors analogy – which blade of the scissors does the cutting, the top or the bottom, cost or utility? Howard Odum's energy-flow understanding of the world has been very influential in ecological-economic theory. Again, this is really interesting work, but it has a fundamentally determinist side to it. This has been a problem with ecological economics: it brings together scientists – often ecologists of a materialist sort – and economists; and when it comes to matters of policy, the scientists dive under the table. Their attitude is descriptive, not prescriptive: 'I'll tell you how things are, but I don't know how they ought to be.'

The critique of determinism raises the question of how historical transformation can take place. If I can play a sort of doctrinaire Marxist for a moment: Engels distinguishes between scientific and utopian socialism, where the utopian form relies on being brought about by an ethical conversion. If we could resuscitate him today, Engels might say that your steady-state economy is too utopian, in the sense that a broad ethical conversion would have to take place to move people in this direction, whereas you don't specify a material or 'scientific' historical process that would effect the change. What do you think about that?

Not just Engels. From what I can tell, that's the official position: it's utopian, and it's not going to happen. I just don't see any alternative to an appeal to morality, whether that's sufficient or not, because I don't believe the story of determinism, and revolutionary attempts to 'help the determined really happen' have often been disasters. Even determinists now seem to have switched their appeals from history to neurobiology.

You don't believe it because you think ethical, moral, religious conversions do have a material effect on how things happen?

Yes. Purpose is causative in the world. If it is not, then we should all go back to sleep.

Right. On that subject, let me read back to you the last few lines of your 1987 essay, 'Alternative to Growthmania'. You wrote that 'the Keynesian revolution did not occur because Keynes's arguments were so compellingly lucid and unanswerable. It was the Great Depression that convinced people that something was wrong with economic theory.' You suggested it would probably take a 'great ecological spasm' to convince people that the current economic paradigm is unsustainable: 'Even in that unhappy event, it is still necessary to have an alternative vision ready to present.' Three decades later, how far down that road do you think we might be?

That's a very important question. Of course, I'm disappointed that things haven't changed, because I thought the evidence was sufficient already: even though we haven't really had a great ecological spasm, we've had plenty of costs. We've entered into an era where economic growth has become uneconomic – it's costing us more in terms of sacrificed ecosystem services than we're gaining in terms of production benefits. We haven't hit a spasm, in the sense that the ecosystem kicks us really hard, but I think maybe that's coming, precisely because we're so resistant to the idea. The Trump Administration is proclaiming it's doubling-down on growth. Maybe the difficulty here is the whole concept of 'us'. Even though growth may be costing more than it's worth in the aggregate, some people are still doing very well – the famous 1 per cent. They don't recognize that growth is hurting 'us', because it's not hurting them.

How does the century ahead look to you? What are the chances of some sort of steady-state social democracy emerging on an adequately wide scale?

My general thought is that we won't take things seriously until they get worse. In global terms, the situation does look bad. Yet, if you look at particular countries, the steady-state model doesn't seem so implausible. Take the case of Japan. Currently, it's a growth economy which is failing. Yet, both in terms of its current situation and its history, it would make sense for Japan to choose to be a successful steady-state economy instead. In pragmatic terms, Japan is declining from a very good economic position. The Japanese people may well be moving towards rejecting the growth mentality: they could decide that they are already well-off and don't need to be better and better-off each year, especially according to a fictitious measure of 'better'. They are also an island country with a scarcity of natural resources and a long history of having to live within limits.

And of being imperialist, I suppose.

Yes, but they had a long history before that of relative isolation from global commerce and the growth race. Japan also has a stable population – even a slightly declining population. Plus, they have a relatively egalitarian distribution of income, a very strong sense of community and nationality, and a tradition – certainly in their recent past – of quality over quantity in their production. Japan is halfway to becoming a steady-state economy already, whether they call it that or not. I think there are possibilities for individual countries and small units to cohere and to do things. But this runs into the great problem that people aren't willing to face today, of borders and immigration. I've gotten into a lot of trouble with my progressive friends because I don't believe in open borders. There have to be reasonable social controls and democratically enacted laws, which can't just be ignored.

What do you make of the de-growth movement in Europe?

I am favourably inclined. I meet a lot of young Europeans questioning growth. But I am still waiting for them to get beyond the slogan and develop something a little more concrete. One of their founders, Serge Latouche, once said the de-growth movement was a slogan in search of a programme. So that is my initial feeling. On the other hand, they have recently produced a compilation containing contributions from many people – *Degrowth: A Vocabulary for a New Era* – and some of the articles in there are good. So I am hopeful that they will go beyond just chanting the word *décroissance*.

From your work, it seems that an adequate programme might be relatively simple – maybe not in its implementation, but in its basic conception, and wouldn't need many institutions.

I am hopeful, and I know Joan Martinez-Alier, a colleague for many years, has been active in the de-growth movement. Josh Farley, with whom I co-authored a book, also contributed an article to their compilation. I had a period in which I was less enthusiastic about the de-growth movement: they seemed to be a little timid on the population question, particularly immigration. They still are somewhat timid, but understandably so – not Martinez-Alier, I make an exception for him. They were quite upset with me because I said that open borders was a bad policy. I said that we should have immigration, but not unlimited immigration: there is the public interest to take into account and questions of selectivity to consider. I have found that there is a general unwillingness to think through these matters. Part of that unwillingness can be attributed to the fact that they have taken Georgescu, my old mentor, as their posthumous patron saint. In one of his articles around 1970, Georgescu gestured towards open borders; and they have jumped on that. He made those remarks in a particular context – to a group of liberal Scandinavians – and he was perhaps goading them just a bit. On the other hand, Georgescu himself was an immigrant from Romania, a refugee basically, and he was quite sympathetic to easy immigration although he never really wrote on the subject in any detail. His personal problem, however, was to escape Communist Romania – emigration not immigration. If you take justice at an individual level as your major goal, then free migration has its appeal. But the economists' usual individualism downplays the social costs to the sending country of losing those young and strong enough to migrate, and the social costs to the receiving country of absorbing immigrants and putting downward pressure on domestic wages. There are a lot of other consequences that we all need to think about honestly without the distractions of either the capitalist cheap-labour lobby or the politically correct libertarians.

We have discussed the failure of steady-state ideas to make inroads in mainstream economics as it is taught to undergraduates and graduate students. Do you think that there is much prospect of that discipline broadening to include thoughts like this in a rigorous way? Or is that work more likely to be done outside of the discipline of economics?

I think it will eventually be done in economics, but only under pressure from outside. You can already see it in some universities. The University of Vermont, particularly, has a good programme now in which this kind of thinking is involved. There was a grant that was received to train perhaps as many as fifty PhD students in ecological economics, across various universities – Vermont was one, Montreal was another. Peter Brown fostered that. There is an effort within universities to broaden economics, and little individual actions will happen. Speaking of Peter Brown, I remember that when his undergraduate institution was after him to donate money, he wrote back saying he was thinking about putting them in his will, but he didn't want to support any university whose economics department taught unlimited economic growth. I don't know that many people will apply that kind of pressure.

My sense is that there was burgeoning interest in ideas of this kind during the seventies, and then they went into hibernation to some extent, until the middle of the last decade. Did that feel like a period in the wilderness, to you?

You certainly could tell that there was a big withdrawal of interest. I do sense that maybe we are coming out of the wilderness now, if for no other reason than that the wilderness is disappearing.

3

To Freeze the Thames

Natural Geo-Engineering and Biodiversity

TROY VETTESE

2018

The idea of a 'steady-state economy', a signal theme in the environmentalist politics of the 1970s with understandable appeal, has been refloated by 'no growth' thinkers in France and, most recently, by Herman Daly, in discussion with Benjamin Kunkel in NLR 109. If, as I shall argue here, steady-state economics is an ambiguous construction that actually offers little to egalitarian environmentalists, then on what foundations might an alternative green political economy be built? Neither population nor GDP will be its fundamental metric, but rather *land scarcity*. This is the concept that emerges – or rather re-emerges – as the most precious resource in any solution that brings the benign possibilities of geo-engineering to bear on the problem of faltering biodiversity and the entailments of an adequate deployment of renewable energy systems. A brisk panorama of the 'Little Ice Age' will help make these airy ideas solid.

'Behold the liquid Thames now frozen o'er / That lately ships of mighty Burthen bore', may seem to be the opening lines of a poet's imagined world, but it recalls the actual freezing of London's great waterway in 1740.[1] Although there are records of the river freezing since the fifteenth century, the frequency of such cold winters increased dramatically during the seventeenth century to about once a decade, often enough for 'Frost Fairs' to become a municipal institution. Between London Bridge and Blackfriars Bridge city-dwellers played skittles, baited bears and feasted atop a strangely solid Thames. Other regions also experienced bizarre shifts in climate during the

---

1 Unknown poet, 'Printed on the River Thames in the Month of January, 1740', in Charles Dickens, William Harrison Ainsworth and Albert Smith, eds, *Bentley's Miscellany*, vol. 7, London, 1841, p. 134.

Little Ice Age, an era of widespread cooling from the sixteenth to nineteenth centuries. Icelanders starved when the frozen sea choked off their ports, Alpine Swiss dreaded glaciers expanding to swallow their villages, and Manhattanites could walk to Staten Island. The poor harvests of the cool, wet seventeenth century have been held responsible for starving peasants and feeding instability: the Thirty Years' War, the Fronde, the English Civil War, the decline of the Ming dynasty, and war between Russia and Poland-Lithuania.[2] Hints of what caused the big chill were to be found in empty towns along the Mississippi.

In 1541 Hernando de Soto travelled along that mighty waterway and encountered a string of densely inhabited, warring settlements: Coosa, Mabila, Pacaha, Chicaza and Cofitachequi. Little is known today about Mississippian society aside from its penchant for moats and mounds; when the next European ventured there in 1682, the region was uninhabited. Most likely, epidemics of Old World origin had broken out between the two expeditions, which was hardly an unusual fate for the time. In 1492, the Americas had teemed with perhaps 60 million inhabitants, a population equalling Europe's; but the ensuing cataract of genocide, enslavement, war and epidemics reduced the indigenous population to fewer than 6 million by the mid-1600s. A slow demographic recovery began in South America a hundred years later, though mass deaths among First Nations have never truly ceased. But the de-peopling of the New World meant millions of hectares of maize, potato, squash and other crops lay fallow in the seventeenth century. Forest encroached on abandoned fields. Much of the verdant splendour of the New World that awed Europeans was the result of nature's reconquest of ancient agricultural land. Botanical regrowth on a bi-continental scale sequestered between 17 and 38 gigatonnes of carbon, lowering the store of atmospheric CO_2 by up to 10 parts per million (PPM). This was a significant share of the total CO_2 – then, 276 PPM; today, 411 PPM – and enough to lower temperatures in the northern hemisphere by 0.6°C.[3]

---

2 Geoffrey Parker, *Global Crisis: War, Climate Change, and Catastrophe in the Seventeenth Century,* New Haven, CT, 2013. The parameters of the Little Ice Age remain hotly disputed. See, inter alia, Emmanuel Le Roy Ladurie, *Les Fluctuations du climat de l'an mil à aujourd'hui,* Paris, 2011, and the discussion of Ladurie's work in Mike Davis, 'Taking the Temperature of History', NLR 110, March–April 2018.

3 Jed Kaplan et al., 'Holocene Carbon Emissions as a Result of Anthropogenic Land Cover Change', *Holocene,* vol. 21, no. 5, December 2010, pp. 775–91; R. J. Nevle et al., 'Neotropical Human–Landscape Interactions, Fire, and Atmospheric CO_2 during European Conquest', *Holocene,* vol. 21, no. 5, August 2010, p. 853.

The Little Ice Age not only provides insight into the far-reaching ecological repercussions of colonialism, it also hints at the possible democratization of Natural Geo-Engineering – accelerating carbon sequestration through natural processes, as a means of safely ameliorating climate change.[4] A rival approach, Artificial Geo-Engineering, would put iron filings or limestone into the oceans and aerosols into the skies to reflect sunlight into space. Given the complexity of the global climate system, this tinkering is terribly risky even if increasingly likely. In a future closer than one expects, entrepreneurial scientists and their private corporations will aim to fire aerosols into the atmosphere by means of artillery, high-flying aeroplanes or balloons. Real-life experiments, despite their illegality, have already been carried out and patents sought.[5] In contrast with this, giving up territory to nature through democratic choice is a safe way to counteract carbon pollution with unambiguously beneficial environmental multiplier effects.

However, Natural Geo-Engineering requires a lot of land. The mere thought of recreating a bloodless second Little Ice Age to avert a climate catastrophe restores the central role of land scarcity to economics after an absence of two centuries. For as it happens, two other goals of the environmental movement – preserving biodiversity and switching to a zero-carbon energy system – also require expanses of continental scope. There are many reasons to forsake nuclear power and fossil fuels and embrace solar- and wind-based energy; but – outside very windy and sunny countries – the latter have extremely low 'power densities'. Power density describes the relationship between energy produced or consumed relative to a system's surface area, measurable in watts per square metre. While the richest deposits of fossil fuels can have power densities near 20,000 W/m^2, even shabby ones like Alberta's tar sands have a power density of 1,000 W/m^2. This is why only half of one per cent of US territory is dedicated to the 'business as usual' energy system.[6] In contrast, the highest power density for solar- and wind-powered infrastructure seems to be about 10 W/m^2, and it is often less than half of that in

---

4   Oswald Schmitz, 'How "Natural Geo-Engineering" Can Help Slow Global Warming', *Yale e360*, 25 January 2016.

5   See Clive Hamilton, *Earthmasters: The Dawn of the Age of Climate Engineering*, New Haven, CT, 2013, pp. 74–84; Philip Mirowski, *Never Let a Serious Crisis Go to Waste*, London, 2013, pp. 325–58.

6   See Vaclav Smil, *Power Density*, Cambridge, MA, 2015, p. 247. A notable exception to this is Appalachian mountain-top removal, which has a power density 'well below' 100 W/m^2: p. 107.

sub-par locations. A fully renewable system would probably occupy one hundred times more land than a fossil-fuel-powered one. In the case of the US, between 25 and 50 per cent of its territory, and in a cloudy, densely populated country such as the UK, *all* of the national territory might have to be covered in wind turbines, solar panels and biofuel crops to maintain current levels of energy production. While ongoing tinkering will improve renewable-energy systems, they will never have the power densities of fossil fuels.[7] It is land scarcity, rather than rare natural resources, that is the ultimate limit to economic growth: energy consumption *must* be cut.

In addition to averting Artificial Geo-Engineering and curtailing fossil-fuel use, perhaps the third most pressing goal of the contemporary global environmentalist movement is to forestall the 'Sixth Extinction'.[8] The current haemorrhaging of flora and fauna species is occurring at a rate one thousand to ten thousand times faster than normal; a speed comparable only to the last great extinction 66 million years ago, when a huge asteroid careened into the earth and set off the volcanic eruptions of the Deccan Traps.[9] Even if the explosion of present-day extinctions remains a quiet catastrophe, it will ultimately prove to be no less deadly to life on Earth. The principal cause of extinction is habitat loss, as underlined by the recent work of E. O. Wilson. Though notorious in the Reagan era as the genetic-determinist author of *Sociobiology*, Wilson is first and foremost a naturalist and conservationist. He estimates that, with a decrease of habitat, the sustainable number of species in it drops by roughly the fourth root of the habitable area. If half the habitat is lost, approximately a tenth of species would disappear, but if 85 per cent is destroyed, then half the species would be extinguished. Humanity is closely tracking this equation's deadly curve: half of all species are expected to disappear by 2100. The only way to prevent this is to leave enough land for other living beings to flourish, which has led Wilson to call for a utopian programme of creating a 'half

---

7 Even eco-optimists, such as Mark Jacobson, assume underwhelming rates of power density for renewables, with only 9 W/m² for wind: Mark Jacobson et al., 'The United States Can Keep the Grid Stable at Low Cost with 100% Clean, Renewable Energy in all Sectors Despite Inaccurate Claims', *PNAS*, vol. 114, no. 26, June 2017.

8 Elizabeth Kolbert, *The Sixth Extinction: An Unnatural History*, New York, 2014.

9 J. M. de Vos et al., 'Estimating the Normal Background Rate of Species Extinction', *Conservation Biology*, vol. 29, no. 2, April 2015, pp. 452–62. Paul Renne et al., 'State Shift in Deccan Volcanism at the Cretaceous-Paleogene Boundary, Possibly Induced by Impact', *Science*, vol. 350, no. 6,256, October 2015, pp. 76–8.

earth', where 50 per cent of the world would be left as nature's domain. Even though much has been lost, he argues that thirty especially rich biomes, ranging from the Brazilian *cerrado* to the Polish–Belarussian Białowieża Forest, could provide the core of a biodiverse, interconnected mosaic extending over half the globe.[10] Yet, at present only 15 per cent of the world's land-area has some measure of legal protection, while the fraction of protected areas in the oceans is even smaller – less than 4 per cent.

Arguably, it is a virtue that these three goals – Natural Geo-Engineering, renewable-energy systems and 'half-earth' habitat protection – are so land-hungry: constraint clarifies thought, and there are simply very few ways to find sufficient space. Furthermore, a focus on land scarcity also reveals new connections and opportunities; after all, cuts in consumption are needed to provide space for both wind farms and rewilded ecosystems, and the latter require a high degree of biodiversity to function effectively as carbon sinks, yet their ability to be effective carbon sinks depends on a rapid transition to renewable-energy systems before climate change irreversibly undermines the integrity of ecosystems. Once land is reclaimed as an integral economic category, and goals of natural preservation and global economic equality are championed, then suddenly a new red–green political economy emerges. What follows, then, explores what such a programme would involve, initially by way of an extended thought-experiment. Extrapolated from the three fundamental aims of Natural Geo-Engineering, biodiversity and renewable-energy systems, the project might take on any number of mantles: 'egalitarian eco-austerity', 'eco-socialism' or, borrowing from Wilson, 'half-earth economics', to emphasize both the necessary scale of ambition and its crucial spatial aspect. First, though, a critical look at some of the most salient alternatives: the 'steady state' of Herman Daly's ecological economics and the possibilities for technological solutions.

Cap-and-trade equilibrium?

In contrast to a strong 'half-earth' programme, Daly's proposals for an ecologically sustainable 'steady-state' economy appear all too modestly reformist, risking capture by neoliberal environmentalism. Repudiating the universal capitalist goal of economic growth – 'growthmania',

---

10   E. O. Wilson, *Half-Earth: Our Planet's Fight for Life*, New York, 2016, pp. 136–51.

in his terms – Daly defines a steady-state economy as one that does not increase in size relative to the overall ecosphere, of which it is a sub-system: the material 'throughput' would remain constant in terms of resources consumed, although the output might improve in quality. The path towards it involves a three-part programme. First, 'depletion quotas', to limit resource use – these would be auctioned by the state, raising public revenues. Second, income redistribution, by way of a maximum-income cap and a minimum-income floor, to limit inequality. Third, a one-child-per-parent cap on human reproduction, regulated through tradable vouchers – the argument being that this would combine aggregate population control with a measure of individual choice. 'Environmental impact is the product of the number of people times per capita resource use', Daly argues, so a steady-state ecological-economic strategy would require both population and resource depletion to be held constant.

Daly's critique of 'growth fetishism' and the macroeconomic pursuit of rising GDP implies that capitalists could be persuaded not to pursue economic expansion. But growth is not the result of a misguided cultural notion. Capitalism is a novel system, emerging only in the early modern era and pitting rival capitals against each other, such that profit-making is a structural imperative, not merely an option. Capital must complete its circuit through the commodity form greater than when it started or there will be a crisis. Profitability, not abstract measurements like GDP, is what matters. The latter's late arrival in the history of capitalism hints that it is mere foam, while the struggle to maintain profitability goes on in the churning depths.[11] Daly underestimates the difficulties of shackling capitalism so as to slow it down.

Despite the egalitarian gesture of restricted income inequality, his approach essentially relies on the market to regulate 'growthmania' – a contradiction in terms. In his steady-state world, the rich would be licensed to breed, while the poor might have to trade their right to a child for the means of subsistence – echoes of Cold War eugenicism. Though 'depletion quotas' would be auctioned by the state, functioning as a sort of extraction tax, their actual operation under conditions of cartelized energy giants and captive state administrations would be no different from current programmes of 'cap and trade', as Daly acknowledges. The cap-and-trade concept was devised in 1968 by

---

11   Adam Tooze, *Statistics and the German State, 1900–1945: The Making of Modern Economic Knowledge,* Cambridge, 2001; Robert Collins, *More: The Politics of Economic Growth in Postwar America*, Oxford, 2002.

John Dales, an economist at the University of Toronto and a Chicago School fellow-traveller, to deal with the environmental degradation of the Great Lakes.[12] He proposed that rather than simply dictate industrial standards, it would be more efficient to impose a limit, or 'cap', on emissions and then have industries buy and trade pollution-permits among themselves. Cleaner factories, for example, could sell permits to dirtier ones, if the latter wanted to avoid upgrades. Dales's idea has proven to be incredibly versatile, seemingly applicable to any environmental problem, including over-fishing, acid rain, climate change and biodiversity loss.

Daly is attracted to cap-and-trade for two reasons. First, it seems to offer a means to impose a 'steady state' – represented by the 'cap' – while still relying on the market to distribute goods efficiently. Second, it provides a way to theoretically reconcile the economy and nature – a problem which has absorbed Daly's attention since he famously doodled the sphere of the 'economy' enclosed by the world's 'ecosystem'. However, cap-and-trade doesn't overcome the binary of nature and the economy; it simply renders the former in market terms, deeming it 'natural capital'. This is why neoliberals admire Daly's solution, just as they admired its neo-classical predecessor, Pigou's 'externalities'. Turning nature into 'natural capital' makes it *easier* to exploit; insisting on the non-fungibility of certain parts of nature by placing it beyond the economy's reach is its surest defence.[13]

Cap-and-trade is the point where the arc of Daly's optimism intersects with the neoliberals' downward-sloping cynicism, for not only does cap-and-trade rarely work, sometimes it is not even intended to. The world's biggest cap-and-trade programme for CO_2 emissions, the European Emissions Trading System (ETS), has largely functioned to forestall meaningful action against climate change since its creation in 2005. At its nadir, in 2013, a tonne of carbon fetched less than €3, and even at the moment of writing (early May 2018) the price is only €10 per tonne. This is a far cry from an effective price for carbon – ExxonMobil estimates that the price would need to be $2,000 per tonne for global warming to be limited to 1.6 degrees centigrade.[14] Even carbon capture and sequestration (CCS) projects need $80 to 150 per tonne to break even, which is why CCS has proven to be such an

---

12   John Dales, *Pollution, Property and Prices,* Toronto, 1968.

13   Andreas Malm makes a similar point in *The Progress of this Storm*, London, 2018.

14   Natasha Lamb and Bob Litterman, 'Tell the Truth, ExxonMobil: A Low-Carbon Future Is Affordable – and Necessary', *Guardian*, 31 January 2016.

unimpressive technology.[15] The problem originated from the European Union's decision to placate industry by setting the number of permits too high, so ensuring prices would remain low. Daly's framework does not address the problem of the class capture of markets.

Furthermore, markets seek markets. With cap-and-trade, money that might have been used productively to alter the energy infrastructure instead, as Philip Mirowski has observed, gets pumped into 'yet another set of speculative financial instruments, leading to bubbles, distortions of capital flows, and all the usual symptoms of financialization'.[16] A similar tactic of delay and destroy can be detected in the burgeoning market for 'biodiversity offsets', a cap-and-trade policy engineered by mining companies in the early 2000s.[17] Potemkin technocracies of this sort are a dead end for the environmentalist movement.

Coal and other questions

As Daly stresses, classical political economy operated with a strong sense of the material limits of land and resources. In *The Coal Question* (1865), William Stanley Jevons – who used the language of Smith and Ricardo while simultaneously introducing marginalist techniques – carefully distinguished between coal's exhaustion in a physical sense and in an economic one, where the cost of extraction would exceed the utility of the coal itself.[18] For a brief period after 1945, petroleum appeared to buck both those limits. First, as Timothy Mitchell notes, oil declined continuously in price – 'although increasing quantities of energy were consumed, the cost of energy did not appear to represent a limit to growth.' Second, 'thanks to its relative abundance and the ease of shipping it across oceans, oil could be treated as something inexhaustible.'[19] While oil-price illusions were shattered by the 1973 OPEC embargo, there still remains a centuries-long total reserve of hydrocarbons, sufficient to fry the planet. Indeed, if there is any chance of capping warming at 2°C, on

---

15   Sean Sweeney, *Hard Facts about Coal: Why Trade Unions Should Rethink Their Support for Carbon Capture and Storage*, New York, 2015, p. 8.

16   Mirowski, *Never Let a Serious Crisis Go to Waste*, pp. 339–40.

17   Sarah Benabou, 'Making Up for Lost Nature: A Critical Review of the International Development of Voluntary Biodiversity Offsets', *Environment and Society*, vol. 5, 2014, pp. 103–23.

18   William Stanley Jevons, *The Coal Question*, London, 1865, Preface, p. 2.

19   Timothy Mitchell, 'Carbon Democracy', *Economy and Society*, vol. 38, no. 3, August 2009, p. 418.

one authoritative estimate three-quarters of fossil-fuel reserves will have to stay in the ground.[20]

Yet even if capitalism is not confronted with an absolute dearth of fossil fuels, it faces the problem predicted by Jevons 150 ago of rapidly increasing marginal costs. In the nineteenth century, the best reserves allowed the retrieval of a hundred barrels for every one used for extraction; an energy return on investment (EROI) of 100:1. The US, long the world's largest producer, still had an energy return of 100:1 in the 1930s, but four decades later this had dropped to 30:1.[21] Already by the 1960s, ultra-cheap Middle Eastern and US petroleum was being supplemented by more expensive production in Siberia, the North Sea, Alaska and the Gulf of Mexico. Since the 1990s, production at many of these second-tier deposits has begun to decline, leading to a new round of exploring ever more marginal reserves. Today's best prospects for future growth, US 'fracked' petroleum and Alberta's tar sands, have the measly energy-return rates of 7:1 and 3:1, respectively.[22] It can't get much lower than this. Nevertheless, 'Peak Oil' in terms of conventional petroleum occurred in 2005, suggesting that the future will resemble Alberta more than Al-Ghawār. Engineers in the Canadian tar sands have been busy sharing their expertise with US, Israeli, Venezuelan, Malagasy, Trinidadian and Chinese counterparts.[23] Relative to conventional petroleum, non-conventional fuel creates more pollution when it is extracted and is much more dangerous to transport, as was manifested by the fire-bombed Québécois town of Lac-Mégantic in 2013 and the desecration of the Kalamazoo River a few years earlier. The massive permanent toxic tailings lakes in Alberta and water-tables contaminated by secret proprietary fracking solvents will multiply globally as the industry transitions from conventional to non-conventional fossil fuels.[24]

---

20 Christophe McGlade and Paul Ekins, 'The Geographical Distribution of Fossil Fuels Unused When Limiting Global Warming to 2°C', *Nature*, vol. 517, pp. 187–90, January 2015.

21 Ugo Bardi et al., 'Modelling eroi and Net Energy in the Exploitation of Non-Renewable Resources', *Ecological Modelling*, vol. 223, no. 1, December 2011, pp. 54–8.

22 Rachel Nuwer, 'Oil Sands Mining Uses up Almost as Much Energy as It Produces', *Inside Climate News*, 19 February 2013.

23 John L. Hallock Jr et al., 'Forecasting the Limits to the Availability and Diversity of Global Conventional Oil Supply', *Energy*, vol. 64, January 2014, p. 130; MacDonald Stainsby, 'New Beginnings: Tar Sands Prospecting Abroad', in Toban Black et al., eds, *A Line in the Tar Sands*, Toronto, 2014, pp. 101–8.

24 The train that destroyed Lac-Mégantic was carrying fracked petroleum, laced with explosive chemicals. Jacquie McNish and Grant Robertson, 'The Deadly Secret

Nor will the seemingly greenest conventional substitutes suffice, for hydropower and methane (i.e., natural gas) are not nearly as 'clean' as advertised. When a forest is flooded to create a dam's reservoir, carbon dioxide is released from the decomposing trees. Algae growth is catalysed by the silt trapped by the dam, creating massive emissions of methane. Some hydropower projects actually produce more greenhouse gas emissions than a fossil-fuel-fired plant would.[25] In addition, dams entail significant destruction of habitats and loss of species. It is worth noting that Mark Jacobson and his co-authors shy from adding new dams to their model because of these costs.[26] The power density of dams can be quite low – an order of magnitude lower than solar or wind-power – if placed on the middle or lower reaches of a river. Ghana's Akosombo Dam has a power density of only 0.1 W/m^2, leading its reservoir to gobble up 4 per cent of the country's landmass.[27] Methane too loses its lustre as a 'bridge fuel' upon closer examination. Fracking has been credited with reducing carbon pollution in the US, as cheaper methane-fired power plants have replaced coal-fired rivals. But this overlooks the fact that, while carbon emissions declined over the dozen years after 2002, any benefit was undone by increased methane pollution, which rose by a third. Although methane decomposes more quickly than carbon dioxide, its 'greenhouse' effect is a hundred times greater in the short term, thirty times greater in the medium term. This is why only a tiny percentage needs to leak before any environmental advantage is nixed. The actual leakage rate is quite high, possibly even 9 per cent.[28]

If no rapid transition away from coal, methane and petroleum is on the cards, then Artificial Geo-Engineering, a dangerous and once-ostracized technology, becomes increasingly likely. It already has

behind the Lac-Mégantic Inferno', *Globe and Mail*, 3 December 2013; Elizabeth McGowan and Lisa Song, 'The Dilbit Disaster: Inside the Biggest Oil Spill You've Never Heard Of', *Inside Climate News*, 26 June 2012; Gillian Steward, 'Tailings Ponds a Toxic Legacy of Alberta's Oilsands', *Toronto Star*, 4 September 2015.

25   Duncan Graham-Rowe, 'Hydroelectric Power's Dirty Secret Revealed', *New Scientist*, 24 February 2005; Bridget Deemer et al., 'Greenhouse Gas Emissions from Reservoir Water Surfaces', *BioScience*, vol. 66, no. 11, 1 November 2016, pp. 949–64.

26   Mark Jacobson, '100% Clean and Renewable Wind, Water, and Sunlight All-Sector Energy Roadmaps for 139 Countries of the World', *Joule*, 6 September 2017, p. 93.

27   Smil, *Power Density*, p. 73.

28   Bill McKibben, 'Global Warming's Terrifying New Chemistry', *Nation*, 23 March 2016; Nathan Phillips et al., 'Mapping Urban Pipeline Leaks', *Environmental Pollution*, vol. 173, February 2013, pp. 1–4.

the blessing of the Intergovernmental Panel on Climate Change. The probable consequences are dystopian sci-fi. 'Solar radiation management' will bleach the sky white, cause tens of thousands of deaths from aerosol pollution, gash the ozone layer and interrupt vital climatic systems like the monsoon and the Gulf Stream. Some of these risks are even acknowledged by its advocates; the world's leading geo-engineer, David Keith, admits that the closest analogue to Artificial Geo-Engineering is nuclear weapons. It is appropriate that the natural habitat of this technology is in Alberta. In the 2000s, Keith was teaching at the University of Calgary; both the institution and city have become inextricably linked to the tar-sands industry. To commodify his dangerous expertise he founded a firm, Carbon Engineering, which counts Bill Gates and tar-sands tycoon Murray Edwards as its billionaire patrons. Keith and his fellow thinkers were ostracized as dangerous quacks only a decade ago, but have become respectable through their embrace by the likes of Harvard (where Keith now teaches) and Oxford. Like nuclear waste, or the gargantuan tailings lakes of the tar-sands industry, Artificial Geo-Engineering will require millennia-long management. Should the 'climate shield' ever fail, if a war or some other disaster interrupts the aerosol cannons, then the world would rapidly overheat. Such an amplified geo-engineered summer could be as devastating to Earth life as a nuclear winter.

Atomic environmentalism

Nor is there much solace to be found in nuclear power, which is nowhere near as environmentally benign as its proponents claim. Studies of the life-cycle of CO_2 emissions of nuclear plants vary widely, since no one knows the total cost of decommissioning a nuclear reactor or permanently storing toxic waste.[29] One can, however, estimate the greenhouse-gas emissions required to process uranium fuel. The use of low-grade ore (<0.01 per cent) may create the same greenhouse-gas footprint as a methane-fired power plant, belying claims that nuclear is a carbon-neutral source of power. More startlingly, perhaps, the use of low-grade ore would give a nuclear-power plant an energy return on investment of 1:1 – literally not worth the effort. This is not an abstract problem: 37 per cent of global

---

29   Benjamin Sovacool, 'Valuing the Greenhouse Gas Emissions from Nuclear Power: A Critical Survey', *Energy Policy*, vol. 36, August 2008, pp. 2940–53. OECD, *Costs of Decommissioning Nuclear Power Plants,* Paris, 2016.

uranium reserves are found in deposits that are only half as rich (<0.005 per cent). Furthermore, the power density of nuclear plants varies tremendously, depending on the size of accompanying radioactive glacis and dedicated cooling lakes. While some projects have a fairly high power density, as Fukushima Daiichi did (1,300 W/m²), others are puny, like the Wolf Creek facility in Kansas (30 W/m²).[30] Economically, of course, nuclear plants are always white elephants: every kilowatt-hour produced by Hinkley Point C will cost double the wholesale rate – and this at a time when prices for wind and solar power continue to plunge.

There have been enough accidents over the past half-century to discredit nuclear power. Without detailing all of these, in their various shades of hubris and incompetence, examination of the most recent will suffice. The clean-up crews at the Fukushima Daiichi plant do not even know where the fuel rods of the three destroyed reactors actually *are*. Six hundred tonnes of still-fissioning uranium melted through their containment vessels and continue even now to sink deep into the earth beneath the plant. Five robots sent to look for the lost fuel rods 'died' during their mission, when radiation destroyed their wiring. The cleanup may take forty years or longer and cost $20 billion, while the total cost of the disaster is estimated at $188 billion.[31] Part of the reason why the destroyed plant is so difficult to clean is that it needs to be inundated daily with 150,000 litres of ocean water. In its early days, the deluge cooled and stabilized the damaged reactors, arresting the core's meltdown; without it, the radiation would have spread much farther, forcing the evacuation of up to 50 million people from Tokyo and its environs, a dislocation the Japanese prime minister compared to 'losing a huge war'.[32] The official stance of the government and the UN is that no one has died because of the disaster at Fukushima Daiichi, but this already defies belief. Some scientists have predicted that there will be 1,000 to 3,000 excess cancer deaths, a figure commensurate with the much smaller release of radioactivity compared to that of Chernobyl in 1986. It was not until twenty years later that the UN admitted there were any deaths at all as a result of the Chernobyl explosion, beyond the 50 in its early

---

30 Keith Barnham, 'False Solution: Nuclear Power Is Not "Low Carbon"', *Ecologist*, 5 February 2015; Smil, *Power Density*, pp. 146–7.

31 Aaron Sheldrick and Minami Funakoshi, 'Fukushima's Ground Zero', *Reuters*, 11 March 2016; Yuka Obayashi and Kentaro Hamada, 'Japan Nearly Doubles Fukushima Disaster-Related Cost to $188 Billion', *Reuters*, 8 December 2016.

32 Andrew Gilligan, 'Fukushima: Tokyo Was on the Brink of Nuclear Catastrophe, Admits Former Prime Minister', *Daily Telegraph*, 4 March 2016.

aftermath. Today, the most conservative estimates put the figure at 9,000.[33]

According to the 'largest statistical analysis of nuclear accidents ever undertaken', another disaster on the scale of Fukushima in 2011 or Chernobyl in 1986 has a 50 per cent chance of occurring before 2050.[34] Yet prominent greens, including George Monbiot, James Hansen and James Lovelock have lined up to declare their support for nuclear power. Monbiot became pro-nuclear *after* the meltdown at Fukushima Daiichi, reasoning that the result wasn't so bad despite the worst possible luck.[35] Writing with the geo-engineer Ken Caldeira, a collaborator of David Keith's, Hansen has called for the world to build a nuclear reactor every five days between now and 2050. These 2,135 new reactors would dwarf the current total of 440 and almost certainly inflate the peril of another meltdown.[36] Yet seemingly not content with the riskiness of common nuclear power, many atomic-environmentalists, including Monbiot, Hansen and Stewart Brand, advocate the even more untested and unstable variant of fast-breeder reactors, which can produce more fissile material than they consume, usually turning uranium or thorium into plutonium, a bomb material *par excellence*.[37] Liquid sodium is used as a coolant, but this has a snag: it combusts upon exposure to air. Most breeders spend nine-tenths of the time offline for repairs, since even the smallest leak causes a fire, making renewable-energy systems seem quite reliable.

---

33   See respectively Jan Beyea et al., 'Accounting for Long-Term Doses in World-wide Health Effects of the Fukushima Daiichi Nuclear Accident', *Energy and Environmental Science,* vol. 6, no. 3, 2013, pp. 1042–5; Frank von Hippel, 'The Radiological and Psychological Consequences of the Fukushima Daiichi Accident', *Bulletin of the Atomic Scientists,* vol. 67, no. 5, September 2011, pp. 27–36; WHO, 'Chernobyl: The True Scale of the Accident', 5 September 2005. Estimates of the number of deaths at Chernobyl vary between 9,000 and 93,000, the Greenpeace figure. Jim Green, 'The Chernobyl Death Toll', *Nuclear Monitor,* no. 785, 24 April 2014.

34   Spencer Wheatley et al., 'Of Disasters and Dragon Kings: A Statistical Analysis of Nuclear Power Incidents and Accidents', *Risk Analysis,* 22 March 2016.

35   George Monbiot, 'Why Fukushima Made Me Stop Worrying and Love Nuclear Power', *Guardian,* 21 March 2011. See also James Lovelock, 'We Have No Time to Experiment with Visionary Energy Sources', *Independent,* 24 May 2004.

36   James Hansen, Ken Caldeira et al., 'Nuclear Power Paves the Only Viable Path Forward on Climate Change', *Guardian,* 3 December 2015. At the 2017 UN Climate Change Conference in Bonn, Hansen shared the podium with Michael Shellenberger, president of the Breakthrough Institute, an outfit that supports 'market solutions', nuclear power and geo-engineering as means to overcome the climatic crisis.

37   Todd Woody, 'Stewart Brand's Strange Trip', *Yale360,* 22 December 2009; Fred Pearce, 'Are Fast-Breeder Reactors a Nuclear Power Panacea?', *Yale360,* 30 July 2012; Jim Green, 'Nuclear Fallacies', *CounterPunch,* 5 October 2017.

The only fast-breeder facility with a better track record was Russia's BN-600 reactor in Zarechny which, uniquely and terrifyingly, continued operating during *fourteen* liquid-sodium conflagrations over seventeen years. Although many trumpet the advantage of breeders in producing little toxic waste from spent fuel, they ignore the fact that the sodium coolant becomes radioactive after use.[38] After wasting $100 billion on decades of experimentation, governments in the US and Western Europe have mothballed their fast breeders. India is one of the few countries that currently has plans to build them, but less as unreliable power plants than as plutonium factories to arm thousands of nukes.[39]

Regreening the land

How would half-earthing work? First, it would be a political economy without the crutches of nuclear power or Artificial Geo-Engineering, which could not rely on economic growth to deal with its problems. Instead, it would have the advantages of a functioning ecosystem, stable climate and egalitarian social order. A sketch of what's envisaged must address three issues: cutting greenhouse-gas emissions as low as possible; finding sufficient land for both a half-earth rewilding programme and a massive expansion of renewable-energy systems; and offering the 'good life' to all.

Natural Geo-Engineering can influence the global climate system quite quickly. Reforestation has had a significant effect in the last decade or two, enough to forestall the worst of climate change's ill effects. The collapse of communist forestry and agriculture in the 1990s allowed the forests in Russia's European half to absorb more carbon, increasing by a third.[40] China, often regarded as bearing the brunt of globalization's environmental costs, actually has an extremely successful state-directed reforestation programme. In the last quarter of the twentieth century, the carbon sequestered by its forests increased fivefold. This was partly due to more tree plantations, but it was the expansion of protected wild forests that was particularly effective. Wild ecosystems generally sequester more carbon per hectare than

38   Thomas Cochran et al., 'It's Time to Give Up on Breeder Reactors', *Bulletin of the Atomic Scientists,* May 2010, pp. 50–6.

39   M. V. Ramana, 'A Fast Reactor at Any Cost', *Bulletin of the Atomic Scientists,* 3 November 2016.

40   Yude Pan et al., 'A Large and Persistent Carbon Sink in the World's Forests', *Science,* 19 August 2011, p. 989.

their managed equivalents.[41] Elsewhere, forests have endured a less happy fate. Rainforests, both the temperate sort found in British Columbia and the tropical kinds strung along the Equator, are capable of sequestering 200–600 tonnes of carbon per hectare – Californian redwood forests can contain an amazing 3,500 tonnes per hectare – and their preservation should be the centrepiece of any climate policy. Species diversity matters among plants, too, as more diverse ecosystems have been found to retain more carbon.[42] Tropical deforestation rates are increasing again, however, after a brief deceleration in the 1990s, with land grabs to establish palm plantations in Indonesia, and soybean and cattle farms in Brazil, the main drivers. Luckily, tropical forest can recover fairly quickly if given the chance.[43] Less studied but no less important are marine biomes. Sea grasses and other marine flora are especially promising means to mitigate climate change, because their weight adds up to less than a twentieth of one per cent of all terrestrial plant biomass, but potentially captures an equal amount of carbon. Marine meadows, however, urgently need protection as they are *the* most endangered ecosystem, facing an annual rate of depletion of 7 per cent.[44]

There isn't much time left to implement Natural Geo-Engineering, for many ecosystems are already on the brink of systemic failure. Wildfires in western North America have doubled their area in the past forty years, as the region has become drier and warmer. The glaciers in the Rocky Mountains that feed the region's many deltas, streams, lakes and bogs have shrunk, some by half in terms of volume. Canada's boreal forest is already close to transitioning from a carbon sink into a source of emissions.[45] The Amazon rainforest is so damp

---

41   Chunhua Zhang et al., 'Disturbance-Induced Reduction of Biomass Carbon Sinks of China's Forests in Recent Years', *Environmental Research Letters*, vol. 10, 2015, p. 3. Jingyun Fang et al., 'Changes in Forest Biomass Carbon Storage in China between 1949 and 1998', *Science*, vol. 292, 2001, p. 2320; Vaclav Smil, *Harvesting the Biosphere: What We Have Taken from Nature*, Cambridge, MA, 2012, p. 19.

42   Smil, *Harvesting the Biosphere*, pp. 18–19; Shiping Chen et al., 'Plant Diversity Enhances Productivity and Soil Carbon Storage', *PNAS*, 17 April 2018, vol. 115, no. 16, pp. 4027–32.

43   Do-Hyung Kim et al., 'Accelerated Deforestation in the Humid Tropics from the 1990s to the 2000s', *Geophysical Research Letters*, 7 May 2015, pp. 3495–501.

44   Nicola Jones, 'How Growing Sea Plants Can Help Slow Ocean Acidification', *Yale e360*, 12 July 2016. See also the report: Grid-Arendal, *Blue Carbon: The Role of Healthy Oceans in Binding Carbon*, Arendal, 2009.

45   Its annual intake of carbon is down by half compared to the 1990s: Pan et al., 'A Large and Persistent Carbon Sink', p. 989. Only 5 per cent of the boreal wetland needs to be drained to counteract any benefit of carbon sequestration by the forest as

because the trees themselves create their own regional climate; trapping water through transpiration contributes half of all rainfall in the forest. This works less well with fewer trees. As the Amazon rainforest has contracted it has endured unprecedented droughts in 2005, 2010 and 2015. If this trend worsens, the rainforest may become a savannah, and a huge source of carbon emissions.[46]

Effective Natural Geo-Engineering is inseparable from biodiversity, which itself is dependent on territoriality, and needs to be upheld in its own right. Kelp, for example, needs to be protected from herbivores by higher predators. The rebound of otter populations in the North Pacific reduced the number of sea urchins, allowing kelp forests to recover to the point where they now absorb a tenth of British Columbia's carbon emissions. Similarly, wolves protect the boreal forest from marauding caribou that would otherwise feed on bark, weakening trees. The great wildebeest herds of the Serengeti regulate the carbon cycle of that vast prairie, as their grazing prevents dead grass from accumulating as kindling for wildfires. Wildebeest herds have quadrupled since the mid-twentieth century, and the Serengeti has returned to its status as a huge carbon sink. Whales can also act as a geological force, accelerating the carbon cycle, delivering plankton from the ocean's surface to its depths through everyday acts of eating, diving and excreting. This mechanism would have a stronger effect if much-depleted whale populations returned to their natural levels.[47] It makes little sense to attempt to preserve biodiversity or to implement Natural Geo-Engineering without linking the two.

Natural Geo-Engineering would still be necessary even if a completely renewable-energy system were to emerge tomorrow, for certain processes still require fossil fuels and thus need to be offset by carbon sequestration. Even an eco-austere society will need steel and cement, if only for hundreds of thousands of wind turbines. For both of these, fossil fuels are indispensable ingredients. Cement production requires kilns at extremely high temperatures to create 'clinker', for which there is as yet no green alternative to coal; it is responsible for some 5 per cent of all greenhouse-gas emissions, about as much as the

a whole. See Peter Lee and Ryan Cheng, 'Bitumen and Biocarbon', Global Forest Watch Canada, Edmonton, 2009, p. 8.

46 Center for International Forestry Research, 'Amazon Forest Could Become an "Impoverished Savannah" under Climate Change', *Reuters*, 18 September 2014.

47 Schmitz, 'How "Natural Geo-Engineering" Can Help Slow Global Warming'; Joe Roman and James McCarthy, 'The Whale Pump: Marine Mammals Enhance Primary Productivity in a Coastal Basin', *PLOS ONE*, vol. 5, no. 10, 2010, p. e13255.

national emissions of Japan and Brazil combined.[48] Steel furnaces may eventually be electrified, but coke is still necessary to smelt limestone and iron ore. Charcoal, a potential biomass alternative, can produce enough heat but cannot bear the weight of metal and rock in the way that coke can.[49] About a third of steel currently produced every year comes from recycled scrap, a proportion that could be raised as overall production is reduced. Intercontinental trade and concourse will still depend to some extent on jet engines for planes and diesel for container ships, even though, with the onset of egalitarian eco-austerity, globalization would be a much reduced force.

Dimming the lights

Half-earthing will involve intensive eco-austerity in land and energy use. The 'Two Thousand Watt Society' proposed by Zürich's Federal Institute of Technology provides a useful starting point. The plan marries environmental and global-economic justice, for it would allow the poorest to double or triple their consumption, while requiring a commensurate reduction by the rich. The average US citizen uses 12,000 watts, or 288 kWh, per day, which is twice as much as a typical Western European, and a dozen times more than an Indian.[50] Once convergence at 2,000 watts has been established, it becomes much easier to fulfil other half-earthing goals, such as conversion to renewable energy. At the present rate of consumption, 6,000 watts per head, the entire land surface of Japan or Germany would have to be covered in solar panels or wind turbines; if this was reduced to 2,000 watts, then less than a third of the land would need to be taken up by renewable-energy systems. Environmentalist programmes have long been criticized for ossifying the inequality between the global North and South. Mahathir bin Mohamad rightly scolded delegates during

---

48   Amazingly, concrete is the most consumed material in the world after water, usage equivalent to about three tons per person every year. See Madeline Rubenstein, 'Emissions from the Cement Industry', *State of the Planet*, 9 May 2012. There is no low-carbon alternative to making clinker according to the Pembina Institute, 'Alternative Fuel Use in Cement Manufacturing: Implications, Opportunities and Barriers in Ontario', Toronto, 2014.

49   Smil, *Power Density*, p. 233.

50   Eberhard Jochem, ed., *Steps toward a Sustainable Development*, Zürich, 2006. In the 1980s the Brazilian environmentalist José Goldemberg argued for a quota of 1,000 watts; he was Brazil's secretary of the environment during the 1992 Earth Summit. See José Goldemberg et al., 'Basic Needs and Much More with One Kilowatt per Capita', *Ambio*, vol. 14, no. 4–5, 1985, pp. 190–200; José Goldemberg et al., *Energy for a Sustainable World*, New York, 1988.

the 1992 Rio Earth Summit: 'When the rich chopped down their own forests, built their poison-belching factories and scoured the world for cheap resources, the poor said nothing. Indeed they paid for the development of the rich. Now the rich claim a right to regulate the development of poor countries.' This charge of hypocrisy has prevented greens from building coalitions across international borders and between social movements, but the half-earthing adoption of the 2,000-watt framework would overcome this history of division.

Although a binding referendum in 2008 committed Zürich to becoming a 2,000-watt city by 2050, even the proponents of the goal baulk at the revolutionary implications of such a low global-energy quota, preferring to believe it will be achievable through greater energy efficiency, electrification and continued reliance on hydro-power. Yet gains from energy efficiency are unlikely to be so spectacular, and the effort will then almost certainly fail.[51] A further difficulty is that of Jevons's Paradox: greater efficiency tends to increase total consumption, because energy becomes relatively cheaper. Effective conservation can be achieved only through state regulation capping total use. Getting down to 2,000 watts cannot happen without sacrifice by consumers and planning by governments, implications that the Swiss have skirted so far.

A more realistic 2,000-watt society would be eco-austere. One would live in a 'passive' house that required little or no energy for heating or cooling, would eat vegan and rarely fly or drive a car, depending instead on free public transport, walking and cycling.[52] Many of these elements of an eco-austere life have matured in the womb of the old society itself, but they require a new political economy to realign them into a coherent whole. Alyssa Battistoni's work on recasting the care economy of teachers and health workers as the nucleus of a future zero-carbon society is exemplary in this

---

51   See François Maréchal et al., 'Energy in the Perspective of Sustainable Development: The 2,000 w Society Challenge', *Resources, Conservation and Recycling*, vol. 44, no. 3, June 2005, pp. 245–62; Thorsten Frank Schulz, 'Intermediate Steps Towards the 2,000-Watt Society in Switzerland: An Energy-Economic Scenario Analysis', PhD dissertation, ETH Zürich, 2007; Dominic Notter et al., 'The Western Lifestyle and Its Long Way to Sustainability', *Environmental Science and Technology*, vol. 47, no. 9, 2013, pp. 4014–21.

52   This echoes many of the recommendations in an influential synthetic review of the climate mitigation literature. Seth Synes and Kimberly Nicholas, 'The Climate Mitigation Gap: Education and Government Recommendations Miss the Most Effective Individual Actions', *Environmental Research Letters*, vol. 12, no. 7, July 2017.

regard. 'To put it plainly,' she writes, 'pink-collar jobs are green.' What would that society look like?

> In general, it will mean less work all around. But the kind of work that we'll need more of in a climate-stable future is work that's oriented toward sustaining and improving human life, as well as the lives of other species who share our world. That means teaching, gardening, cooking and nursing: work that makes people's lives better without consuming vast amounts of resources, generating significant carbon emissions, or producing huge amounts of stuff.[53]

Battistoni's vision could be supplemented by renewable energy, clean public transport and state action on housing – so far, only the municipality of Brussels requires all new construction to meet passive standards, as opposed to offering modest subsidies or supporting one-off experimental houses or neighbourhoods.[54]

Roads and urban sprawl are leading causes of ecosystem fragmentation; a serious reduction in car use would free up huge amounts of space. In many US cities, for example, approximately 60 per cent of municipal land area is dedicated to car use in the form of roads, car parks and easements.[55] Even if energy efficiency gains mean that cars are not as polluting as one might have expected, reducing their use is important to free up scarce land. Air travel will need to be rationed, too. Although planes have doubled their fuel efficiency since 1978, flying is the fastest growing sector of transportation and, in the short term, the greenhouse-gas pollution emitted by planes has an effect 20 times greater than all the world's cars, because of the sensitivity of the atmosphere's upper reaches.[56] Substitutes, such as solar-powered planes, will not be able to compete with kerosene-fuelled rivals for many decades. Here, there is no technological fix in sight.

---

53   Alyssa Battistoni, 'Living, Not Just Surviving', *Jacobin*, 15 August 2017.

54   Lenny Antonelli, 'How Brussels Went Passive', *Passive House+*, 26 October 2016. For a summary of international subsidy regimes, see Tom-Pierre Frappé-Sénéclauze et al., *Accelerating Market Transformation for High-Performance Building Enclosures*, Pembina Institute, Calgary, 2016, pp. 119–26.

55   Charlie Gardner, 'We Are the 25%: Looking at Street Area Percentages and Surface Parking', *Old Urbanist*, 12 December 2011.

56   Duncan Clark, 'The Surprisingly Complex Truth about Planes and Climate Change', *Guardian*, 9 September 2010.

Euthanize the carnivore

Agriculture is by far the most profligate sector of the economy in its greenhouse-gas emissions and land-use; its expansion, especially over the past half-century, has had terrible effects. Most deforestation occurs when new land is opened up for ranching and plantations, a process responsible for one-eighth of greenhouse-gas production. Industrial agriculture is heavily dependent on fossil fuels for pesticides, mechanical equipment, fertilizers and irrigation. Much of its prodigious waste stems from raising and slaughtering billions of animals every year. The energy losses entailed in transmuting grain into animal flesh generally result in an efficiency of only 10 per cent, as is generally the case when trophic levels are crossed. If the US alone redirected the grains currently fed to livestock to human consumption, it could feed 800 million more people. Since extreme carnivorousness is closely linked to income, it is the bourgeois slivers of humanity that devour the lion's share of global meat production. The leading cause of the Sixth Extinction is manifest in the statistics of the world's terrestrial vertebrate biomass: one third is human, two-thirds is livestock, and only a few percentiles remain for all the world's wild animals.[57]

Food production would have to be completely transformed to realize the goals of half-earth economics, but this should be predicated on *less* technology, not more. Organic vegan agriculture can achieve yields comparable to industrial farming, though it requires more labour and a different diet.[58] If agriculture were to be deindustrialized and livestock farming eliminated, then emissions could be reduced and new swathes of land used for parks or energy facilities. Solar panels and wind turbines could largely overlap with cities and the remaining farms. Given that about half of all territory in Europe and the US is currently dedicated to agriculture – a ratio that would drastically shrink in a meatless society – this would free up enough land to achieve all the goals of half-earthing. The average omnivore

---

57   Nadia El-Hage Scialabba and Maria Müller-Lindenlauf, 'Organic Agriculture and Climate Change', *Renewable Agriculture and Food Systems*, vol. 25, no. 2, March 2010, pp. 158–69; 'US Could Feed 800 Million People with Grain that Livestock Eat, Cornell Ecologist Advises Animal Scientists', *Cornell Chronicle*, 7 August 1997; Smil, *Harvesting the Biosphere*, p. 299.

58   David Pimentel et al., 'Environmental, Energetic, and Economic Comparisons of Organic and Conventional Farming Systems', *BioScience*, vol. 55, no. 7, 2005, pp. 573–82.

requires 1.08 hectares to grow enough food for herself, but a vegan needs only 0.13 hectares.[59] Vegetarianism is a half-measure, as egg and cheese-eaters still need about 0.4 hectares per head.

It is from pasture, necessarily, that an eco-austere world will derive the land needed for Natural Geo-Engineering. Nearly half the world's non-mountainous land is already dedicated to agriculture. Of these 5 billion hectares, 3.5 billion are pasture, which vegans would not require at all, while of the remaining 1.5 billion dedicated to crops, 400 million are used to grow animal feed and 300 million for industrial purposes such as biofuels and bioplastics. Only 800 million hectares of land are devoted to growing food directly for people. One study estimates that if 800 million hectares of land were reforested, the billions of new trees would sequester 215 gigatonnes of carbon over the next century. Natural Geo-Engineering at this scale would decrease atmospheric carbon pollution at the scale of 85 PPM, bringing it to a much safer range in the low 300s PPM.[60] This feat would be relatively easy to accomplish in a mostly vegan world, even though a reforestation of this scale would be five times greater than the last massive rewilding during the Little Ice Age.

A global Cuba

There is cause for some optimism, however, for a great experiment in creating a nearly fossil-fuel-free society has already taken place. Cubans had to make do with much less in the 1990s during the *Período Especial*, when Soviet petroleum exports vanished along with the superpower itself. During the 1980s, known locally as the 'years of the fat cow', Cuba depended on a massive, industrialized, export-oriented sugar sector, grew few crops for sustenance and catered to extremely carnivorous tastes; its agriculture at the time was even more reliant on fossil-fuel inputs than its US counterpart. Due to the severity of US sanctions, far harsher than Saddam Hussein's Iraq ever faced, and the distortions introduced by two decades of Soviet 'support', Cuba's transition away from fossil fuels was a painful one, accomplished during a severe recession. But if this relatively poor and isolated island could refashion itself in this way, then no society

---

59   Christian Peters et al., 'Carrying Capacity of US Agricultural Land: Ten Diet Scenarios', *Elementa*, 22 July 2016.

60   Sebastian Sonntag et al., 'Reforestation in a High-CO$_2$ World – Higher Mitigation Potential than Expected, Lower Adaptation Potential than Hoped For', *Geophysical Research Letters*, vol. 43, 2016, p. 6548.

has an excuse for inaction. Indeed, despite economic contraction and the tightening of the US embargo, universal healthcare and education were maintained in Cuba.[61]

Getting by without petroleum or petroleum-based products (fertilisers and pesticides, for example) forced the largest and most compressed experiment in organic and urban gardening in history. The early 1990s saw the creation of 26,000 public gardens in Havana alone, turning the city into a big urban farm that supplied enough produce for about half of its nutritional needs. Although the notion will surely horrify work-shy futurists, the substitution of labour intensity for power intensity is in itself not a bad thing. If half-earthing were ever implemented, agriculture could usefully soak up unemployed workers from defunct industries that were dependent on high fossil-fuel consumption. During the *Período Especial,* Cuba bought over a million bicycles from China to replace the idle buses and cars. Eating less meat and more vegetables, combined with cycling or walking to get around led to improved health in the general population. Plantation monocultures could not be managed without massive fossil-fuel inputs, so Cubans cultivated less land more intensively, returning about a third of farmland to wilderness. This has helped Cuba maintain its incredible biodiversity (it is listed among Wilson's global hotspots) and led the World Wildlife Fund to recognize it as the world's *only* 'sustainable' country.[62] With its effective and low-cost social policy and post-fossil-fuel economy, the experience of Cuba in the 1990s offers the outline of a feasible, eco-egalitarian half-earth society.

The argument for half-earthing is predicated upon the clear and present danger of nuclear power, Artificial Geo-Engineering and fossil fuels. Capitalism *can* continue 'business as usual', but only at an ever greater cost to nature and the world's poor. An effective and desirable

---

61 Julia Wright, 'The Little-Studied Success Story of Post-Crisis Food Security in Cuba', *International Journal of Cuban Studies,* vol. 4, no. 2, Summer 2012, p. 132; Emily Morris, 'Unexpected Cuba', NLR 88, July–August 2014. The major crisis of the period was the effect on eyesight caused by nutritional deficiencies, alleviated by mass distribution of vitamin supplements once diagnosed. Christina Mills, 'In the Eye of the Cuban Epidemic Neuropathy Storm', *MEDICC Review*, vo. 13, no. 1, January 2011, pp. 10–15.

62 Gustav Cederlof, 'A Farewell to Oil: Low-Carbon Ecology and Social Power in Cuban Urban Agriculture', master's thesis, Lund University, 2013, p. 67; Sarah Boseley, 'Hard Times behind Fall in Heart Disease and Diabetes in 1990s Cuba', *Guardian*, 9 April 2013; Elisa Botella-Rodríguez, 'Cuba's Inward-Looking Development Policies: Towards Sustainable Agriculture', *Historia Agraria,* no. 55, December 2011, p. 160; World Wildlife Fund, *Living Planet Report 2006*, Gland, 2006, p. 19.

half-earth political economy must offer a better life for most people. If egalitarian eco-austerity is to work, resources must be rationed for the sake of fairness and efficacy; asceticism cannot be a mere 'lifestyle choice'. An eco-austere life may mean fewer consumerist trifles and less work, but it would guarantee rights to shelter, healthcare, leisure and education. There is a vast literature on the uselessness of private consumption, beyond a certain point.[63] A solution to global environmental crises requires the humbling of the global bourgeoisie, the richest several hundred million. The bourgeoisie cannot pretend that the society they have created can solve its own problems; a green veneer would signify little in a biologically impoverished world with a corporate-controlled climate. While this minority must adjust to relatively modest living standards, the very same ceiling to their consumption would imply a greatly raised floor for the majority. Most importantly, this egalitarian limit would protect the global climate system that everyone depends upon and preserve millions of other species.

To avert a neoliberal future that would entail the desecration of irreplaceable biomes and the climatic system, the environmentalist left needs new concepts, goals and tactics, along with a realistic reckoning of sacrifices. This is a costly programme in terms of the land required – giving up half the world to nature – but it is a price worth paying to prevent capitalism from continuing to enrich a few million rentiers while impoverishing billions, and irrevocably turning the planet into a factory farm and garbage dump. It is only within an eco-austere society that Londoners may perhaps one day enjoy another Frost Fair: 'This transient scene, a Universe of Glass / Whose various forms are pictur'd as they pass / Here future Ages may with wonder view / And what they scarce could think, acknowledge true.'[64]

63   See Kim Humphery, *Excess: Anti-Consumerism in the West*, Hoboken, 2013.
64   *Bentley's Miscellany*, p. 134.

4

Degrowth vs a Green New Deal

ROBERT POLLIN

2018

Climate change necessarily presents a profound political challenge in the present historical era, for the simple reason that we are courting ecological disaster by not advancing a viable global climate-stabilization project.[1] There are no certainties about what will transpire if we allow the average global temperature to continue rising. But as a basis for action, we only need to understand that there is a non-trivial possibility that the continuation of life on Earth as we know it is at stake. Climate change therefore poses perhaps the ultimate 'what is to be done' question. There is no shortage of proposals for action, including, of course, the plan to do nothing at all advanced by Trump and his acolytes. In recent numbers of NLR, Herman Daly and Benjamin Kunkel have discussed a programme for a sustainable 'steady-state' economy, and Troy Vettese has proposed re-wilding as a means of natural geo-engineering. In this contribution, I examine and compare two drama-tically divergent approaches developed by analysts and activists on the left. The first is what I variously call 'egalitarian green growth' or a 'green new deal'.[2] The second has been termed 'degrowth' by its proponents.

1 I am grateful to John O'Neill at Manchester University for generously bringing me up to date on the degrowth literature, despite our differences on this question; Mark Lawrence of the Institute for Advanced Sustainability Studies, Potsdam, for sharing his current research findings on CO_2 removal proposals; and especially to Mara Prentiss at Harvard for patiently instructing me on the land-use requirements for building a 100 per cent renewable energy economy. A shorter version of this text appeared in the 'Debating Economics' strand of the *Review of Radical Political Economics*, vol. 51, no. 2, 2019.
2 My approach is developed in Robert Pollin, *Greening the Global Economy*, Cambridge, MA, 2015. Underlying the results in that monograph are two more detailed studies: Robert Pollin, Heidi Garrett-Peltier, James Heintz and Bracken Hendricks, *Green Growth*, Center for American Progress, 2014; and Robert Pollin, Heidi Garrett-Peltier, Heintz and Shouvik Chakraborty, *Global Green Growth*, UN

Versions of degrowth have been developed in recent work by Tim Jackson, Juliet Schor and Peter Victor. A recent collection, *Degrowth: A Vocabulary for a New Era*, offers a good representation of the range of thinking among degrowth proponents. As the editors put it: 'The foundational theses of degrowth are that growth is uneconomic and unjust, that it is ecologically unsustainable and that it will never be enough.'[3] As is evident from the fifty-one distinctly themed chapters in their collection, degrowth addresses a much broader range of questions than climate change alone. In fact, as I will discuss, a major weakness of the degrowth literature is that, in concerning itself with such broad themes, it gives very little detailed attention to developing an effective climate-stabilization project. This deficiency was noted by Herman Daly himself, without question a major intellectual progenitor of the degrowth movement, in his interview with Benjamin Kunkel. Daly said he was 'favourably inclined' towards degrowth, but nevertheless demurred that he was 'still waiting for them to get beyond the slogan and develop something a little more concrete.'

Let's dispose of some red herrings at the outset. First, I share virtually all the values and concerns of degrowth advocates. I agree that uncontrolled economic growth produces serious environmental damage, along with increases in the supply of goods and services that households, businesses and governments consume. I also agree that a significant share of what is produced and consumed in the current global-capitalist economy is wasteful, especially by high-income people. It is obvious that growth per se, as an economic category, makes no reference to the distribution of the costs and benefits of an expanding economy. As for Gross Domestic Product as a statistical construct, aiming to measure economic growth, there is no disputing that it fails to account for the production of environmental bads, as well as consumer goods. It does not account for unpaid labour, most

---

Industrial Development Organization and Global Green Growth Institute, 2015. Further country-specific studies are Robert Pollin and Shouvik Chakraborty, 'An Egalitarian Green Growth Program for India', *Economic and Political Weekly*, vol. 50, no. 42, 17 October 2015, pp. 38–51; Robert Pollin, Heidi Garrett-Peltier and Shouvik Chakraborty, 'An Egalitarian Clean Energy Investment Program for Spain, 2015, Political Economy Research Institute Working Paper no. 390; and Amanda Page-Hoongrajok, Shouvik Chakraborty and Robert Pollin, 'Austerity vs Green Growth for Puerto Rico,' *Challenge*, 2017, vol. 60, no. 6, pp. 543–73. Unless otherwise indicated, the research findings that I report here can be found in these references.

3 Giacomo D'Alisa, Frederico Demaria and Giorgos Kallis, *Degrowth: A Vocabulary for a New Era*, London, 2015, p. 6.

of which is performed by women, and GDP per capita tells us nothing about the distribution of income or wealth.

One further general point. Introducing his NLR interview with Daly, Kunkel states that 'fidelity to GDP growth amounts to the religion of the modern world'. A large number of degrowth proponents express similar views. This perspective makes the critical error of ignoring the reality of neoliberalism in the contemporary world. Neoliberalism became the predominant economic-policy model with the military coup of Pinochet in Chile in 1973, and the elections of Thatcher in 1979 and Reagan in 1980. It has been clear for decades that, under neoliberalism, the real religion is maximizing profits for business in order to deliver maximum incomes and wealth for the rich. The financialization of the global economy under Wall Street's firm direction has been central to the neoliberal project. As is well known, the concentration of income and wealth in the advanced economies has proceeded apace under neoliberalism even while average economic growth has fallen to less than half the rate that was sustained during the initial postwar 'golden age of capitalism' that ended in the mid-1970s. If economic growth were really the 'religion of the modern world', then its high priests would be concentrating on how to put capitalism back on the leash that prevailed during the 'golden age' rather than on consolidating the victories achieved under neoliberalism.[4]

Returning to climate change, it is in fact absolutely imperative that some categories of economic activity should now grow massively – those associated with the production and distribution of clean energy. Concurrently, the global fossil-fuel industry needs to contract massively – that is, to 'degrow' relentlessly over the next forty or fifty years until it has virtually shut down. In my view, addressing these matters in terms of their specifics is more constructive in addressing climate change than presenting broad generalities about the nature of economic growth, positive or negative. I develop these points in what follows.

Absolute decoupling

To make real progress on climate stabilization, the single most critical project is to cut the consumption of oil, coal and natural gas dramatically and without delay. The reason why this is so crucial is because producing and consuming energy from fossil fuel is responsible for

---

4 This 'unleashing' of capitalism through the ascendance of neoliberalism is powerfully documented in the late Andrew Glyn's *Capitalism Unleashed,* Oxford, 2006.

generating about 70 per cent of the greenhouse gas emissions that are causing climate change. Carbon dioxide emissions from burning coal, oil and natural gas alone produce about 66 per cent of all greenhouse gas emissions, with another 2 per cent caused mainly by methane leakages during extraction. The most recent worldwide data from the International Energy Agency (IEA) indicate that global CO_2 emissions were around 32 billion tons in 2015.[5] The reports of the Intergovernmental Panel on Climate Change (IPCC), which provide conservative benchmarks for what is required to stabilize the average global temperature at no more than 2°C above the pre-industrial average, suggest that global CO_2 emissions need to fall by about 40 per cent within twenty years, to 20 billion tons per year, and by 80 per cent as of 2050, to 7 billion tons.[6]

The global economy is nowhere near on track to meet these goals. Overall global emissions rose by 43 per cent between 2000 and 2015, from 23 to 32 billion tons per year, as economies throughout the world continued to burn increasing amounts of oil, coal and natural gas to produce energy. According to the IEA's 2017 forecasting model, if current global policies remain on a steady trajectory through 2040, global CO_2 emissions will rise to 43 billion tons per year. The IEA also presents what it terms a 'New Policies' forecast for 2040, with the global 'new policies' corresponding closely to the agreements reached at the UN-sponsored 2015 Paris Climate Summit. Coming out of the conference, all 196 countries formally recognized the grave dangers posed by climate change and committed to substantially lowering their emissions. Nevertheless, the IEA estimates that, under its New Policies scenario, global CO_2 emissions will still rise to 36 billion tons per year as of 2040. Moreover, the IEA's forecast takes no account of the fact that the Paris commitments were non-binding on the signatory governments, nor that the United States under Trump has renounced the agreement. In short, there is at present nothing close to an international project in place capable of moving the global economy onto a viable climate-stabilization path.[7]

---

5 International Energy Agency, *World Energy Outlook 2017*, OECD/IEA, pp. 650–1.

6 The IPCC presents its benchmarks in terms of ranges and probabilities, but this would be a fair summary of its *Fourth Assessment Report* (2007) and *Fifth Assessment Report* (2014), both available from the IPCC website.

7 These projections refer only to net increases in CO_2 emissions through the ongoing combustion of fossil fuels. The climate-stabilization project becomes more challenging still once we recognize that a significant share of the accumulated stock of CO_2 in the atmosphere will need to be removed – that is, the CO_2 removal rate will

People still need to consume energy – to light, heat and cool buildings; to power cars, buses, trains and planes; to operate computers and industrial machinery, among other uses. As such, to make progress towards climate stabilization requires a viable alternative to the existing fossil-fuel infrastructure for meeting the world's energy needs. Energy consumption, and economic activity more generally, therefore need to be *absolutely decoupled* from the consumption of fossil fuels – that is, fossil-fuel consumption will need to fall steadily and dramatically in absolute terms, even while people must still be able to consume energy resources to meet their various demands. The more modest goal of *relative decoupling* – through which fossil-fuel consumption and CO_2 emissions continue to increase, but at a slower rate than GDP growth – is therefore not a solution. Economies can continue to grow – and even grow rapidly, as in China and India – while still advancing a viable climate-stabilization project, as long as the growth process is absolutely decoupled from fossil-fuel consumption. In fact, between 2000 and 2014, twenty-one countries, including the US, Germany, the UK, Spain and Sweden, all managed to absolutely decouple GDP growth from CO_2 emissions – that is, GDP in these countries expanded over this fourteen-year period, while CO_2 emissions fell.[8] This is a positive development, but only a small step in the right direction.

Basics of a green new deal

The core feature of the Green New Deal needs to be a worldwide programme to invest between 1.5 and 2 per cent of global GDP every year to raise energy-efficiency standards and expand clean renewable-energy supplies. Through this investment programme, it becomes realistic to drive down global CO_2 emissions relative to today by 40 per cent within twenty years, while also supporting rising living standards and expanding job opportunities. CO_2 emissions could be eliminated altogether in forty to fifty years through continuing this clean-energy investment project at roughly the same rate of about 1.5

---

need to exceed gross emissions, at least by 2050. For careful discussions on this issue, see Mark Lawrence et al., 'Evaluating Climate Geoengineering Proposals in the Context of the Paris Agreement Temperature Goals', *Nature Communications*, vol. 9, 2018; and Kevin Anderson and Alice Bows, 'Beyond "Dangerous" Climate Change: Emission Scenarios for a New World', *Philosophical Transactions of the Royal Society*, vol. 369, no. 1934, January 2011, pp. 20–44.

8   Nate Aden, 'The Roads to Decoupling: 21 Countries Are Reducing Carbon Emissions while Growing GDP', World Resources Institute blog, 5 April 2016.

to 2 per cent of global GDP per year. It is critical to recognize that, within this framework, a higher economic growth rate will also accelerate the rate at which clean energy supplants fossil fuels, since higher levels of GDP will correspondingly mean a higher level of investment being channelled into clean-energy projects.

In 2016, global clean-energy investment was about $300 billion, or 0.4 per cent of global GDP. Thus, the increase in investments will need to be in the range of 1 to 1.5 per cent of global GDP – about $1 trillion at the current global GDP of $80 trillion, then rising in step with global growth thereafter – to achieve a 40 per cent emissions reduction within twenty years. The consumption of oil, coal and natural gas will also need to fall by about 35 per cent over this same twenty-year period – an average rate of decline of 2.2 per cent per year. Pursuing this same basic investment pattern beyond the initial twenty-year programme, along with the continued contraction of fossil-fuel consumption, could realistically achieve a zero-emissions standard within roughly the next fifty years. Of course, both privately owned fossil-fuel companies, such as ExxonMobil and Chevron, and publicly owned companies like Saudi Aramco and Gazprom have massive interests at stake in preventing reductions in fossil-fuel consumption; they also wield enormous political power. These powerful vested interests will have to be defeated.

Investments aimed at raising energy-efficiency standards and expanding the supply of clean renewable energy will also generate tens of millions of new jobs in all regions of the world. In general, building a green economy entails more labour-intensive activities than maintaining the world's current fossil fuel-based energy infrastructure. At the same time, unavoidably, workers and communities whose livelihoods depend on the fossil-fuel industry will lose out in the clean-energy transition. Unless strong policies are advanced to support these workers, they will face layoffs, falling incomes and declining public-sector budgets to support schools, health clinics and public safety. It follows that the global green-growth project must commit to providing generous transitional support for workers and communities tied to the fossil-fuel industry.

There are major variations in the emissions produced by burning oil, coal and natural gas. To produce a given amount of energy, natural gas will generate about 40 per cent fewer emissions than coal, and 15 per cent less than oil. It is therefore widely argued that natural gas can be a 'bridge fuel' to a clean-energy future, through switching to it from coal. Such claims do not withstand scrutiny. At best, an implausibly large 50 per cent global fuel switch to natural gas would reduce emissions by only 8 per cent. But even this calculation does not take account of the methane gas that leaks into the atmosphere when natural gas is extracted through fracking. Recent research has shown that when more than about 5 per cent of the gas extracted by fracking leaks into the atmosphere, the impact eliminates any environmental benefit from burning natural gas relative to coal. Various studies have reported a wide range of estimates as to what leakage rates have actually been in the United States, as fracking operations have grown rapidly. A recent survey puts that range between 0.18 and 11.7 per cent for different sites in North Dakota, Utah, Colorado, Louisiana, Texas, Arkansas and Pennsylvania. It would be reasonable to assume that if fracking expands on a large scale in regions outside the US, leakage rates would fall closer to the higher-end figures of 12 per cent, at least until serious controls were established. This would diminish, if not eliminate altogether, any emission-reduction benefits from a coal-to-natural gas fuel switch.[9]

For some analysts, 'clean energy' includes nuclear power and carbon capture and sequestration (CCS) technologies. Nuclear power does generate electricity without producing CO_2 emissions. But it also creates major environmental and public-safety concerns, which have only intensified since the March 2011 meltdown at the Fukushima Daiichi power plant in Japan. CCS presents hazards, too. These technologies aim to capture emitted carbon and transport it, usually through pipelines, to subsurface geological formations, where it would be stored permanently. But such technologies have not been proven at a commercial scale. The dangers of carbon leakage from flawed transportation and storage systems will only increase if CCS technologies are commercialized and operating under an incentive structure where maintaining safety standards will reduce profits. An appropriately cautious clean-energy transition programme requires investment in technologies that are well understood, already operating at large scale and, without question, safe.

---

9   Ramon Alvarez et al., 'Greater Focus Needed on Methane Leakage from Natural Gas Infrastructure', *Proceedings of the National Academies of Sciences,* vol. 109, no. 17, 9 April 2012; Joe Romm, 'Methane Leaks Wipe Out Any Climate Benefit of Fracking, Satellite Observations Confirm', *Think Progress,* 22 October 2014; Robert Howarth, 'Methane Emissions and Climactic Warming Risk from Hydraulic Fracturing and Shale Gas Development: Implications for Policy', *Energy and Emission Control Technologies,* vol. 3, 2015, pp. 45–54; and J. Peischl et al., 'Quantifying Atmospheric Methane Emissions from Oil and Natural Gas Production in the Bakken Shale Region of North Dakota', *Journal of Geophysical Research,* vol. 121, no. 10, 2016, pp. 6101–11.

Thus, the first critical project for a global green-growth programme is to dramatically raise energy-efficiency levels – that is, using less energy to achieve the same, or higher, levels of energy service through the adoption of improved technologies and practices. Examples include insulating buildings more effectively to stabilize indoor temperatures, driving more fuel-efficient cars – or, better yet, relying on well-functioning public-transport systems – and reducing the amount of energy wasted through generating and transmitting electricity, and through operating industrial machinery. Expanding energy-efficiency investment supports rising living standards because, by definition, it saves money for energy consumers. A major study by the US Academy of Sciences found that, for the US economy, 'energy-efficient technologies . . . exist today, or are expected to be developed in the normal course of business, that could potentially save 30 per cent of the energy used in the US economy while also saving money'. Similarly, a McKinsey study focused on developing countries found that, using existing technologies only, energy-efficiency investments could generate savings in energy costs in the range of 10 per cent of total GDP, for all low- and middle-income countries. In *Energy Revolution: The Physics and Promise of Efficient Technology*, Mara Prentiss argues further that such estimates understate the realistic savings potential of energy-efficiency investments.[10]

Raising energy-efficiency levels will generate 'rebound effects' – that is, increased energy consumption resulting from lower energy costs. But such rebound effects are likely to be modest within the context of a global project focused on reducing CO_2 emissions and stabilizing the climate. Among other factors, energy-consumption levels in advanced economies are close to saturation point in the use of home appliances and lighting – we are not likely to clean dishes more frequently because we have a more efficient dishwasher. The evidence shows that consumers in advanced economies are more likely to heat and cool their homes and drive their cars when they have access to more efficient equipment – but again, these increased consumption levels are usually modest. Average rebound effects are likely to be significantly larger in developing economies. It is critical, however, that all energy-efficiency gains be accompanied by complementary policies (as discussed below), including setting a price on

---

10 National Academy of Sciences, 'Real Prospects for Energy Efficiency in the United States', 2010; McKinsey & Co., 'Energy Efficiency: A Compelling Global Resource', 2010; Mara Prentiss, *Energy Revolution: The Physics and Promise of Efficient Technology,* Cambridge, MA, 2015, passim.

carbon emissions to discourage fossil-fuel consumption. Most significantly, expanding the supply of clean renewable energy will allow for higher levels of energy consumption without leading to increases in CO_2 emissions. It is important to recognize, finally, that different countries operate at widely varying levels of energy efficiency. For example, Germany presently operates at an efficiency level roughly 50 per cent higher than that of the United States. Brazil is at more than twice the efficiency level of South Korea and nearly three times that of South Africa. There is no evidence that large rebound effects have emerged as a result of these high efficiency standards in Germany and Brazil.

As for renewable energy, the International Renewable Energy Agency (IRENA) estimated in 2018 that, in all regions of the world, average costs of generating electricity with clean, renewable-energy sources – wind, hydro, geo-thermal, low-emissions bioenergy – are now roughly at parity with fossil fuels.[11] This is without factoring in the environmental costs of burning oil, coal and natural gas. Solar-energy costs remain somewhat higher on average but, according to IRENA, as a global-weighted average, solar photovoltaic costs fell by over 70 per cent between 2010 and 2017. Average solar photovoltaic costs are likely to fall to parity with fossil fuels as an electricity source within five years. Adnan Amin of IRENA summarizes the global cost trajectory: 'By 2020, all mainstream renewable power generation technologies can be expected to provide average costs at the lower end of the fossil-fuel cost range. In addition, several solar PV and wind power projects will provide some of the lowest-cost electricity from any source.'[12]

Land-use requirements

In the last number of NLR, Troy Vettese argued that it is unrealistic to expect that a global renewable-energy infrastructure could be the foundation for a viable climate-stabilization project because, at present consumption levels, it would take up enormous amounts of the earth's land surface. Vettese writes: 'A fully renewable system will

---

11   IRENA, *Renewable Capacity Statistics*, Abu Dhabi, 2018.
12   The figures I am citing from the 2018 IRENA study are for 'Levelized Costs of Electricity', which include levelized capital costs; fixed operations and maintenance; variable operations and maintenance, including fuel costs; transmission; and the capacity factor for the equipment in use. IRENA reports ICOE figures on a national, regional and global basis.

probably occupy a hundred times more land than a fossil-fuel-powered one. In the case of the US, between 25 and 50 per cent of its territory, and in cloudy, densely populated countries such as the UK and Germany, all of the national territory might have to be covered in wind turbines, solar panels and biofuel crops to maintain current levels of energy production.' Vettese's primary focus is not renewable energy and land use. Instead he presents an extended case for what he terms 'natural geo-engineering' as a climate solution, with global 'afforestation' being the main driver. This involves increasing forest cover or density in previously non-forested or deforested areas, with 'reforestation' – the more commonly used term – as one component. The case Vettese makes for afforestation is valuable, but it is undermined by his initial discussion of renewables and land use.

Vettese provides virtually no evidence to support his claims about the land-use requirements for renewables. In fact, his claims cannot be supported, as a review of the relevant evidence makes amply clear. A critical contribution here is Mara Prentiss's *Energy Revolution*, which offers a rigorous account. Focusing on the US economy to illustrate the main issues, Prentiss shows that, relying on existing solar technologies, the US could meet its entire energy consumption needs through solar energy alone, while utilizing just 0.8 per cent of the total US land area. If we allow that energy-efficient investment, as described above, can cut US per capita energy consumption by roughly 50 per cent over twenty years, this would then mean that solar energy could supply 100 per cent of US energy demand through utilizing 0.4 per cent of the country's total landmass. Moreover, with the US as a high-efficiency economy, more than half of the necessary surface area could be provided through locating solar panels on rooftops and parking lots throughout the country.[13] If this is taken into account, solar-energy sources using existing technologies could supply 100 per cent of US energy demand while consuming somewhere between 0.1 and 0.2 per cent of additional US land area.

Wind power does require more land. Prentiss estimates that wind power could provide 100 per cent of existing US energy demand through using 15 per cent of the country's land area. Again, assuming investment in energy efficiency lowers per capita energy consumption by half, then only 7.5 per cent of total US land area would be needed to produce 100 per cent of energy demand through wind power.

---

13 For a detailed analysis, see the US National Renewable Energy Research Laboratory study, *Rooftop Solar Photovoltaic Technical Potential in the United States*, 2016.

Further, wind turbines can be placed on land currently used for agriculture with only minor losses of agricultural productivity. The turbines would need to be located on about 17 per cent of the existing farmland to generate 100 per cent of US energy supply with high efficiency. Farmers should welcome this dual use of their land, since it would provide them with a major additional income source. At present, the states of Iowa, Kansas, Oklahoma and South Dakota generate more than 30 per cent of their electricity supply through wind turbines.

Of course, neither solar nor wind power need to be the sole energy source, in the US or elsewhere. The most effective renewable-energy infrastructure would combine solar and wind, along with geothermal, hydro and clean bioenergy as supplemental sources. Overall land-use requirements can be minimized through an integrated renewable-energy infrastructure. For example: roughly half of all US energy supply could be provided by solar panels on rooftops and parking lots, another 40 per cent by wind turbines mounted on about 7 per cent of US farmland and the remaining 10 per cent by geothermal, hydro and low-emissions bioenergy. This is without including contributions from solar farms in desert areas, solar panels mounted on highways or offshore wind projects, among other supplemental renewable-energy sources.

Moreover, it is through combining these sources that we can effectively address some of the real challenges in building a renewable-energy infrastructure: intermittency, transmission and storage. Intermittency refers to the fact that the sun does not shine and the wind does not blow twenty-four hours a day. Moreover, on average, different geographical areas receive different levels of sunshine and wind. As such, the solar and wind power that are generated in the sunnier and windier areas of the US – such as Southern California, Florida and the Midwest farm belt – will need to be stored and transmitted at reasonable cost to the less sunny and windy areas. Investments in advancing storage and transmission technologies therefore need to be included in the overall clean-energy investment programme of roughly 1.5 per cent of annual GDP.

It is true that conditions in the United States are more favourable than those in some other countries. Germany and the UK, the two countries cited by Vettese, have population densities seven or eight times greater than the US and receive less sunlight over the course of a year. As such, these countries, operating at high efficiency levels, would need to use about 3 per cent of their total land area to generate 100 per cent of their energy demand through domestically produced solar energy. Wind power would require a significant share of their land area. But here again, farmlands could be converted to dual use with only minor reductions in productivity. The UK and Germany could also supplement their solar and wind supply with domestically produced geothermal, hydro and clean bioenergy. Using cost-effective storage and transmission technologies, they could also import energy generated by solar and wind power in other countries, just as, in the United States, wind power generated in Iowa could be transmitted to New York City. Any such import requirements are likely to be modest. Both the UK and Germany are already net energy importers in any case. With respect to population density and the availability of sunlight to harvest, and factoring in likely global energy consumption levels over the next forty years, average requirements for renewables are much closer to those in the US than to Germany and the UK. Overall then, the work by Prentiss and others demonstrates that, in fact, requirements for land use present no constraint on developing a global clean-energy infrastructure.[14]

Vettese is correct to emphasize the importance of afforestation as a climate-stabilization project because forested areas naturally absorb significant amounts of CO_2. He does not present estimates as to how much of the CO_2 already accumulated in the atmosphere afforestation would be able to sequester, nor for how far it could offset newly generated emissions produced by ongoing fossil-fuel consumption. Recent analysis by Mark Lawrence and colleagues at the Institute for Advanced Sustainability Studies in Potsdam concluded that afforestation could realistically reduce CO_2 levels by between 0.5 and 3.5 billion tons per year through 2050, with the figure rising to 4 to 12 billion tons per year from 2051 to 2100.[15] As noted above, current global CO_2 emissions levels are at 32 billion tons per year, and the IEA estimates this figure rising through 2040, even if the Paris Agreement is fully implemented. As such, the figures provided by Lawrence demonstrate that afforestation can certainly serve as a critical complementary intervention within a broader clean-energy transition programme, because it is a natural and proven method of absorbing a significant share of the accumulated stock of CO_2 in the

---

14 The late David MacKay provided the most detailed arguments on the heavy land-use requirements associated with renewable energy in his *Renewable Energy without the Hot Air* (2009). But, as Prentiss has pointed out (private correspondence), some of MacKay's key assumptions – including those on solar conversion rates and costs – are significantly in error.

15 Lawrence et al., 'Evaluating Climate Geoengineering Proposals'.

atmosphere. But afforestation cannot bear the major burden of a viable climate-stabilization project in the absence of global clean-energy investments at the scale I have described above – that is, about 1.5 per cent of global GDP per year until emissions have been driven to near-zero within roughly forty years.

Job creation and a just transition

Countries at all levels of development will experience significant gains in job creation through clean-energy investments relative to maintaining their existing fossil-fuel infrastructure. Our research at the Political Economy Research Institute, cited below, has found this relationship to hold in Brazil, China, Germany, India, Indonesia, Puerto Rico, South Africa, South Korea, Spain and the United States. For a given level of spending, the percentage increases in job creation range from about 75 per cent in Brazil to 350 per cent in Indonesia. For India, we found that increasing clean-energy investments by 1.5 per cent of GDP every year for twenty years would generate a net increase of about 10 million jobs per year. This is *after* factoring in job losses resulting from retrenchments in the country's fossil-fuel industries. There is no guarantee that the jobs generated through clean-energy investments will provide decent compensation to workers. Nor will they necessarily deliver improved workplace conditions, stronger union representation or reduced employment discrimination against women, minorities or other under-represented groups. But the fact that new investments will be occurring will create increased leverage for political mobilization across the board – for improving job quality, expanded union coverage and more jobs for under-represented groups.

At the same time, workers and communities throughout the world whose livelihoods depend on oil, coal and natural gas will lose out in the clean-energy transition. In order for the global clean-energy project to succeed, it must provide adequate transitional support for these workers and communities. Brian Callaci and I have developed a 'just transition' policy framework in some detail for the US economy; and Heidi Garrett-Peltier, Jeannette Wicks-Lim and I have developed more detailed approaches around these issues for the US states of New York and Washington.[16] Considering the US as a whole, Callaci

---

16   Robert Pollin and Brian Callaci, 'A Just Transition for Us Fossil Fuel Industry Workers', *American Prospect,* 2016; Robert Pollin and Brian Callaci, 'The Economics of Just Transition: A Framework for Supporting Fossil Fuel-Dependent Workers and

and I estimate that a rough high-end cost for such a programme would be a relatively modest $600 million per year, which is less than 0.2 per cent of the 2018 US Federal budget. This level of funding would provide strong support in three areas: income, retraining and relocation for workers facing retrenchments; guaranteeing the pensions for workers in the affected industries; and mounting effective transition programmes for fossil-fuel dependent communities. Comparable programmes will need to be implemented in other country settings.

Industrial policies and ownership forms

Increasing clean-energy investment by 1.5 per cent of global GDP will not happen without strong industrial policies. Even though, for example, energy-efficiency investments generally pay for themselves over three to five years, and the average costs of producing renewable energy are at rough parity with fossil fuels, it is still the case that some entities – public enterprises, private firms or a combination of both – will have to advance the initial capital and bear the project risk. Depending on specific conditions within each country, industrial policies will be needed to promote technical innovation and, more broadly, adaptations of existing clean-energy technology. Governments will need to deploy a combination of policy instruments, including research and development support, preferential tax treatment for clean-energy investments and stable long-term market arrangements through government-procurement contracts. Clean-energy industrial policies also need to include emission standards for utilities and transport, and price regulation for both fossil fuel and clean energy. The widely discussed tool of pricing carbon emissions through either a carbon tax or a cap on permissible emissions certainly needs to be a major component of the overall industrial policy mix. A carbon tax in particular can raise large amounts of revenue that can then be used to help finance clean-energy investments as well as redistributing funds to lower-income households. Germany's experience of financing is valuable here, since it has been the most

Communities in the United States', *Labor Studies Journal*, 2018, pp. 1–46; Robert Pollin, Heidi Garrett-Peltier and Jeannette Wicks-Lim, *Clean Energy Investments for New York State, Political Economy Research Institute (PERI)*, Amherst, MA, 2017; Robert Pollin, Heidi Garrett-Peltier and Jeannette Wicks-Lim, *A Green New Deal for Washington State*, PERI, 2017. Sasha Abramsky reports on the progress of the Green New Deal movement in Washington State in 'This Washington State Ballot Measure Fights for Both Jobs and Climate Justice', *Nation*, 20 July 2018.

successful advanced economy in developing its clean-energy economy. According to the International Energy Agency, a major factor in Germany's success is that its state-owned development bank, KfW, 'plays a crucial role by providing loans and subsidies for investment in energy efficiency measures in buildings and industry, which have leveraged significant private funds'.[17] Germany's development banking approach could be adapted throughout the world.

Another critical measure in supporting clean-energy investments at 1.5 per cent of annual global GDP will be to lower the profitability requirements for these investments. This in turn raises the issue of ownership of newly created energy enterprises and assets. Specifically: how might alternative ownership forms – including public ownership, community ownership and small-scale private companies – play a role in advancing the clean-energy investment agenda? Throughout the world, the energy sector has long operated under a variety of owner-ship structures, including public or municipal ownership, and forms of private cooperative ownership as well as private corporations. Indeed, in the oil and natural gas industry, publicly owned national companies control approximately 90 per cent of the world's reserves and 75 per cent of production, as well as many of the oil and gas infrastructure systems. These national corporations include Saudi Aramco, Gazprom, China National Petroleum Corporation, the National Iranian Oil Company, Petroleos de Venezuela, Petrobras in Brazil and Petronas in Malaysia. There is no evidence to suggest that these publicly owned companies are likely to be more supportive of a clean-energy transition than the private corporations. National development projects, lucrative careers and political power all depend on continuing the flow of fossil-fuel revenues. In and of itself, public ownership is not a solution.

Clean-energy investments will nevertheless create major new oppor-tunities for alternative ownership forms. For example, community-based wind farms have been highly successful for nearly two decades in Germany, Denmark, Sweden and the UK. A major reason for their success is that they operate with lower profit requirements than large-scale private corporations. On this point, my Green New Deal perspective converges with positions supported by degrowth propo-nents. For example, Juliet Schor describes in *True Wealth* (2011) what she calls 'a prima facie case that the emerging green sector will be powered by small and medium-size firms, with their agility, dynamism

---

17   International Energy Agency, *Energy Efficiency Market Report, 2013: Market Trends and Medium-Term Prospects*, OECD-IEA, Paris, 2013.

and entrepreneurial determination'. Over time, Schor writes, 'these entities can become a sizeable sector of low-impact enterprises, which form the basis of animated local communities and provide livelihood on a wide scale.'[18]

It is one thing to conclude that all countries – or at least those countries with either large GDPs or populations – should invest about 1.5 per cent of GDP per year in energy efficiency and renewable investments. It is another matter to determine what standard of fairness should be applied in allocating the costs of such investments among the various people, countries and regions of the globe. What would be a fair procedure? If the global clean-energy investment project sketched here were successful, average per capita CO_2 emissions would fall within twenty years from its current level of 4.6 tons to 2.3 tons. This corresponds to a fall in total emissions from 32 to 20 billion tons. Still, at the end of this twenty-year investment cycle, average US emissions would be 5.8 tons per capita, nearly three times the averages for China and the world as a whole, and five times the average for India. At a basic level, this is unfair – particularly given that, over the past century of the fossil-fuel era, US emissions have exceeded those in India and China combined by around 400 per cent. On grounds of fairness, one could, with good reason, insist that the United States and other rich countries be required to bring down per capita CO_2 emissions to the same level as low-income countries. We could also insist that high-income people – regardless of their countries of residence – be permitted to produce no more CO_2 emissions than anyone else.

There is a solid ethical case for such measures. But there is absolutely no chance that they will be implemented. Given the climate-stabilization imperative facing the global economy, we do not have the luxury to waste time on huge global efforts fighting for unattainable goals. Consider the US case: on grounds of both ethics and realism, it would be much more constructive to require that, in addition to bringing its own emissions down to about six tons per capita within twenty years, the US should also provide large-scale assistance to other countries in financing and scaling up their own transformative clean-energy projects.

---

18   Juliet Schor, *True Wealth: How and Why Millions of Americans Are Creating a Time-Rich, Ecologically Light, Small-Scale, High-Satisfaction Economy*, London, 2011, pp. 156–7. This aspect of the clean-energy investment project is very much in the spirit of E. F. Schumacher's classic *Small Is Beautiful* (1973).

Problems with degrowth

As I emphasized at the outset, degrowth proponents have made valuable contributions in addressing many of the untenable features of economic growth. But on the specific issue of climate change, degrowth does not provide anything like a viable stabilization framework. Consider some very simple arithmetic. Following the IPCC, we know that global CO_2 emissions need to fall from their current level of 32 billion tons to 20 billion tons within twenty years. If we assume that, following a degrowth agenda, global GDP contracts by 10 per cent over the next two decades, that would entail a reduction of global GDP four times greater than during the 2007–09 financial crisis and Great Recession. In terms of CO_2 emissions, the net effect of this 10 per cent GDP contraction, considered on its own, would be to push emissions down by precisely 10 per cent – that is, from 32 to 29 billion tons. It would not come close to bringing emissions down to 20 billion tons by 2040.

Clearly then, even under a degrowth scenario, the overwhelming factor pushing emissions down will not be a contraction of overall GDP but *massive growth* in energy efficiency and clean renewable-energy investments – which, for accounting purposes, will contribute towards increasing GDP – along with similarly dramatic cuts in fossil-fuel production and consumption, which will register as reducing GDP. Moreover, the immediate effect of any global GDP contraction would be huge job losses and declining living standards for working people and the poor. During the Great Recession, global unemployment rose by over 30 million. I have not seen a convincing argument from a degrowth advocate as to how we could avoid a severe rise in mass unemployment if GDP were to fall by twice as much.

These fundamental problems with degrowth are illustrated by the case of Japan, which has been a slow-growing economy for a generation now, even while maintaining high per capita incomes. Herman Daly himself describes Japan as being 'halfway to becoming a steady-state economy already, whether they call it that or not'. Daly is referring to the fact that, between 1996 and 2015, GDP growth in Japan averaged an anaemic 0.7 per cent per year. This compares with an average Japanese growth rate of 4.8 per cent per year for the thirty-year period between 1966 and 1995. Nevertheless, as of 2017, Japan remained in the ranks of the large, upper-income economies, with average GDP per capita at about $40,000. Yet despite the fact that Japan has been close to a no-growth economy for twenty years, its

CO_2 emissions remain among the highest in the world, at 9.5 tons per capita. This is 40 per cent below the figure for the United States, but it is four times higher than the average global level of 2.5 tons per capita that must be achieved if global emissions are to drop by 40 per cent by 2040. Moreover, Japan's per capita emissions have not fallen at all since the mid-1990s. The reason is straightforward: as of 2015, 92 per cent of Japan's total energy consumption comes from burning oil, coal and natural gas.

Thus, despite 'being halfway to becoming a steady-state economy', Japan has accomplished virtually nothing in advancing a viable climate-stabilization path. The only way it will make progress is to replace its existing, predominantly fossil-fuel energy system with a clean-energy infrastructure. At present, hydro power supplies 5 per cent of Japan's total energy needs, and other renewable sources only 3 per cent. Overall then, like all large economies – whether they are growing rapidly or not at all – Japan needs to embrace the Green New Deal.

A green great depression?

The majority of degrowth proponents pay almost no attention to emission levels. Thus the introduction to a special issue of *Ecological Economics* focused on degrowth, edited by leading contemporary degrowthers Giorgos Kallis, Christian Kerschner and Joan Martinez-Alier devoted precisely one paragraph to the issue. This described a proposal for 'cap-and-share' which, the authors explained, would involve placing 'a declining annual global cap on the tonnage of CO_2 emitted by fossil fuels' and 'allocating a large part of each year's tonnage to everyone in the world on an equal per capita basis'.[19] Kallis, Kerschner and Martinez-Alier recognize that the political economy of such a proposal would be highly complex; but they do not take it upon themselves to examine any of these complexities. In the same issue of *Ecological Economics* Peter Victor, author of *Managing without Growth* (2008), did develop a series of models for evaluating the relationship between economic growth and CO_2 emissions for the Canadian economy. Under Victor's baseline scenario, Canadian GDP would grow by an average of 2.3 per cent between

---

19   Giorgos Kallis, Christian Kerschner and Joan Martinez-Alier, 'The Economics of Degrowth', *Ecological Economics*, vol. 84, 2012, p. 4. The special issue of *Ecological Economics* collected contributions from the second International Conference on Economic Degrowth, held in Barcelona in 2010.

2005 and 2035, resulting in a doubling of per capita GDP, while CO_2 emissions would rise by 77 per cent. Victor then presented both low-growth and degrowth scenarios for the same period. He reports that, under degrowth, greenhouse-gas emissions would fall by 88 per cent, relative to the 2035 'business-as-usual' growth scenario. But he also concludes that Canada's per capita GDP under degrowth would fall to 26 per cent of the business-as-usual scenario by 2035.[20]

Victor does not flesh out his results with actual data on the Canadian economy, but it is illuminating to do so. In 2005, Canada's per capita GDP was $53,336 (expressed in 2018 Canadian dollars). Thus, under the business-as-usual scenario, per capita GDP rises to about $107,000 as of 2035. Alternatively, under the degrowth scenario, Canada's per capita GDP in 2035 would plummet to $28,000. This per capita GDP level for 2035 is 48 per cent below Canada's actual per capita GDP for 2005. In other words, under Victor's degrowth scenario, the emissions reduction achieved over a thirty-year period would be only modestly greater than what would be achieved under a clean-energy investment programme at 1.5 per cent of annual GDP, but with this fundamental difference: under the clean-energy investment project, average incomes would roughly double, while under degrowth, average incomes would experience a historically unprecedented collapse. Victor doesn't ask whether an economic depression of this magnitude under degrowth, in Canada or elsewhere, is either economically or politically viable. He doesn't examine what impact this loss of GDP would have on funding for healthcare, education or, for that matter, environmental protection. Nor does he explain what policy tools would be deployed to force Canada's GDP to halve within thirty years. Victor's article is further remarkable in that, in an analysis focused on the relationship between economic growth and climate change, it includes only one brief mention of renewable energy and no reference whatsoever to energy efficiency.

Perhaps the most influential contemporary discussion of the economics of climate change and degrowth is Tim Jackson's *Prosperity without Growth*.[21] Jackson begins by emphasizing that a viable climate-stabilization path requires absolute decoupling between

20   Peter Victor, 'Growth, Degrowth and Climate Change: A Scenario Analysis', *Ecological Economics*, vol. 84, 2012, p. 212. Victor's *Managing without Growth: Slower by Design, Not Disaster*, Cheltenham, 2008, presented his models in a broader degrowth framework.

21   Tim Jackson, *Prosperity without Growth: Economics for a Finite Planet*, London, 2017 [2009].

growth and emissions on a global scale, not merely relative decoupling. This point is indisputable. Jackson then reviews data for 1965–2015, showing that absolute decoupling has not occurred either at a global level or among, respectively, low-, middle- or high-income countries. Again, there is no disputing this evidence – although, as noted above, several individual countries did achieve absolute decoupling between GDP growth and CO_2 emissions for 2000–14. In fact, there are only two major issues to debate with Jackson. The first is whether absolute decoupling is a realistic possibility, moving forward. Jackson is dubious, writing that 'the evidence that decoupling offers a coherent escape from the dilemma of growth is, ultimately, far from convincing. The speed at which resource and emissions efficiencies have to improve if we are going to meet carbon targets are at best heroic, if the economy is growing relentlessly.'[22]

But is it really the case that absolute decoupling requires 'heroic' advances in building a clean-energy economy? It is true that absolute decoupling on a global scale is a highly challenging project. But we can be fairly precise in measuring the magnitude of the challenge. As discussed above, it will require an investment level in clean renewables and energy efficiency at about 1.5 to 2 per cent of global GDP annually. This amounts to about $1 trillion at today's global economy level and $1.5 trillion on average over the next twenty years. These are large but realistic investment goals which could be embraced by economies at all levels of development, in every region of the globe. One reason why this is a realistic project is that it would support rising average living standards and expanding job opportunities, in low-income countries in particular. For nearly forty years now, the gains from economic growth have persistently favoured the rich. Nevertheless, the prospects for reversing inequality in all countries will be far greater when the overall economy is growing than when the rich are fighting everyone else for shares of a shrinking pie. How sanguine, for example, would we expect affluent Canadians to be about the prospect of their incomes being cut by half or more in absolute dollars over the next thirty years? In political terms, the attempt to implement a degrowth agenda would render the global clean-energy project utterly unrealistic.

The second issue to raise with Jackson is still more to the point: does degrowth offer a viable alternative to absolute decoupling as a climate-stabilization project? As we have seen, the answer is 'No.' Jackson himself provides no substantive discussion to demonstrate

---

22   Jackson, *Prosperity without Growth*, p. 87.

otherwise. Indeed, on the issue of climate stabilization, Jackson offers no basis for disputing Herman Daly's characterization of degrowth as a slogan in search of a programme. Overall, then, if the left is serious about mounting a viable global climate-stabilization project, it should not be losing time seeking to build an all-purpose, broad-brush degrowth movement – which, for the reasons outlined, cannot succeed in actually stabilizing the climate. This is even more emphatically the case when a fair and workable approach to climate stabilization lies right before us, by way of the Green New Deal.

5

Degrowth: A Defence

MARK BURTON AND PETER SOMERVILLE

2019

Degrowth, or a 'green new deal'? Robert Pollin's contribution to the recent debate on environmental strategy in *New Left Review* counterposes the two paths that currently dominate radical discussion of this issue. That they do not exhaust it is clear from the other contributors: Herman Daly, the Grand Old Man of ecological economics, reiterates his call for a 'steady-state' economy in his interview with Benjamin Kunkel. Troy Vettese, drawing on the example of the seventeenth century's Little Ice Age, argues for a 'natural geo-engineering project' to lower global temperatures through reforestation, and against mooted artificial geo-engineering solutions, which propose to manipulate the earth's cloud cover, alter the chemical composition of the oceans or release a 'solar shield' of sunlight-reflecting sulphate particles into the upper atmosphere. At the same time, Mike Davis's discussion of the painstaking archival research by Emmanuel Le Roy Ladurie into the evidence for the Little Ice Age in France illuminates the limits of our knowledge of climate history.[1] What follows will focus on Pollin's trenchant criticisms of degrowth and the version of 'green growth' he offers as an alternative.

Pollin's starting point is the urgent need for emissions reduction to stabilize global temperatures, as set out by the International Panel on Climate Change. Other environmental issues – biodiversity, clean air and water, liveable cities – as well as political questions – social and international equality, for example – are subordinated to the imperative of moderating climate change. 'There are no certainties about what will transpire if we allow the average global temperature to continue rising. But as a basis for action, we only need to understand that there is a non-trivial possibility that the continuation of life on Earth as we know it is at stake.' His programme calls for a 1.5 to 2

---

1 Mike Davis, 'Taking the Temperature of History', NLR 110, March–April 2018.

per cent of global GDP to be invested annually in a fast-growing programme of clean, non-nuclear, renewable-energy provision, while fossil-fuel industries will be shrunk by 35 per cent over the next twenty years, an annual 2.2 per cent. Taking aim at proponents of degrowth, he argues:

> It is in fact absolutely imperative that some categories of economic activity should now grow massively – those associated with the production and distribution of clean energy. Concurrently, the global fossil-fuel industry needs to contract massively – that is, to 'de-grow' relentlessly over the next forty or fifty years until it has virtually shut down.[2]

This scenario is based on the 'absolute decoupling' of economic growth from fossil-fuel consumption – the former can expand while the latter contracts. Pollin claims this will drive down CO_2 emissions 'by 40 per cent within twenty years, while also supporting rising living standards and expanding job opportunities'. He provides costings for the social support and retraining of fossil-fuel workers: for the US as a whole this amounts to $600 million a year, or 0.2 per cent of the Federal budget. There are no costings for compensating the giant oil, gas and coal corporations; instead, Pollin notes in passing that these behemoths 'will have to be defeated'. Although he concedes the moral case for rich countries to reduce their per capita emissions to the level of poorer ones, he considers this politically unrealistic. Under his programme, US emissions will fall from 16.5 to 5.8 tons per capita after twenty years, but they would still be three times the world average and three times higher than China's per capita emissions, which would fall to 2.3 tons. To compensate, Pollin hopes the US will provide poorer countries with financial help for the transition.

Taking issue with Kunkel's opening flourish, that 'fidelity to GDP growth amounts to the religion of the modern world', Pollin counters that, under financialized neoliberalism, the real religion is not growth but maximizing profits 'in order to deliver maximum incomes and wealth for the rich'. While agreeing with the degrowth movement that much global-capitalist production is wasteful and that GDP is a

---

2 The 'degrowth movement' has been organized through the Research & Degrowth network, founded in 2001 by Joan Martinez-Alier (Universitat Autònoma de Barcelona) and Serge Latouche (University of Paris-Sud). Since 2008 it has held biennial international conferences in Paris (2008), Barcelona (2010), Montréal/Venice (2012), Leipzig (2014), Budapest (2016) and Malmö (2018). For an early analysis from this viewpoint, see J. Martinez-Alier, 'Political Ecology, Distributional Conflicts and Economic Incommensurability', NLR I/211, May–June 1995.

flawed metric, he argues that degrowthers have not produced a viable set of policies to cut greenhouse-gas emissions enough to stabilize global temperatures. Most damningly, it would seem, Pollin charges that degrowth would create soaring levels of poverty and unemployment, while failing to arrest climate change. According to his calculations, a 10 per cent contraction of the global economy, following a degrowth agenda, would create a world-historic slump, with global unemployment rocketing and declining living standards for poor and working-class people, but would still miss IPCC targets.

Limits of decoupling

How well do these claims stand up? Pollin's argument that the drive for profits, not GDP growth, is the real 'religion' of financialized neoliberalism fails to acknowledge that both neoliberalism and financialization are part of capitalism's response to the crisis of profitability that arose following the breakdown of the postwar settlement between capital and labour. The underlying problem is not 'neoliberalism' but the self-expanding system of capitalism, which turns everything into a commodity (real or fictitious), and so threatens the basis for the social and physical reproduction of human society at a variety of levels. Perhaps it is this misidentification of the villain(s) – targeting neoliberalism, not the capitalist mode of production – that helps Pollin to propose what is essentially a social-democratic approach of mitigated capitalism. At the same time, there is no doubt that the imaginary of GDP growth remains a powerful ideological force in its own right, mystifying the real economic processes at stake and instead focusing debate on the idea of expansion as an inherent good. It has a significant influence on decisions regarding production, distribution and consumption, and on the financial system that facilitates each of these elements.

Pollin is partially right to argue that the degrowth movement has not prioritized the formulation of detailed policy proposals on reducing greenhouse-gas emissions; its contributions have generally concentrated on showing how GDP growth makes such reduction harder. However, there are degrowthers who have addressed this question. Kevin Anderson, certainly an ally of degrowth, has proposed a Marshall Plan to decarbonize energy supplies, as well as shifts in 'behaviour and practices' such as frequent flying.[3] Energy and

---

3 See for example Kevin Anderson, 'Manchester, Paris and 2C: Laggard or Leader', presentation available on the Greater Manchester Combined Authority

resource caps feature in the work of ecological economist Blake Alcott, for example, and the 'cap and share' variant of this approach has been taken up by Brian Davey and the Irish NGO FEASTA.[4] Again, Pollin is right to call for a specific sectoral analysis of what needs to happen to make the 'dirty' sectors contract and the clean sectors – the 'replacement economy' – expand. Proponents of degrowth have never argued that *some* sectors should not grow, and shutting down fossil-fuel industries has been a strong strand in their work; it was, for example, the main extra-academic project of the Leipzig degrowth conference in 2014. Crucially, however, this sectoral adjustment needs to take place within an overall envelope that contracts, so that aggregate human activity remains within safe planetary limits and its ecological footprint does not exceed the available bio-capacity. This is not just a matter of carbon; it involves water, air, forests, croplands and fishing grounds, as affected by the processes of production, consumption and trade.

Pollin's argument is premised on the 'absolute decoupling' of economic activity from fossil fuels. He rightly emphasizes that the more modest goal of 'relative decoupling' – 'through which fossil-fuel consumption and CO_2 emissions continue to increase, but at a slower rate than GDP growth' – is not a solution. He goes on to argue that it's fine for economies to continue growing as rapidly as China and India have been doing, so long as the growth process is completely delinked from fossil fuels. However, Pollin doesn't confront the difficulties involved in ensuring that this absolute decoupling will occur. It's implausible that Chinese and Indian growth rates could have been so high *without* soaring fossil-fuel consumption – not to mention the carbon emissions caused by changed land-use and the production of concrete and steel. Pollin appeals to a World Resources Institute study which claimed to show that in a number of advanced economies, including the US, Germany and the UK, GDP growth had indeed been decoupled from CO_2 emissions for the period 2000–14.[5] On closer inspection, however, there are serious problems of data quality in the

---

website. In the assessment of Anderson and his co-author Alice Bows, 'only the global economic slump has had any significant impact in reversing the trend of rising emissions': 'Beyond "Dangerous" Climate Change: Emission Scenarios for a New World', *Philosophical Transactions of the Royal Society*, vol. 369, no. 1934, 2011.

4   Blake Alcott, 'Impact Caps: Why Population, Affluence and Technology Strategies Should Be Abandoned', *Journal of Cleaner Production,* vol. 18, no. 6, 2010; Brian Davey, ed., *Sharing for Survival*, Dublin, 2012.

5   Nate Aden, 'The Roads to Decoupling: 21 Countries Are Reducing Carbon Emissions while Growing GDP', World Resources Institute blog, 5 April 2016.

WRI paper, including the use of different reporting protocols by different countries, missing data – emissions from international shipping and aviation are not counted in the national totals, for example – and the 'construct validity' of proxy measures: whether they actually measure what they purport to. The observed effects may reflect one-off or reversible changes – such as the impact of the 2008 economic crisis.[6]

In addition, these supposedly 'decoupling' countries have also been de-industrializing, switching to financialized-capitalist economies with large service sectors, and importing commodities manufactured elsewhere. This creates further problems on both sides of the 'economic growth/carbon emissions' equation. First, through outsourcing production, firms headquartered in the rich countries obtain goods produced at poor-country wage costs, but sold at rich-country consumer-market prices, the sales then figuring in the rich country's GDP.[7] In other words, part of the GDP growth attributed to the supposedly 'decoupling' advanced economies is the result of labour processes in poorer countries. The GDP of rich countries is inflated through this neo-colonial value capture, but the emissions are counted in the emerging economies in which the commodities were produced. This would appear to qualify, if not invalidate, the decoupling claim. The problem is compounded by the fact that the GDP figures enter into both sides of the comparison, since as well as being one of the two variables considered, GDP is used to compute consumption-based emissions which are not directly measured. In any event, the rate of emissions reduction in the apparently decoupling countries would be nowhere near sufficient to avert climate catastrophe. As Kevin Anderson and Alice Bows have shown, the developed economies – known as 'Annex 1' parties in the Kyoto Accord – need to be cutting emissions at 8 to 10 per cent a year, whereas in the 'decoupling' countries emissions were falling at a mere 2 per cent.[8] Meanwhile, global emissions for the period 2000–14 actually increased by 45 per cent, with the world economy as a whole showing no signs of decoupling.

Moreover, when the full picture of material flows through national economies is considered – the 'physical throughput' emphasized by

---

6   For a more detailed critique, see Mark Burton, 'New Evidence on Decoupling Carbon Emissions from GDP Growth: What Does It Mean?', Steady State Manchester blog, 15 April 2016.

7   This is not the only mechanism by which the core countries' income is inflated; transfer pricing by multinationals is another.

8   Anderson and Bows, 'Beyond "Dangerous" Climate Change'.

Herman Daly – it turns out that there is no decoupling at all between resource use and GDP growth.[9] While Pollin is right to emphasize carbon emissions, it's also clear that present levels of production-consumption (let alone their growth) require materials which are, to varying extents, becoming scarcer.[10] The cost of obtaining them has risen, putting a growing strain on the global economy – the dynamic that underpinned the *Limits to Growth* business-as-usual scenario, with its system crash in the mid-twenty-first century. Their extraction entails the destruction of livelihoods and ecosystems across the world, particularly in the global South.[11] All this would seem to put degrowth firmly back on the agenda.

The scale of the world economy exceeds the earth's biological and physical capacity to absorb the impacts and restore the resources used. The Global Footprint Network currently estimates human-kind's collective material footprint at 1.7 times the available biocapacity. Daly is correct to argue that population size is an impor-tant part of environmental impact. However, while global emissions are still rising, the rate of population growth has slowed signifi-cantly – increasing from 4 billion to 7 billion between 1975 and 2010, but only projected to reach 8 billion by the mid-2020s and around 9 billion by 2050.[12] The main driver of the slow-down is the declining rate of fertility, already below replacement level in Europe, though higher in India and sub-Saharan Africa. Historically, rising living standards, urbanization and education, particularly for women, have been associated with falling fertility, while poorer and more unequal

---

9   Thomas Wiedmann, Heinz Schandl et al., 'The Material Footprint of Nations', *Proceedings of the National Academy of Sciences*, vol. 112, no. 20, May 2015.

10   Carlos de Castro, Margarita Mediavilla et al., 'Global Wind Power Potential: Physical and Technological Limits', *Energy Policy*, vol. 39, no. 10, October 2011; 'Global Solar Electric Potential: A Review of Their Technical and Sustainable Limits', *Renewable and Sustainable Energy Reviews*, vol. 28, December 2013.

11   Post-extractivism – the movement against extractivism in the global South – has been closely allied with degrowth. See Alberto Acosta, 'Post-Growth and Post-Extractivism: Two Sides of the Same Cultural Transformation', *Alternautas*, March 2016; Alberto Acosta and Ulrich Brand, *Salidas del laberinto capitalista. Decrecimiento y postextractivismo,* Barcelona, 2017.

12   Projections beyond 2050 involve a high degree of uncertainty. In a 2014 paper Patrick Gerland and his colleagues estimate a global population between 9.6 and 12.3 billion in 2100. See Gerland et al., 'World Population Stabilization Unlikely This Century', *Science*, vol. 346, no. 6206, 10 October 2014; see also K. C. Samir and Wolfgang Lutz, 'The Human Core of the Shared Socioeconomic Pathways: Population Scenarios by Age, Sex and Level of Education for All Countries to 2100', *Global Environmental Change*, vol. 42, January 2017, pp. 181–92.

countries tend to have higher rates. If these conditions were tackled, and primary healthcare as well as modern contraception made freely available, the global population could stabilize and even begin to decline before 2050.

Green expansion?

What of Pollin's proposal to stabilize the climate by investing an annual 2 per cent of global GDP in clean energy? His argument is that this switch to renewables can cut global emissions by 40 per cent within twenty years 'while also supporting rising living standards and expanding job opportunities'. So far, however, the expansion of renewables has come as an addition to fossil-fuel supplies, rather than as a replacement for them (see Table 1, below). The countries that are most advanced in developing renewable energy, such as Denmark and Germany, have also expanded their consumption of fossil fuels, particularly coal; the same applies to the US, China, India, Canada and Australia. To replace oil, coal and gas with other sources of energy would take something like an eighteen-fold increase in renewables deployment, at current levels of energy consumption. If worldwide energy usage were to increase, as Pollin indicates, then the challenge would be even greater.

Table 1: Primary Energy Consumption By Fuel, Million Tonne Equivalents

	1970	1980	1990	2000	2010	2020
Oil	2,253	2,986	3,153	3,580	4,021	4,564
Gas	890	1,291	1,767	2,182	2,874	3,534
Coal	1,483	1,813	2,246	2,385	3,636	3,697
Nuclear	18	161	453	584	626	674
Hydro	266	385	487	601	779	1,015
Renewables	2	7	35	59	234	794
Total	4,912	6,642	8,142	9,390	12,170	14,278

Source: BP Energy Outlook, 2018.

The contradiction of the 'green new deal' is that GDP growth makes reducing emissions far harder. Expanding the economy inevitably means more extraction, production, distribution and consumption, and each of these processes produces emissions. If Pollin's renewable-energy investment plan also succeeded in generating tens of millions of new jobs and raising living standards worldwide, as he hopes, that would mean a further increase in the consumption of carbon-intensive services and products – unless the relevant industries were thoroughly decarbonized, probably in conjunction with caps on energy use, extraction and land-use conversion.

In theory, contracting the world economy need not hurt the relatively poor, since high emissions are strongly correlated with concentrations of wealth and income: globally, the top 10 per cent of emitters contribute approximately 45 per cent of greenhouse-gas emissions, while the bottom 50 per cent contribute only 13 per cent.[13] Deep economic retrenchment can be managed equitably, as was demonstrated during the hardship of the Special Period in Cuba in the early '90s, when punitive US sanctions exacerbated the impact of the collapse of the Soviet Union. The possibility that contraction might take place in a properly democratic fashion was explored by André Gorz – acclaimed as a forerunner by the degrowth movement – who called for forms of workers' self-management as a means to 'restore the correlation between less work and less consumption, on one hand, and more autonomy and more existential security on the other'.[14] Pollin's proposals for a 'just transition' to renewable energy that would also contribute to greater global equity are welcome; but so far work in this area, including Pollin's, has tended to concentrate on the fossil-fuel industry.[15]

Finally, Pollin argues that a degrowth agenda to shrink global GDP by 10 per cent over the next twenty years would entail a slump four times deeper than the 2008 recession, with world unemployment soaring amid steep spending cuts, yet the net effect would be to push CO_2 emissions down by a mere 10 per cent – from 32 to 29 billion tons – nowhere near the necessary fall to 20 billion tons by 2040. This is correct. On its own, managed economic contraction – which isn't the same as degrowth, but is a component of it – will not bring about the kind of emissions cuts we need. But as we have seen, maintaining

---

13   Lucas Chancel and Thomas Piketty, 'Carbon and Inequality from Kyoto to Paris: Trends in the Global Inequality of Carbon Emissions (1998–2013) and Prospects for an Equitable Adaptation Fund', Paris School of Economics, November 2015, p. 50.

14   André Gorz, 'Political Ecology: Expertocracy versus Self-Limitation', NLR I/202, November–December 1993; see also Ecology as Politics, London, 1987.

15   See the examples of local outcomes for energy workers in Europe, China, Australia, Argentina and the US cited in Anabella Rosenberg, 'Strengthening Just Transition Policies in International Climate Governance', Stanley Foundation, Muscatine, IA, 2017.

aggregate expansion of the economy, tracked by GDP growth, will add to the hill that has to be climbed. Besides, even the elimination of fossil fuels may not be enough to ensure the future of life on Earth, given the increasing pressures on ecosystems and scarce resources. Capitalism's relentless quest for new forms of profit-making, and for natural resources to exploit and extract, is not limited to oil, coal and gas.

An ecologically sustainable world economy would have to be delinked from the drive for profits, and ordered instead around the principle of deploying human capabilities to meet human needs, within the limits of Earth's biocapacity. In other words, it would be a socialist mode of production of some sort. This would need to involve the equitable control and reduction of the material scale of the global economy, together with targeted curtailment of emissions.[16] That means drastic action to cut industrial production (of goods that are not needed, that involve high energy consumption, that do not last) as well as industrial construction (roads, airports, speculative skyscrapers and shopping malls), industrial agriculture (fossil-fuel-dependent monocultures that destroy soils and water supplies, and require huge energy inputs to bring food to the table) and industrial distribution (sea, air and road transportation systems, all highly dependent on fossil-fuel combustion). The working week would be much shorter, and consumption in the developed world, and by elites in the developing world, severely circumscribed. Heating would be provided entirely by electricity generated from renewable sources. Transport would largely be public, powered by electricity or hydrogen fuel cells. Construction would no longer involve the use of cement or steel. Agriculture would be guided by the principles of agroecology: biodiversity and complexity as the foundation for soil quality, plant health and crop productivity; diversified farming practices, including crop rotation, polycultures, agroforestry, green manures, crop-livestock mixtures, cover crops and mulching.[17]

None of this suggests that it would be easy to steer the world economy towards its ecologically consistent size. Indeed, it perhaps hardly seems likely that this will happen, at least in the immediate

---

16   Decreasing the scale of the global material economy is proposed here as a means to an end, emissions reduction – a necessary condition for strong sustainability. Arguably, this voluntary downscaling, one dimension of degrowth, may be a desirable end in itself.

17   Third World Network, *Agroecology: Key Concepts, Principles and Practices*, Penang and Berkeley, 2015.

future. Yet that does not mean there is any escape from the fundamental problem that the global economy now far exceeds the capacity of Earth's systems to sustain its demands; expanding it further can only make matters worse. The mitigated capitalism of a 'green new deal' will be little help, because it leaves the overall system of commodification, and the motors of expansion, firmly in place. How degrowth might happen we don't know. A fortuitous combination of popular struggle and collapse of the capitalist system is perhaps the only route. That isn't to say that good governmental action, including investment in clean energy and demand-reduction measures, can't help. But for it to work, government policy would have to break from its normal mode of handmaiden to global capital. Unrealistic? Implausible? Probably, but no more than Pollin's imaginary of green accumulation to the rescue.

6

Green Questions

LOLA SEATON

2019

As time rolls on and the IPCC's deadlines for reducing the rise in global temperatures get closer, the prospect of climate catastrophe looms larger, and the problem of how to avert it becomes ever more pressing. This is the question that has been under discussion in recent numbers of NLR. The debate has featured interventions from a number of distinct positions, on both sides of the Atlantic and across different political generations. Herman Daly, a pioneer in the field of ecological economics, was quizzed on his programme for a steady-state system by Benjamin Kunkel. Canadian environmental historian Troy Vettese argued for a pollution-shrinking 'half-earth' project of natural geo-engineering and eco-austerity. Taking the opposite tack, the radical economist Robert Pollin called for massive global investment in renewable energy. UK-based scholar-activists Mark Burton and Peter Somerville replied with a defence of 'degrowth'.

Sacrifice?

One way of comparing the contributions so far is to regard them as providing different answers to the question: what does the world need to cut, or cut out, in order to avoid global disaster? Herman Daly defines 'environmental impact' as 'the product of the number of people times per capita resource use', and so argues that we need both to reduce our use of resources, especially fossil fuels, and to limit population growth through some kind of cap-and-trade system. In the case of resources, there would be a 'limit on the right to deplete what you own', and that right would be purchasable 'by auction from the government'. In the case of population, everyone would be given the right to reproduce once, but since not everyone can, or wants to, have children, those rights could be reallocated 'by sale or by gift'. Daly also advocates a minimum and maximum income. These redistributive policies are critical accompaniments to his caps on resource use and population growth since without setting a limit on inequality too, the distribution of the rights to consume and to have children could be drastically uneven and unfair (the rich could, for example, monopolize reproduction).

Taking land scarcity as the 'fundamental metric' for his 'alternative green political economy', Troy Vettese's 'eco-austere' answer is that we must reduce our energy consumption and cut out meat and dairy. Mandatory veganism would free up farmland for 'land-hungry' clean-energy infrastructure like wind turbines and solar panels, which could then become the world's primary way of meeting its energy needs. The extra land could also be used for natural geo-engineering projects like large-scale rewilding ('half-earthing') to create eco-systems that would act as carbon sinks.

Robert Pollin takes issue with Vettese's 'fundamental metric': he thinks Vettese's estimates about how much land renewable-energy systems would require are inflated. With land scarcity not a limiting factor in Pollin's account, cutting our energy consumption – beyond reducing energy wastage – becomes unnecessary. So, unlike Daly and Vettese, Pollin is almost exclusively concerned with reducing not energy use but fossil-fuel use: 'To make real progress on climate stabilization, the single most critical project is to cut the consumption of oil, coal and natural gas dramatically and without delay.' Through concerted global investment in both clean-energy infrastructure and more energy-efficient 'technologies and practices', we can eradicate fossil fuels while continuing to 'achieve the same, or higher, levels of energy service'.

Degrowth scholar-activists Mark Burton and Peter Somerville agree with Pollin about the necessity for 'targeted curtailment of emissions' through a transition to clean energy. But, whereas Pollin is sceptical about the political viability and wary of the economic consequences of shrinking the economy – he fears this would result in soaring unemployment and plunging living standards ('a green great depression') – Burton and Somerville argue that a drastic contraction of the material size of the economy through cutting industrial production, construction, agriculture and distribution is the essential complement to a switch to renewables. They calculate that meeting current energy needs without recourse to oil, coal or natural gas would require 'an eighteen-fold increase in renewables deployment', and so argue that if energy consumption were to increase further – as it will if the economy continues to expand, barring major efficiency breakthroughs – weaning ourselves off fossil fuels would only be more difficult.

Pollin's vision of the transition to clean energy is distinguished by its mostly not being felt by individual consumers, whose energy use could in principle continue as normal (and whose energy bills might even be cheaper thanks to efficiency improvements). This prompts a second question that may highlight the distinctiveness of Pollin's contribution: how much sacrifice do the different proposed cuts require? However costly Pollin's proposals – he estimates they would suck up 'between 1.5 and 2 per cent of global GDP every year' – and however temporarily painful the transition (job losses in shuttered fossil-fuel industries, for example), the question of sacrifice in Pollin's text is largely out of frame.[1] By using clean-energy resources, and using them more efficiently, we don't have to use less energy; we can even use more. Far from climate change 'changing everything', as Naomi Klein suggested, so long as 'energy consumption, and economic activity more generally' are *absolutely decoupled* from the consumption of fossil fuels', both can go on largely as before.[2] The key figure in Pollin's proposal sounds small – a mere 1.5 per cent – but the scale of the projected changes is huge. This combination obscures their impact, which can appear negligible or at least abstract. Predominantly affecting large industries and to be enforced by remote bureaucracies, Pollin's solutions release us from significantly altering our lifestyles and call for little curtailment of individual freedom.

Vettese's prescription, by contrast, deprives everyone of meat and requires 'the global bourgeoisie' to use a lot less energy, especially in the US, where people would have to reduce their energy consumption by more than 80 per cent: the average US citizen uses about 12,000 watts per day, whereas in Vettese's 'eco-austere' society each person could use no more than 2,000. Though neither local nor small in scale ('half-earthing'), Vettese's proposals prescribe behavioural changes at the level of the individual – which Daly's programme in particular is designed to avoid – and he makes no secret of the relative hardship

---

1   A recent editorial in *n+1* argues that the emphasis on sacrifice in green solutions is misplaced: 'The most radical and hopeful response to climate change shouldn't be, What do we give up?', but 'How do we collectively improve our overall quality of life? It is a welfare question, one that has less to do with consumer choices – like changing light bulbs – than with the spending of trillions and trillions of still-available dollars on decoupling economic growth and wealth from carbon-based fuels and carbon-intensive products, including plastics': 'The Intellectual Situation: The Best of a Bad Situation', *n+1*, no. 33, winter 2019, p. 8.

2   Naomi Klein, *This Changes Everything: Capitalism vs. the Climate*, Harmondsworth, 2014.

these changes might entail ('eco-austerity'). Though Pollin mentions job losses and the need for a 'just transition', his emphasis is on net job creation, and our imaginations are not seriously engaged in thinking through the personal loss and upheaval that would surely accompany the elimination of whole industries around which communities have grown and on which they depend.

Daly's proposals provide something of a bridge between Pollin's technology-enabled business-as-usual consumption and Vettese's compulsory asceticism. In Daly's steady state, the rights to deplete resources and to have children are both exchangeable. This means that the inverse deprivations can be traded too: the seller of a right is buying an obligation to make a sacrifice – though, crucially, this may not feel like a sacrifice (the seller of their right to reproduce may not want children). Cushioning the iron fist of state-mandated sacrifice is thus the glove of flexibility about how that sacrifice is distributed: privileges and privations would be allocated according to individual need and personal choice. This is why Daly is fond of cap-and-trade systems: they combine aggregate control – over the total amount of carbon we collectively emit or the total number of children born – with as much personal autonomy as is compatible with such macro-restrictions.

Pollin's appeal

Pollin's proposal stands out because it has a kind of *prima facie* plausibility that the others lack. Its eschewal of the necessity of personal sacrifice no doubt accounts for much of this impression. Particularly in the US – with its fanatical enshrinement of freedom, conceived in highly individualistic terms – it is hard to imagine either Daly or Vettese's policies, let alone those of Burton and Somerville, gaining much traction. Daly's wealth restrictions seem perhaps more quixotic than his ecological ones. At one point in the interview, Kunkel observes that, anecdotally, Daly's population proposal is the one that people tend to 'find most difficult to contemplate', but the prospect of America's oligarchic governing class overseeing the implementation of Daly's maximum income is equally unimaginable.

Pollin's circumvention of the logic of personal sacrifice also appeals because it speaks to the scepticism some feel about the efficacy of small-scale, local efforts to reduce humankind's ecological footprint. Unlike households' switching to energy-efficient light bulbs or avoiding plastic-wrapped goods, the global ambition of Pollin's proposal seems adequate to the size of the problem.[3] His programme is attractive on account of its narrow focus, too. Daly and Vettese's platforms are multi-pronged, and their concerns are several and broader. Pollin is ruthlessly focused on curtailing fossil-fuel use, which, he has elsewhere noted, 'is responsible for generating about 74 per cent of overall global greenhouse gas emissions'.[4] Past effective environmental action – against ozone-destroying CFCs for example – suggests that single-issue or single-substance initiatives, which attract public support more easily and are more conducive to targeted legislation, have a greater chance of success (although a resource as pervasive in and essential to the global economy as fossil fuel admittedly poses a quite different political and practical challenge to prohibiting a refrigerant).

Unlike Vettese, who argues biodiversity ought to be 'upheld' not just because it increases carbon retention but 'in its own right', in Pollin's more anthropocentric, pragmatic contribution, climate change is the sole focus and nature is scarcely imagined outside of its human use. The other contributions contain extra-ecological reflections, too, or carry extra-ecological implications – social, economic and political ones about how we could organize ourselves better and more fairly, and particularly about whether continuing to produce and circulate increasing quantities of commodities constitutes a social good. Though here prompted by the climate crisis, these questions about value and fairness nevertheless exceed it. Except for Pollin – who admits current consumption can be 'wasteful', but doesn't advocate seeking to limit or transform it – all the contributors are critical of the amount we consume. But these criticisms frequently stem from concerns that go beyond sustainability. Vettese, for example, approvingly quotes Alyssa Battistoni's reflections on the pursuit of a 'climate-stable future' as an opportunity to re-think which kinds of work are truly socially useful and improve people's lives 'without consuming vast amounts of resources'.[5] Likewise, Burton and Somerville suggest in a footnote that the 'voluntary downscaling' of the material economy might be 'a desirable end in itself'.

---

3   George Monbiot has argued that citizens need governments to regulate their ecological behaviour for them because 'self-enforced abstinence is both ineffective' and 'unattractive': 'Environmental Feedback: A Reply to Clive Hamilton', NLR 45, May–June 2007, p. 113.

4   Robert Pollin, 'Global Green Growth for Human Development', UNDP Human Development Report, 2016, p. 3.

5   Alyssa Battistoni, 'Living, Not Just Surviving', Jacobin, 15 August 2017.

This extra-ecological critique of the untrammelled consumption on which economic expansion depends is most pronounced in the interview with Daly, who, in Kunkel's words, believes 'that life, or a society, ought to have some purpose beyond economic growth'. Kunkel suggests that some of Daly's readers might 'detect a certain religious orientation' in this notion that societies ought to be guided by more enlightened values than mere enthusiasm for material increase. Whether or not this conviction implies a 'religious' framework, it is not an *economic* rationale for degrowth, nor, significantly, an exclusively ecological one. This is not purely an objection to the environmental havoc unlimited growth wreaks, but to its meaninglessness and its disconnection from social needs.

Pollin's text is distinctive for its relative silence on these matters. He does not articulate a broader socioeconomic vision within which his global clean-energy programme might fit. In the short passage where Pollin does discuss the possibility of forcibly equalizing emissions between rich and poor regions of the world, he is categorical: though there is 'a solid ethical case' for measures that would allow the wealthy to pollute no more than everyone else, 'there is absolutely no chance that they will be implemented', and 'we do not have the luxury to waste time on huge global efforts fighting for unattainable goals'.

Strategy in the second sense

Pollin dismisses these social and ethical questions on the grounds of political realism. He thinks it is 'more constructive' to concentrate on specific, concrete goals than to 'present broad generalities about the nature of economic growth, positive or negative'. Pollin's strategic reticence about problems of value and fairness is part of what makes his text persuasive – and distinctive, since his pragmatic attitude, and overt engagement with the limits of the politically possible, are largely missing from the other contributions. This series is about, as Pollin puts it baldly, 'what is to be done'. But the question of how to avert planetary disaster does not only call for prescriptive technical strategizing that weighs the efficacy and viability of green technologies and behaviours. It is also a question about *political* strategy, which calls for descriptive analysis of the present moment, and for attempts to identify what kind of political obstacles sit in the way of implementing those technical solutions, rapidly and comprehensively, with a view to asking how those obstacles might be overcome.

We have little trouble envisaging greener futures – one powered by wind turbines and solar panels, with more wilderness and fewer cars and so on – but what we can't seem to answer adequately is this second political question about how to get from our carbon-intensive present to that green future; how, in Daly's words, to map the route between 'how things are' and 'how things ought to be'. This question is to different degrees unaddressed in all the contributions, including Pollin's. The absence is perhaps most conspicuous in the interview with Daly, where Kunkel gently presses him on it. Averse to the 'story of determinism' he discerns in historical materialist accounts, Daly fails to provide any rival theory of what motors change, or to identify an agent or force that could secure the uptake of his policies, instead trusting in 'an appeal to morality, whether that's sufficient or not'. 'Purpose is causative in the world', Daly says. 'If it is not, then we should all go back to sleep.' Which purposes, and whose, prove causative, he doesn't specify. Moral awakenings may have material consequences, but they do not necessarily outweigh the self-interested purposes of, for example, the coal lobby. In the absence of robust theorizing about how desired changes might come about – beyond hoping for an epiphany among elites – Daly's policies risk appearing utopian and politically impotent, since it's not clear how they would come to seem attractive or necessary to the people in a position to implement them. The same could apply to Vettese's suggestions, to Burton and Somerville's – and even to Pollin's harder-headed platform.

For Pollin, too, despite his unsentimental *realpolitik*, doesn't explain how the intergovernmental bureaucracy his global investment plan presumably requires would obtain enough political clout to override the interests of the fossil-fuel industries or petrostates. Pollin registers this issue only to drop it swiftly:

> Of course, both privately owned fossil-fuel companies, such as Exxon-Mobil and Chevron, and publicly owned companies like Saudi Aramco and Gazprom have massive interests at stake in preventing reductions in fossil-fuel consumption; they also wield enormous political power. These powerful vested interests will have to be defeated.

The passive construction – 'to be defeated' – is symptomatic of his leaving this critical question of agency and power unanswered.

Growth as such

In his introduction to the interview with Daly, Kunkel suggested in passing that 'fidelity to GDP amounts to the religion of the modern world'. The claim launched a particularly contentious strand of the debate, about whether increasing GDP is in fact essential to contemporary capitalist societies and, if so, whether this is a result, as Kunkel's claim implies, of the 'ideological' sway it holds (as a 'religion'), or whether growth is a 'structural imperative', as Vettese put it, which inheres in the economy and is reducible to the logic of capital.

Vettese takes issue with both parts of Kunkel's remark, reminding us, first, that GDP is just an 'abstract measurement', and as such 'mere foam' to 'what goes on in the [economy's] churning depths', and second, that growth is not a 'religion' insofar as it is not, primarily, an ideological phenomenon (or epiphenomenon). What drives capitalist economies and their perpetual expansion is not a theoretical commitment to increasing their size, but the competitive dynamics that compel capitalists to pursue ever-increasing profits. This is not, at root, a subjective preference that could be easily ditched for some other priority.

Pollin agrees with Vettese that 'the real religion' of the modern world – at least since 'neoliberalism became the predominant economic-policy model' in the mid-'70s – is not growth, but 'maximizing profits for business in order to deliver maximum incomes and wealth for the rich'. The massive concentration of wealth effected by neoliberal policies has in fact come at the expense of growth in the advanced economies, the average rate of which has fallen to well below that sustained during the *trente glorieuses*.

Burton and Somerville also argue that growth is ultimately an effect of the accumulation of capital, and that fixating on GDP risks missing this underlying reality. Yet unlike Vettese they also allow that growth is an influential 'cultural notion', which has a determining effect on economic behaviour: 'growth remains a powerful ideological force in its own right'. Burton and Somerville emphasize the material economic effects of this GDP 'imaginary': it 'has a significant influence on decisions regarding production, distribution and consumption'. This imaginary also influences electoral politics. The stamp of economic strength, a steadily increasing GDP is also a prerequisite for electoral success, and failure to sustain growth is punished at the polls. An expanding economy and rising living standards are what citizens of advanced economies expect, and growth is, as its incessant rhetorical invocation suggests, what politicians in capitalist democracies must promise to secure majorities. Michael Mann reminds us of this dynamic when he writes that 'the political treadmill is not imposed by states on unwilling subjects, for these measure their own success by material consumption, and they will support politicians who they think will deliver this'.[6] The *sine qua non* of electoral viability, growth is thus not just a side-effect of profit-seeking, but the traditional cornerstone of capitalism's social legitimacy. 'GDP growth', Mann observes, 'is why capitalism is seen as a great success story', and 'political success is actually measured by economic growth'.[7]

But when electorates demand growth, what is the content of their demand? Perhaps 'material consumption', as Mann suggests, but only if under this rubric he includes not simply the latest Apple gadgets but those goods – like food and shelter and central heating – essential to a decent quality of life. In that case, to believe in growth is to subscribe to the notion that sustaining profitability for private companies is ultimately a public good because it enables higher living standards – the classic basis of capitalism's claim to legitimacy, famously captured in the slogan 'what's good for General Motors is good for America'. Then one could see GDP as the symbolic marker of capitalism's putative conversion of 'private vices' into 'public benefits'.[8] This is where Daly's critique of GDP as an empirical measure becomes relevant. He argues that the supposed connection between profit and welfare institutionalized by GDP barely holds: 'the coupling of GDP and welfare is loose, or even non-existent beyond some sufficiency threshold.' A figure that records how much we collectively produce and consume does not tell us much about our quality of life.

But, as Pollin points out, self-sustaining growth is no longer a reality in capitalist economies in the West. As Robert Brenner explains: 'The capitalist system long ago lost the capacity to realize its ostensible historic comparative advantage and justification – to drive unceasing capital accumulation, which makes for self-sustaining economic growth and creates the potential for rising living standards.' As growth has slowed, Brenner contends, so has people's belief in it. 'In

---

6 Michael Mann, *The Sources of Social Power: Globalizations, 1954–2011*, vol. 4, New York, 2013, p. 364.

7 Ibid., pp. 325, 365.

8 These phrases are Wolfgang Streeck's. See his 'How Will Capitalism End?', NLR 87, May–June 2014.

the last thirty years or so', as 'upward redistribution' of wealth has increasingly displaced its production, even the notion that healthy profits lead to higher living standards has lost its purchase on the public imaginary: the 'cliché has ceased to hold – and the world's capitalist classes no longer really proclaim it'.[9] According to Brenner's account, it is not just the rate of growth that is in decline, but the ideological aura surrounding it.

Degrees of capitalism

Burton and Somerville offer an alternative understanding of financial-ized neoliberalism, which, they observe, was 'capitalism's response to the crisis of profitability' that ensued after the postwar boom. In other words, neoliberal policies – including massive deregulation of a surging financial sector – were not simply instruments of upward redistribution in flagging economies that had abandoned the pursuit of growth, but were rather symptoms of an ongoing commitment to growth insofar as they were improvised reactions to the falling rate of return on productive investment. Burton and Somerville complete their criticism by wondering whether Pollin's 'misidentification of the villain(s)' – his blaming financialized neoliberalism and thus the stagnation of growth, rather than growth itself – is what allows him to make ecological proposals that operate essentially within 'miti-gated capitalism'.

It is perhaps no coincidence that Daly, the other contributor whose proposals ostensibly operate within capitalism, also insists on gradations of that mode of production: 'Capitalism in the sense of financialized monopoly capitalism, geared towards continuous growth and concentration of incomes, is really bad', but it also has more benign incarnations: a 'small-scale capitalism, operating within scale and distributive limits', to which, he implies, we can revert while saving the planet.

Whereas Daly's eco-friendly capitalism would be small-scale and stationary, under Pollin's 'green new deal', a bigger economy may be better. This is a key difference. Ironically, the name 'green new deal' was popularized by the *New York Times* columnist and ardent free-marketeer Thomas Friedman in 2007.[10] 'There is only one thing as big as Mother Nature', Friedman enthused recently, 'and that is Father

---

9   The editors, 'Introducing Catalyst', *Catalyst*, vol. 1, no. 1, spring 2017.
10   Thomas Friedman, 'A Warning from the Garden', *New York Times*, 19 January 2007.

Greed – a.k.a., the market. I am a green capitalist. I think we will only get the scale we need by shaping the market.'[11] Pollin, on the other hand, although no 'green capitalist', nonetheless believes in the social value of healthy growth rates. This is his priority, and his sense of the urgency of the climate crisis means that while he does discuss how different ownership forms might advance his renewables agenda, he is prepared to postpone the question of an alternative economic order.

Why is growth such a priority for Pollin? Growth is a cornerstone of his programme's funding mechanism: since investment comes from a portion of global GDP, 'a higher economic-growth rate will also accelerate the rate at which clean energy supplants fossil fuels'.[12] Although he does not dwell on them here, it becomes clear that there are at least two, connected reasons Pollin is committed to growth. First, he regards it as politically non-negotiable: 'most political leaders remain convinced that significantly cutting fossil-fuel dependency will slow economic growth and cost jobs – a price they are unwilling to pay.'[13] Author of *Back to Full Employment* (2012), Pollin argues growth is politically compulsory because it is connected to employment, and he believes that 'the single best form of protection' for workers in all countries who are displaced by the switch to clean energy – more than 'adjustment assistance programmes', like retraining and relocating workers – is 'a full-employment economy' in which 'there is an abundance of decent jobs available for all people seeking work'.[14] Accordingly, Pollin's central objection to degrowth is to its 'immediate effect': 'huge job losses and declining living standards for working people and the poor'. Pollin writes that he has 'not seen a convincing argument from a degrowth advocate' about how to avoid this eventuality. Can Burton and Somerville be said to supply one? They support Pollin's call for a 'just transition' – though who would oppose it? – and suggest that the rich world and high-income consumers ought to bear the brunt. But in the short term at least, the effects of their 'drastic' cuts in industrial food and goods production, construction and international trade would send prices soaring, while millions would be thrown out of work.

---

11   Thomas Friedman, 'The Green New Deal Rises Again', *New York Times*, 8 January 2019.

12   Burton and Somerville argue that Pollin ignores the fact that a faster-growing economy will be using more energy, thus annulling the progress made by a speedier transition: though moving faster up it, we will simply be adding 'to the hill that has to be climbed' by renewable-energy systems.

13   Pollin, 'Global Green Growth for Human Development', p. 3.

14   Ibid., p. 15.

Displacement

Another implicit fault line in the series separates those who envisage stabilizing the climate within the framework of a mitigated capitalism (Pollin, and, somewhat half-heartedly, Daly), from those who think averting climate catastrophe means transcending the prevailing political-economic order (Vettese, Burton and Somerville). The contributors mostly do not explicitly categorize their proposals in these terms: Daly doesn't think 'we should just abandon capitalism and opt for eco-socialism', yet he also says that if you want to call his more egalitarian vision of capitalism 'eco-socialism, that's fine with me'.

Those in the post-capitalist camp are similarly casual about how to classify their policies politically. Vettese's 'project might take on any number of mantles: "egalitarian eco-austerity", "eco-socialism" or, borrowing from Wilson, "half-earth economics".' And though Burton and Somerville speak of the 'collapse of the capitalist system', they also slightly hedge their invocation of socialism: 'an ecologically sustainable world economy' would require 'a socialist mode of production of some sort'.

This evasion of binding political distinctions has consequences. Instead of debating whether the planetary rescue operation can be conducted within the capitalist system – or, if not, what would be required to establish a different economic order within which it could – much of the argument becomes focused on growth, and its compatibility with ecological recovery. In other words, the crux of the disagreement is not exactly about the benefits of untrammelled growth – which no one, including Pollin, appears unequivocally in favour of – but about whether or not growth as such is inherently ecologically destructive. If, like Daly, Burton and Somerville and other degrowth advocates, you think the answer to this question is 'yes', then the question becomes whether or not stationary or even shrinking economies can remain capitalist (Daly, yes; Burton and Somerville, probably not).

Is capitalism capable of averting the ecological disaster it has helped to precipitate, or does it need to be jettisoned, along with fossil-fuelled growth, if the planet is to remain habitable? Broadly speaking Daly and Pollin seem to converge in thinking capitalism can prevent the worst of the oncoming climate crisis – as long as capitalism is prevented by massive state intervention from doing *its* worst. Daly and Pollin do not believe that markets will be the sole agent of the transition to clean energy; if they did, they would presumably have nothing to add to the debate, since the problem of 'what is to be done' would magically dissolve: we could simply sit back and let capitalism autopilot itself to ecological repair.

Vettese believes that solutions to the climate crisis like those offered by Daly 'underestimate the difficulties of shackling capitalism so as to slow it down'. Taking the view that the curtailment of economic activity necessary to protect the planet is unlikely to take place within a capitalist economy that 'leaves the overall system of commodification, and the motors of expansion, firmly in place', Burton and Somerville possibly put it more strongly, suggesting that the necessary downsizing will probably happen only after some kind of breakdown of the prevailing economic order.

There are reasons to doubt the idea that the collapse of capitalism is the answer to the ecological crisis we face. First, though we must surely acknowledge the minimum fact that 'there is a link between capitalism and emissions of carbon dioxide', at least since the adoption of coal by early-industrializing nations, it's not clear that this correlation between economic activity and ecological impact is unique to capitalism.[15] Communism, too – famously, in both the Soviet and Chinese cases – has been no less devastating for the environment in recent times, if over a briefer historical period. The industrialization of the USSR and the PRC was not at all different, in ecological terms, from that of their capitalist counterparts with whom they were trying to catch up. 'All modern states', Michael Mann writes, 'have sacrificed the environment to GDP, regardless of regime type.' Mann is convinced that 'if we all had state socialism, the problem would be just the same'. Perhaps this is partly why the contributors have mostly preferred to concentrate on the basic principle of cutting consumption, rather than on the broader picture of who owns the means of production.

Instrumentalizing the crisis?

Mann identifies three 'fundamental social actors of our time' who he thinks are responsible for climate change: capitalism, nation-states and individual consumers. For Mann, avoiding planetary disaster is a matter of curbing the impact and autonomy of all three. He makes two other important points about the kind of problem climate change poses: since it is 'a genuinely global issue' – 'emissions in all countries

---

15   Andreas Malm, 'Long Waves of Fossil Development: Periodizing Energy and Capital', *Mediations*, vol. 31, no. 2, spring 2018, p. 17.

affect everyone's climate' – 'legislation must be international', and, notwithstanding its urgency, it is a long-term problem.[16] These factors combine to make solving the climate crisis particularly difficult: short-termism characterizes the thinking of both politicians, beholden to the rhythm of election cycles, and the capitalist class, impelled by the profit-making imperative, while the nation-state remains the fundamental political and jurisdictional unit, and national security and the performance of the national economy, the overriding political priorities. Everyone's problem and no one's problem, it is an international crisis that has not yet become any nation's foremost concern. Until it is, it seems clear that the necessary transformations will not be undertaken.

Bearing in mind Mann's pointers about the specific difficulties climate change presents, can any conclusions be drawn from this comparative survey of the debate so far about the kind of strategies required? It seems unarguable that an essential component of any viable green strategy must be the existence of a global, intergovernmental body with genuine legislative capabilities and practical powers of enforcement. The problem with Pollin's programme is that it assumes that this kind of truly effective international organization either already exists, or could easily be created. Recent UN climate talks do not inspire confidence in this regard. The central strategic question, then, is how to mobilize global green coalitions that would make such a transnational body genuinely cooperative, productive and powerful – which might require governments to accept limitations on their national sovereignty.[17]

Aside from the ecological harm of ceaseless economic expansion, does capitalism also entrench geopolitical arrangements that thwart climate action? In *Climate Leviathan*, Geoff Mann and Joel Wainwright suggest that globalized capitalism is itself an impediment to cooperation on a world scale, since – though it gives rise to economic interdependence – it also heightens inter-state competitiveness and exacerbates global inequality, which 'undermines the capacity for collective action by reducing willingness to share sacrifices'.[18] This economic inequality is intensified by an acute form of ecological inequality: the skewed geographical distribution of where global

---

16   Mann, *The Sources of Social Power*, pp. 366, 362, 380.

17   To increase 'the power of the collectivity of nation-states', it might be necessary to reduce their individual autonomy: ibid., p. 380.

18   Geoff Mann and Joel Wainwright, *Climate Leviathan: A Political Theory of Our Planetary Future*, London, 2018, p. 101.

heating is predominantly caused, and where its impacts are most keenly felt. While Michael Mann is right to point out that 'carbon emissions anywhere affect everywhere' since 'the climate knows no boundaries', it is also true, as Mike Davis notes, that these effects are uneven: rich, high-emitting nations of the global North continue to bear most of the responsibility for the warming of the planet, while poorer countries in the global South are most likely to suffer the unpredictable consequences of the changes to the climatic system they did least to bring about, and to which they are less able to adapt. This economic and ecological unevenness is part of what makes the problem so intractable: how to compel high-consuming countries to accept sacrifices to secure the safety of more exposed regions? As Davis wryly observed: 'Coordinated global action on their behalf thus presupposes either their revolutionary empowerment – a scenario not considered by the IPCC – or the transmutation of the self-interest of rich countries and classes into an enlightened "solidarity" with little precedent in history.'

Vettese is alert to these issues: he discusses the way environmental-ist programmes can 'ossify the inequality between the global North and South', and argues that the 'hypocrisy' of the former 'has pre-vented greens from building coalitions across international borders and between social movements'. The 'half-earthing adoption of the 2,000-watt framework', Vettese suggests, 'would overcome this history of division', since 'it would allow the poorest to double or triple their consumption, while requiring a commensurate reduction by the rich'. But Vettese does not explain how this drastic reduction in consump-tion would be accomplished in advanced economies without the hemispheric 'division' he identifies *already* being overcome; the impo-sition of such radical policies implies the existence of the powerful international green alliances the current order forecloses.

Moral and ecological arguments abound for consuming less and organizing our economies more thoughtfully and fairly, and in ways that show greater respect for nature, as well as each other. But, as Mann writes, though 'eco-socialist arguments are morally valid, morality does not rule the world' – even if it does, as Daly and Kunkel discuss, have some 'material effect on how things happen'.[19] If Pollin's contribution disappoints because it sets aside ethical consid-erations, more radical proposals can encounter the opposite problem, which is that the concern for social and economic justice can seem to predominate over ecological considerations, which can seem tacked

---

19   Mann, *The Sources of Social Power*, p. 390.

on or subsidiary. Rather than presenting robust arguments for why we must combat capitalism and climate change simultaneously, eco-socialist visions can leave one with the impression that they are instrumentalizing the climate crisis – co-opting its urgency in order to expedite socialist transformation.[20] However sympathetic one is to the latter aspiration, there is a danger that such overt opportunism can make eco-socialist proposals seem utopian and partisan rather than grounded in objective analysis.

Given this, are there political projects which not only combine social and economic justice with ecological rescue, but integrate them so tightly that they become structurally dependent?[21] It may be true that 'it is easier to imagine the end of the world than to imagine the end of capitalism', but can it be shown that we need to attempt the latter – the hardly imaginable – in order to prevent the former – the easily imaginable – from befalling us in reality?[22]

Pragmatic impossibilism vs utopian realism

Pollin's ruling out of individual sacrifice and fairness measures, his exclusive focus on cleaning our energy supply, and his refraining from making normative claims about how we ought to live, is, as we saw, what makes his proposal seem plausible. But is this lean approach as pragmatic as it seems in the context of a crisis of such magnitude and urgency? In 'Who Will Build the Ark?' Mike Davis begins by evoking his own psychological oscillations 'between ana-lytic despair and utopian possibility', and concludes with the conviction that 'taking a "realist" view of the human prospect, like seeing Medusa's head, would simply turn us into stone'. It can be

---

20   Consider, for example, how Naomi Klein describes her awakening to environ-mentalism: 'I began to understand how climate change . . . could become a galvanizing force for humanity, leaving us all not just safer from extreme weather, but with socie-ties that are safer and fairer in all kinds of other ways as well . . . This is a vision of the future that goes beyond just surviving or enduring climate change, beyond "miti-gating" and "adapting" to it in the grim language of the United Nations. It is a vision in which we collectively use the crisis to leap somewhere that seems, frankly, better than where we are right now': *This Changes Everything*, p. 7. The instrumentalism – 'use the crisis' – is here undisguised.

21   See, for example, George Monbiot's 'scheme for tackling climate change', which aims to be 'fair and progressive' only because 'that is what would make it politically plausible . . . Let us hammer the rich by other means, but let us not confuse this programme with an attempt to cut carbon emissions': 'Environmental Feedback', p. 112.

22   Quoted by Fredric Jameson in 'Future City', NLR 21, May–June 2003.

necessary and, in a certain way, expedient, to make unrealistic demands, as Davis explains: 'Only a return to explicitly utopian thinking can clarify the minimal conditions for the preservation of human solidarity in face of convergent planetary crises.' Realism and utopianism are thus not always simple opposites: utopianism can be strategic, in some version of what *n+1* founding editor Mark Greif once called 'calculated impossibilism' – 'asking for what is at present impossible, in order to get at last, by indirection or implausible directness, the principles that would underlie the world we'd want rather than the one we have'.[23]

Propelling Davis's lurches between hopelessness and utopianism is the perception that reality – the all too real prospect of global disaster – has become, so to speak, unrealistic. What is scientifically 'necessary' to avert this disaster may be politically 'impossible': 'Either we fight for "impossible" solutions to the increasingly entangled crises of urban poverty and climate change, or become ourselves complicit in a de facto triage of humanity.'

During the latest dispiriting episode of the UN climate talks, held in Katowice in Poland in December, Wells Griffith, Trump's international energy and climate adviser, insisted: 'We strongly believe that no country should have to sacrifice their economic prosperity or energy security in pursuit of environmental sustainability.'[24] This is what devotion to GDP also means: as an index of the size of national economies, it is not just a commitment to the economy over the environment, it is a commitment to the nation over the rest of the world – and not just to the national economy, but to national security.[25] And economic strength is critical for the industrial militarization that helps ensure geopolitical dominance. Meanwhile, as Michael Mann writes: 'The more militarized a country is, the more it damages the environment.' Among the ways, Mann points out, of enhancing national security – 'currently the most sacred goal of American politicians' – is to achieve 'resource independence', by, for example, seeking out new fossil-fuel reserves on home soil in order to reduce dependence on imported energy. The irony, then, is that what countries do in the name of 'national

---

23   Francis Mulhern, 'A Party of Latecomers', NLR 93, May–June 2015, pp. 82–3.
24   Editorial, 'Trump Imperils the Planet', *New York Times*, 26 December 2018.
25   J. R. McNeill writes that 'among the swirl of ideas, policies and political structures of the twentieth century, the most ecologically influential probably were the growth imperative and the (not unrelated) security anxiety that together dominated policy around the world': *Something New Under the Sun: An Environmental History of the Twentieth-Century World*, Harmondsworth, 2000, p. 355.

security' frequently imperils the ecological security of the planet they share.[26]

In the month before the Katowice talks, a US climate report warned that global warming could reduce America's GDP by 10 per cent by the end of the century.[27] Climate change is not only set to undo decades of economic progress in developing (and comparatively ecologically innocent) countries, but to shrink the world's largest and most ecologically culpable economies, too. If advanced economies don't degrow now by choice, in other words, they will be degrown later by force. The bloodless logic of the warning – save the planet to save (America's) GDP – suggests that if 'fidelity to GDP amounts to the religion of the modern world', the faith of the modern world's largest economy shows no sign of waning. Even if the rich world's GDP idols are not to be smashed, the ecological gods may still punish its devotion to them.

26   Mann, *The Sources of Social Power*, pp. 365, 376.
27   Coral Davenport and Kendra Pierre-Louis, 'US Climate Report Warns of Damaged Environment and Shrinking Economy', *New York Times*, 23 November 2018.

7

An Eco-Feminist Proposal

Sufficiency Provisioning and Democratic Money

MARY MELLOR

2019

Two features stand out in the NLR debate on eco-strategy. First, whether arguing for a Green New Deal, like Robert Pollin, or for degrowth, half-earthing or a 'steady-state' economy to limit humanity's impact on the planet, as Herman Daly, Troy Vettese and Mark Burton and Peter Somerville do, the contributors all advance a view of the relation between the productive economy and the biosphere that is largely gender-blind.[1] They fail to recognize the role of reproductive work in mediating between nature and 'the economy', through the daily regeneration of human (and non-human) life. Steady-state and degrowth proposals often ignore the fact that reproductive work will probably increase if energy for labour-saving appliances is less readily available. Even ending the alienation of paid work would not mean freedom from the unrelenting nature of care work throughout the life cycle. Historically – and still, for the most part, today – this labour has mainly been undertaken by women, though colonized and exploited peoples also bear the costs and burdens of socially and ecologically unsustainable economies.

Eco-socialist utopians such as the degrowther Serge Latouche in *Farewell to Growth* (2009) or the eco-Marxist Michael Löwy in his recent essay 'Why Eco-socialism' tend to leap over these problems to hail a genderless 'kingdom of freedom'.[2] But as socialist-feminists

---

1   See also Christine Bauhardt, 'Solutions to the Crisis? The Green New Deal, Degrowth, and the Solidarity Economy: Alternatives to the Capitalist Growth Economy from an Ecofeminist Economics Perspective', *Ecological Economics,* vol. 102, June 2014, pp. 60–8.

2   Michael Löwy, 'Why Ecosocialism: For a Red–Green Future', *Great Transition Initiative* website, December 2018.

have long pointed out, in such dreams of a coming age in which one can hunt in the morning, fish in the afternoon and be a critic after dinner, there is rarely any mention of who cooks the dinner. Second, as Lola Seaton points out, these thinkers offer bold global strategies for solving climate change and rescuing biodiversity, but they don't tell us how to get there from here – from our privatized, neoliberal economies with their indebted public sectors and political systems at the mercy of corporate lobbyists.

This contribution aims to cut the Gordian knot of austerity politics, on the one hand, and environmental destruction on the other, by proposing the democratization of money as a catalyst in the transition from current patterns of exploitation and unsustainability to an eco-feminist model of 'sufficiency provisioning'. Both terms require a word of explanation. 'Sufficiency', as an organizing principle, is most clearly defined by what it is not – neither 'too much' nor 'too little'. As Daly and others have suggested in an earlier work, sufficiency is 'enough', the minimum that enables people to flourish.[3] There can be no absolute prescriptions for it; what counts as enough must be continually debated, as social and environmental conditions change. Sufficiency is an egalitarian concept: sufficiency for one must be sufficiency for all, or else some will have more than enough and others too little. The 'sacrifices' demanded by ecological sustainability, as Seaton puts it, should therefore be met first by those who have more than enough, rather than falling on those with less than they need.

The concept of provisioning is rooted in feminist economics, with its concern for both productive and reproductive labour; it is critical to the development of a radical political economy that is both socially just and ecologically sustainable.[4] The notion of provisioning is more comprehensive than the standard categories of political economics, embracing an understanding of human beings as themselves bodily creatures, metabolically related to the environment and embedded in the natural conditions of the planet. As such, provisioning addresses the entire life course of each person, not just those aspects of production and consumption defined by market economics. By contrast, the *homo economicus* of mainstream thinking is assumed to be fit, mobile, able-bodied and unencumbered by domestic or other responsibilities. 'He' transcends the real world of the body, which lives

---

3   See Herman Daly's preface to Rob Dietz and Dan O'Neill, *Enough Is Enough: Building a Sustainable Economy in a World of Finite Resources*, Abingdon, 2013.

4   Marilyn Power, 'Social Provisioning as a Starting Point for Feminist Economics', *Feminist Economics*, vol. 10, no. 3, 2004, pp. 3–19.

in biological time – the time it takes to rest, recover, grow up and grow old; the daily cycle and the life cycle itself. Economic man is also disconnected from ecological time – that is, the time it takes to restore the environmental effects of human activity, the life cycle of renewal and replenishment within the ecosystem. 'He' is also alienated from the life cycle of products and processes, seeing them only as traded commodities or consumable conveniences; they appear and are discarded, vanishing from 'his' gaze.[5]

'Women's work' and nature

Just as the capitalist mode of production treats natural resources and ecosystems – fossil fuels, water systems, forests, soils, the atmosphere, the climate system – as inexhaustible, 'costless externalities', so also it relies on the 'costless externality' of the work, historically assigned to women in the gendered division of labour, of producing healthy, adaptable members of the labour force, whose needs for bodily and emotional sustenance are met outside the workplace. This is not to identify an essentialized concept of 'woman' with nature, as in Romantic theory. The relations of nature and of 'women's work' to the capitalist-patriarchal economy are not simply parallel – both equally exploited. To the contrary, reproductive work stands between 'the economy' and the natural world, grappling with the consequences of ecological destruction. It is this historically gendered work that enables *Homo economicus* to assume a position of transcendence towards the space and time of the natural world – and towards other creatures, human or otherwise – rather than to acknowledge the immanence of embodied creaturely existence.

By contrast, the labour of social reproduction associated with women – child-bearing and rearing; provisioning, cooking, cleaning; caring for the old, the young, the sick – is spatially centred around a specific environment, the home, and characterized by presence, by 'being there'. The sick must be tended when ill, children clothed and fed when they wake. Temporally, as noted above, the labour of reproduction is structured by daily, recurring needs and by the generational rhythms of the life cycle. Thus, while capitalist productive processes aspire to expand globally and operate 24/7, social-reproductive work restores the embodiedness of humankind, subject to the same processes

---

5 I develop this argument in 'Women, Nature and the Social Construction of "Economic Man"', *Ecological Economics*, vol. 20, no. 2, February 1997, pp. 129–40; see also *Breaking the Boundaries*, London, 1992.

of metabolic growth and decay as other forms of life on Earth, and embedded in the same environmental framework. For environmental strategy, social-reproductive labour also offers a way to connect ecological sustainability to social justice, through the project of sufficiency provisioning.

Sufficiency provisioning thus implies a dual objective: the provision of the goods and services necessary for social reproduction – housing, food, drinking water, childcare, health needs – governed by the twin principles of environmental sustainability and social justice. The question would be to define the limits of what the biosphere can sustain, and to treat all equally within that constraint. This could imply a move from agro-industry to agro-ecology, a choice for local supply chains, a shift to environmentally friendly construction methods and, more generally, to forms of production that help promote the regeneration of the environment. In terms of macroeconomic relations, the concept of provisioning helps break down the formal distinction between paid and unpaid work. Aspects of the current economy would become part of the provisioning framework – contributing to sufficiency provisioning through a market mechanism. But since such a market system would need to operate according to principles of social justice and ecological sustainability, this would involve much more local and social production: co-operative businesses and so forth. At the same time, self-organized social-economy structures can only address a limited range of provisioning. There would remain an important role for the public economy, whether local, national or international; ultimately, only collective, democratic, universal provisioning can guarantee social justice. Sufficiency provisioning thus also requires the revaluation of the public sector as a provider of goods and services, through re-gendered and non-oppressive relations. This would entail an expansion of high-quality public-sector social provision, funded at least in part by public money.

This approach contrasts with two alternative perspectives for addressing the problems of reproductive labour and ecological sustainability. The first aimed to bring both bodywork and ecological considerations into current economic frameworks by attaching a monetary value to them: make the market pay. Socialist feminists long debated the idea of 'wages for housework', but the proposal faced a major problem: even if the contribution of domestic work to capital accumulation could be calculated, payment would not end women's unequal burden and might well reinforce it.[6] Green proposals for

6   Jean Gardiner, *Gender, Care and Economics*, London, 1997, pp. 82–98.

imposing environmental constraints within market structures also faced the problem that this was no guarantee of more sustainable practices and could arguably – as with the EU's cap-and-trade systems – make things worse. The opposite solution would be an environmentalism that would abandon the use of money altogether. Proponents such as Veronika Bennholdt-Thomsen and Maria Mies acknowledge that this would entail a return to subsistence production and argue explicitly that this should be the aim.[7] Anitra Nelson and Frans Timmerman see non-monetary local production building up to a more integrated economic structure through a 'nested' sequence of productive decisions.[8] In my view, neither version is feasible: the level of urbanization today would make returning to a primarily rural economy highly problematic, and a system of production without the use of money would be unwieldy on any but the most local level. What is needed is a money system that can support sufficiency provisioning.

Greening the mints

The case for seeing money as a key agent of change might not appear obvious.[9] For socialists, money is often seen as an epiphenomenon masking the real conflicts and contradictions of the capitalist productive process. For feminists and greens, it's sometimes viewed as an agent of oppression – women trapped and exploited through their unpaid or underpaid labour – or destruction, in the case of the commodification of nature. Money should instead be seen as a commons, a public resource.[10] This is not a utopian idea; it exists in modern economies, but it has been obscured by the myths and distortions propounded by capitalist, and particularly neoliberal, economics. This has allowed control of the production of money to be privatized, in theory as well as practice. If whole-life provisioning is to be addressed, the idea of public money – a money for the people – needs to be reclaimed, along with the idea of a public economy. What is needed is a democratic politics of money.

---

7   Veronika Bennholdt-Thomsen and Maria Mies, *The Subsistence Perspective: Beyond the Globalized Economy*, London, 1999.

8   Anitra Nelson and Frans Timmerman, *Life Without Money: Building Fair and Sustainable Economies*, London, 2011.

9   Mary Mellor, 'Could the Money System Be the Basis of a Sufficiency Economy?', *Real-World Economics Review*, no. 54, September 2010, pp. 80–9.

10   Mary Mellor, *The Future of Money: From Financial Crisis to Public Resource*, London, 2010.

Mainstream economics has tended to see money solely in relation to the market, as a means for the efficient allocation of resources, reflected in prices. It views money as a convenience whose primary functions are to express value (unit of account) and to transfer value (medium of exchange). What is less often examined are the relations of ownership and control over the production and circulation of money itself. Money does not just appear in societies; it has to be created and circulated, its producer enjoying the advantage of seigniorage, the benefit of first use of the money.[11] In capitalist economies, the perception of money is subject to a particular ideological confusion. Monopoly control over the creation of public currency, and responsibility for its efficacy, lies with the state, or with publicly authorized monetary authorities. Unauthorized creation of the public currency is punished as counterfeiting; on a large scale, it would intimate that the state had lost control of a major lever of governance.

However, the phrase 'making money' is generally taken to imply that the market is the source of money – or rather, that while the state creates money as a medium, the market turns it into wealth. This leads to the conundrum that, while the currency is a public institution, the public economy is dependent on the market for access to that currency. As a result, the money available for public services and structures is dependent upon what the market claims it can afford. Proposals for public spending are often quashed with the rhetorical question, 'Where is the money to come from?' Implicitly this reflects a zero-sum assumption that public expenditure must always be at someone's expense – the taxpayer, commercial profitability; there is a presumption that money is in short supply. This form of 'handbag economics' is, of course, highly ideological: the public economy is portrayed as a dependent that must live on a 'house-keeping allowance' from the market. Money is seen as a scarce and limited resource: if the state spends money, then someone else – the 'hard-pressed taxpayer' – must be out of pocket. This is the logic of austerity: if wealth is to be maximized, public expenditure must be cut to the bone, to leave as much money as possible free for the market.

This conception of money is largely based on myth. Money is obviously not in short supply; the paper, inks, base metals and electronic blips that constitute a currency are not themselves subject to scarcity. Central banks' quantitative easing in response to the 2008

---

11   See Josh Ryan-Collins et al., *Where Does Money Come From? A Guide to the UK Monetary and Banking System*, New Economics Foundation, London, 2011; see also Joseph Huber, *Sovereign Money: Beyond Reserve Banking*, Basingstoke, 2017.

financial crisis showed that states can, and do, 'print money', increasing the money supply – although, following the tenets of neoliberalism, only to meet the needs of the financial sector; calls for 'quantitative easing for the people' were ignored.

Myths of scarcity

The claim that money originates in market transactions rests on the myth that money was invented to overcome the limitations of barter. This narrative was famously promulgated by the Austrian economist Carl Menger, who built on the work of Smith to argue that money emerged spontaneously from an earlier form of economy, the era of barter.[12] By projecting individualistic market-like behaviour back onto pre-market societies, the myth of barter naturalizes this behaviour – presents it as a defining human feature. In fact, anthropological studies of pre-state and pre-market communities have found that, while most communities already had some form of money, this was mainly used in a social context: to celebrate important events or to quell conflicts – to compensate for injuries or placate antagonistic groups.[13] Moreover, there is scant historical evidence of barter economies, or even individual bartering on any scale in these societies.

The myth of barter is the result of a thought experiment. Instead of exploring empirically what types of economy preceded the market, Menger's theory works backwards from the experience of how money operates in market economies. The question then becomes, 'How would markets operate if money had not been invented?' The presumption is that people would barter, and that the inconvenience of bartering would lead to the invention of money. As the original form of money was assumed to be gold or silver, a 'commodity theory' of the origin of money was born. This led directly to the notion that, ideally, money should be valuable in itself: scarcity gives it its value, therefore money is, or should be, necessarily in short supply. But even if precious metal had been the original form of money (which it was not), or coinage had been an invention of the market (which it was not), precious-metal money has not been in general circulation for generations. It is accepted that all money is now fiat money – that is,

---

12   Carl Menger, 'On the Origin of Money', *The Economic Journal*, vol. 2, no. 6, June 1892, pp. 239–55.

13   The *locus classicus* is Alison Hingston Quiggin, *A Survey of Primitive Money: The Beginnings of Currency*, London, 1949; see also David Graeber, *Debt: The First 5,000 Years*, New York, 2011.

valueless in itself, and not pegged to any sort of 'real' money with intrinsic value, such as gold, but guaranteed only by the word of the state. This appears to make modern money no less useful. Today, most money exists only as bank records, refuting the argument that money should be made of something rare, or of any 'thing' at all.

Radical money theorists have long argued that it was commercial banks, rather than market transactions, that were creating new public currency out of thin air. No existing bank deposits are raided when a loan is made.[14] Bank loans add to the overall money supply by creating new accounts, or adding numbers to existing accounts, designated in the national currency. When the loans are paid back with interest, the overall money supply shrinks. Mainstream banking theory has conventionally claimed that this bank-produced money was not really public currency, it was only 'credit' money. This illusion was shattered by the 2008 financial crisis, when governments had to guarantee money in bank accounts to preserve the integrity of their currencies. With transactions increasingly becoming cashless, bank transfers are clearly as 'real' as any other form of money, and are commonly understood as being no different to a cash payment.

Bank loans do create public currency, but this is a form of money supply based on debt and therefore subject to crises. As long as the circuit of loans and repayment with interest is flowing well – and preferably expanding with increased lending – there will be no problem. However, if there are no new borrowers, or the banks cannot identify viable loans, the money supply will contract as old loans are repaid. Debt as the basis for the supply of money is socially divisive – only the credit-worthy can access new money – and economically unsustainable: bank lending in a financialized economy rapidly results in vertiginously high levels of leverage, pumping up the financial markets, funding speculative gambles, buyouts and takeovers, often leaving the targeted companies burdened with debt. A money system based on debt is also likely to be ecologically damaging: the need to repay with interest requires an expanding economy, putting pressure upon natural resources beyond the biosphere's ability to regenerate.

The advent of commercial banking, and the ability of those banks to create debt-based money, was central to the emergence of capitalism.[15] For thousands of years before that, the creation and circulation

---

14   John Kenneth Galbraith, *Money: Whence It Came, Where It Went*, London, 1975.

15   John Smith, *Money, Enterprise and Income Distribution: Towards a Macroeconomic Theory of Capitalism*, London, 2009.

of money was the prerogative of the sovereign. In the same way that capitalism as a system of production eclipsed the role of feudal elites, so capitalist credit money can be seen as wresting monetary power from autocratic rulers.[16] However, capitalist money had its own contradictions and limitations. The new system of commercial credit that emerged did not fully displace sovereign money but fused with it, creating a hybrid. Rather than using the state-generated, debt-free circulating currency, people began to circulate the private credit notes issued by commercial lenders. Thus, for example, the Bank of England was set up as a private bank in 1694 to lend money, via paper loans, to the state. Over time, the Bank of England credit notes became the authorized national currency. Even today, sterling notes still 'promise to pay the bearer' the value of the note in sovereign money, although they circulate as cash. The commercial banks' role in creating public money is not acknowledged in more recent currencies: the dollar bill states that it must be accepted as 'legal tender', and the euro says nothing other than the numerical value of the note. As a result, the politics of money – and particularly the banks' role in its creation and circulation – is occluded.

Money as commons

If a public-money system is to operate as a mechanism of ecological sustainability and social justice, we need to socialize and democratize the production of money – and to argue that it is not necessary always to defer to the market. There are pressing political questions to raise. By what right are the commercial banks creating public currency – dollars, sterling, euros – as debt? To whom are the banks accountable for being able to create currency out of nothing? Who are the beneficiaries of this largesse? Should bank lending continue to be seen as a private matter? As they are issuing new public currency, shouldn't banks be seen as an arm of the state and made democratically answerable? Should all the banks be nationalized or socialized? Should their power to create money through debt be curtailed? Why should they be bailed out by the state if they end up in a crisis?

At the same time, we need to re-evaluate the use of sovereign power to create debt-free money. If bank loans and their repayment increase and reduce the overall money supply, a similar process occurs within the public economy: currency is created and circulated as the government

---

16   I elaborate on this history in Mary Mellor, *Money: Myths, Truths and Alternatives*, Bristol, 2019.

spends, adding to the money supply, while taxation removes money from circulation. Both bank lending and repayment, and public spending and tax-collecting, are continuous circuits, with money flowing in and out. For mainstream economics, higher taxes are the driving force of public expenditure. But there are strong arguments for seeing public spending as the driving force instead, with citizens' ability to pay taxes dependent on access to public money in the first place – on public investments in infrastructure, health and education, for example. A substantial portion of the tax take comes from people in the public sector, who could not pay their taxes unless they had first been paid from the public budget. Nor can the public sector itself be funded entirely by the 'wealth-creating' private sector; even in the low-spending United States, public expenditure reached 45 per cent of GDP following the 2008 crisis. Rather than states relying on privately generated, debt-based money, recent experience has shown the markets to be reliant on the circulation of public money.

The market domination of the creation of money needs to be challenged if sufficiency provisioning is to be achieved. There is a political choice to be made between debt as the main driver of the economy and the explicit exercise of the sovereign power to create and circulate money – the power, not of an autocratic ruler, but of a sovereign people. Through the democratic exercise of this power, the public would be able to create debt-free money that could be directly allocated or spent in the public economy. It could be used to recognise the needs of the sphere of reproduction and to secure the future of the environment. This is not as daunting a project as it might seem. The sovereign power to create money has not gone away: as noted, it has been used on a grand scale in quantitative easing, and it is at work, more discreetly, in general public spending.

As new money in the economy is effectively produced out of thin air, there is an overwhelming case for putting this 'commons' into the hands of the people as a whole rather than into the commercial market. This would transform economic priorities. Instead of seeking private profits, money would be issued to meet needs within the limits of ecological sustainability. Identifying those needs would require public participation to draw up a people's budget. Participatory approaches to budgeting are already well established. The method was pioneered in 1989 in the southern Brazilian city of Porto Alegre, where citizens' assemblies debated and determined public-spending priorities – an initiative of the Workers' Party. The assemblies then elected budget delegates to put their proposals forward to higher levels of decision-making. Since that time, more than two thousand examples of participatory budgeting have been explored or established around the world.

All public and private organizations that received a direct or indirect allocation of public money would need to have clear mechanisms for democratic accountability and transparency in place. The efficiency and efficacy of public spending would need to be monitored on a regular basis by citizens, workers and user-groups – another important focus of democratic participation. However, participation should not just be about how to spend a given amount of money. Most importantly, a people's budget would determine how big the public economy should be. There are no 'natural' limits on public spending. The first major decision would therefore be the long-term balance between public provisioning and the market.

What of inflation? While there is no 'natural' shortage of money for public spending, there is the problem of issuing too much. A high level of public expenditure could cause inflation by creating a money flow that overwhelms finite provisioning capacity, particularly in the market sector. This is where taxation comes in. As we have seen, taxation does not *raise* the money to spend, but it does *retrieve* the money already spent. The monetary role of taxation in this regard is to remove excess money. Calculating the likely impact of public expenditure on the overall money supply would require technical expertise to assess the level of monetary retrieval needed, through taxation and other government charges, for a particular level of public expenditure. The monetary assessors need have no role in determining how much public expenditure there should be, nor what taxes should be applied. In contrast to neoliberal attempts to reduce public spending to 'balance' tax income, the balance here is between public expenditure and provisioning capacity, with taxation serving as an instrument of that balance.

Taxation is not the only mechanism of monetary retrieval. State borrowing also removes money from the economy, technically referred to as 'sterilizing' public expenditure. The key point is that all sectors that benefit from money creation in the public-spending circuit need to contribute to the retrieval process, in a socially just way. Much of the money generated by bank lending and state spending in recent years has gravitated to the internationalized financial sector and tech giants. This makes retrieval of that money by individual states more difficult, while taxation pressures then fall on captive groups such as employees and consumers. Rather than being seen as major contributors to the economy, large tax-avoiding and speculative companies should be seen as a drain on the public resource of money.

The balance in provisioning between the public sector, the market and other social and community structures is not fixed, but something that is open to debate. And while recognizing public money as a public resource is a direct challenge to the domination of the market, it does not automatically lead to sufficiency provisioning or to the recasting of reproductive labour. It does, however, provide a framework within which the case for sufficiency provisioning as a route to ecological sustainability, gender equality and social justice can be made. The critical point is that monetization does not necessarily mean commodification. On the contrary, the democratization of money challenges the assumption that its use must entail profit-seeking market exchange. If sufficiency provisioning is to be the aim, the starting point should instead be human needs and those of the planet. Rather than two-step provisioning – in which money has to be earned by wage labour, no matter how exploitative or unsustainable, in order to provide for personal needs – this would encourage a shift to one-step provisioning, in which most people can work directly to fulfil those needs.

8

Hot-Earth Rebels

ZION LIGHTS

2019

Over the past year, Extinction Rebellion (XR) has drawn a new gene-
ration into mass civil disobedience over climate change – literally
bringing the London traffic to a halt. Could you tell us about your
background, and how you got involved in XR?

I was born in 1984 and grew up in an industrial suburb of Birming-
ham. My parents were from India – a little village in the Punjab – and
came over to get factory jobs. I actually began thinking about
environmental issues as a child – we learnt about the Amazon
rainforest and global warming in school; this was around the time
of the '90s Rio Earth Summit. There was a TV advertising campaign
about taking care of the planet – turn the taps off, switch out the
light when you leave the room – which had the tagline 'It's not too
late'. I remember watching it with a horrible feeling: what if we *are*
leaving it too late? I used to get my parents to collect all our glass
bottles and take them down to the bottle bank for recycling when
we went shopping on a Saturday. And I turned vegetarian too. At
university I was part of a campaign to switch the campus to renewable energy, which we won. And later I was involved in the Climate
Action Camp, which focused on corporations rather than public
disruption.

Then my children were born, which was a turning point. The
stakes seemed higher: what situation were they going to inherit? I'd
moved to Devon and was doing a lot of freelance writing about
environmental politics and sustainable lifestyles, including a book
called *The Ultimate Guide to Green Parenting*, put out by *New Inter-*
nationalist – it's a science-based approach to green birth, baby
essentials, greening your home. So, like a lot of people, I was chipping
away on my own. When I first saw Extinction Rebellion come into
being, I was excited, of course, and got in touch with my local

group – but I thought it might be another movement that would just fizzle out, like the Climate Camps or Occupy. With the April Rebellion this spring, when we blocked five sites in London – Oxford Circus, Marble Arch, Parliament Square, Piccadilly Circus, Waterloo Bridge – I realized this was different. I helped take Waterloo Bridge, which turned into a sort of festival, with huge numbers of people turning up after seeing us on television, many of whom had never been involved in protest before. We ended up staying there for two weeks. That's when I thought, if anything works, it's this. I gave up my other work and ended up switching over full-time to Extinction Rebellion.

So how did Extinction Rebellion get started?

What really galvanized XR was the 2018 IPCC report, *Global Warming of 1.5°C* – just as it did Greta Thunberg and the school-students who protested in the Fridays for Future campaign. The International Panel on Climate Change is very careful in its formulations to avoid anything scientifically contentious – it always seeks a broad consensus among the international climate scientists whose work it draws on. They agree that the global mean surface temperature now is around 0.87° higher than the 1850–1900 average, the proxy for the 'pre-industrial level'. Over the last thirty years, as carbon emissions have soared, it's been rising at roughly 0.2°C per decade. This warming has already brought loss of ice, rainfall changes – increased droughts and floods – and ocean acidification, as the seawater absorbs carbon. The southern Arctic permafrost is already softening, the northern tundra and boreal forests are changing, sea levels are rising and marine ecosystems have already been affected – 70 per cent of warm-water coral reefs are dying off and fish populations are migrating to cooler regions. At 1.5°C hotter – and the greenhouse effects of past emissions guarantee we'll reach it by 2040 – these present problems will be intensified, with the Arctic ecosystems, high mountain ranges and coastal regions most affected. But the IPCC report warned that simply limiting global warming to 1.5°C will require 'rapid, far-reaching and unprecedented changes in all aspects of society' – and if we don't make those changes now, cutting emissions by 40 per cent in the next twelve years, global temperatures will increase well above that, with terrifying effects.

XR was launched in October 2018, the same month as the IPCC report?

Yes. Its precursor was a group called Rising Up, started eighteen months before by some long-standing direct-action campaigners. There was Gail Bradbrook, who'd been involved in environmental campaigns since she was a teenager and had led anti-fracking protests around Stroud in Gloucestershire. There was Simon Bramwell, a builder and bush-craft teacher, who founded the Stroud-based Compassionate Revolution group in 2015 with Gail and George Barda, an Occupy and Greenpeace activist. Roger Hallam was studying civil disobedience at King's College, London; originally he'd been an organic farmer in Wales, but he could see the impact of climate change on his crops and began reading up about it. Clare Farrell was a fashion designer, she does a lot of XR's art work – the block printing, for example. Robin Boardman was a student from Bristol, a bit younger than the rest.

It's striking that so many of the original Extinction Rebels seem to come from the West Country – the Cotswolds, mid-Wales, down to Somerset and Devon – a region of small towns, hills and moors, and mixed farming, compared to the flat fields of East Anglia. It used to be seen as majority-conservative, though since the seventies, counter-cultural networks have been flourishing there.

Yes, it's interesting – you get painted as middle class, yet Gail is a Yorkshire miner's daughter, and I'm the child of immigrant factory workers. My parents certainly weren't hippies – though some people think they must have been, to call me Zion. They're very hardworking, very pro-capitalist, because that enabled them to get out of poverty – although I tell them, actually, capitalism is the reason you're in poverty. But they do care about ecological issues, because they know what's going on in India – the droughts, the terrible smog.

So what motivated Rising Up?

The starting point was the need to find a more effective form of protest than what we'd all been doing to date. Pretty much none of this came out of our own innovative thinking. It was about looking at the research, adding up the facts. Conventional A-to-B marches don't work: millions of us demonstrated against the Iraq War and it didn't make any difference. A key piece of research was Erica Chenoweth and Maria Stephan's *Why Civil Resistance Works*. They take data from hundreds of twentieth-century social movements and analyse what they did right and what they did wrong. The most successful ones, those that had their demands met, used forms of decentralized, non-violent civil disobedience – large-scale direct action. The tipping-point, Chenoweth and Stephan found, was to get 3.5 per cent of the population involved. That's not a huge number – it's about two million in the UK. But it's not just about getting them to demonstrate, because unfortunately that doesn't make any difference. It's about getting them involved at a higher level. If two million people bring the capital city to a stand-still, what can the government do? They can't arrest that many people. We saw that in the April and October Rebellions this year: even when the number of people arrested was in the thousands, the police and the judicial system were overwhelmed.

It's interesting that Extinction Rebellion borrows from this US 'colour revolutions' tradition. Although Chenoweth herself started from a slightly different area of expertise, in counter-terrorism and advice to Homeland Security about US financial-sector vulnerabilities, her work on civil disobedience chimes broadly with the Albert Einstein Institute approach. Maria Stephan works for the US State Department at NATO HQ and in Afghanistan. But how did the Rising Up activists put this approach into practice?

It's not a blueprint, but the research is useful. So, in May 2018, about fifteen Rising Up people met in a cafe in Bristol and agreed on a strategy. They set themselves the target of addressing a hundred meetings of potential activists up and down the country, giving people the facts about the climate emergency, explaining that, in face of government inaction, they were going to declare a rebellion on 31 October 2018 in Parliament Square and asking people to ask themselves what role they would like to play. The Declaration of Rebellion was drafted by Simon Bramwell. It's a really beautiful piece of prose, declaring that it's our duty to rebel against our failing government – 'We act in peace, with a ferocious love of these lands in our hearts.' Some one thousand five hundred people turned up for the declaration – far more than expected. That was followed by a spate of civil-disobedience actions in central London – sit-ins on bridges, planting trees outside Parliament, people super-gluing themselves to Buckingham Palace – which really caught the public's attention. That was when Extinction Rebellion erupted into the headlines, in November 2018. The April 2019 Rebellion was much bigger, as I said, and the October 2019 Rebellion bigger still in terms of numbers, though the police prevented us from taking the bridges and kept us in Trafalgar Square.

This mode of organizing suggests a radical break with Occupy's approach to operating by consensus?

XR uses a self-organizing system based on features of the holacracy model. The idea is to be able to harness group wisdom while still being able to set clear targets and respond quickly in fluid situations. Local groups are the basic community-organizing structures, but we recommend that, as they grow, they should split into smaller working groups or circles, each focusing on its own specialist area. Each circle can choose its own coordinator; the coordinators then meet to decide key local issues. Local groups can connect with each other through regional and national coordination.

Nationally, there are a whole series of different circles, each with its own mandate, and they work pretty much autonomously of each other. The Actions and Logistics circle decides on the dates and frames for actions. The Media and Messaging circle decides about organizing press conferences and press releases, covering relations with TV and the press; we've also set up our own paper, *The Hourglass*, which now has its own branch. There's a Political circle that meets with politicians; a Finance circle which takes care of donations and fundraising, and checks everything with the Legal team; a Regenerative Culture circle, a Communities circle, a Tech circle and so on. Some of the circles are quite large and have lots of teams branching off, but each has its own clearly defined role. All the circles have at least two coordinators, one internal, the other external – feeding back information to the coordinators of other circles. The Anchor circle encompasses all the others. We organize discussions through WhatsApp and Zoom video-conferencing calls.

Coordinators from different circles have to work together: for planning the big rebellions, the Action and Political circles formulate demands, the Arts circle needs to know what the Action circle needs, and the Action circle needs to know how much money there is from Finance. Media and Messaging is one of the bigger circles: we have between fifteen and twenty key coordinators, though that shifts around as different branches develop. The Social Media team decides on the hashtags, like #EverybodyNow before the rebellion and #WheresYourPlan. The idea for a funeral march, to stage the extinction of our future, came from brainstorming in the Arts circle. It was first performed in London with people solemnly burying a coffin marked 'Nature'. But then the local and regional groups picked it up, and it very quickly caught on in other countries around the world.

As we understand it, the holacracy model is a management structure derived from the 'holarchies' – the natural hierarchies – in Arthur Koestler's Ghost in the Machine?

Well, again, we don't practise that model, we just derive some features from it where they seem to be useful for building an inclusive, participatory movement. The important thing is that anyone can start a local group and take action in the name of Extinction Rebellion, as long as they adhere to XR's principles and values, and work towards realizing its three demands. As you can see from the map on our website, over two hundred XR groups have been set up across the UK, so it seems to be working!

Could you talk us through XR's three demands?

Number one is for the government to tell the truth about the climate and ecological emergency; we need the state to mobilize all-out, like in wartime, to halt the crisis. The second demand is to reduce greenhouse gas emissions to net zero by 2025 and to halt biodiversity loss – the 2019 IBPES Report on biodiversity says that one in seven species is now at risk of extinction. Third, a Citizens' Assembly on climate and ecological justice, to decide which policies to push forward. This would be a jury-like structure, chosen by lot to get a cross-section of society. Parliament will remain, but it will play an advisory role to the Citizens' Assembly.

These are quite general demands. Might it not be more effective to call for three more concrete actions, like legislating and budgeting for a mandatory switch to renewable energy, or making public transport free and strictly limiting the use of private vehicles or air travel?

I don't think we should pretend to be experts on all the factors involved. Of course there are things that I would like to see, like blue-green infrastructure – using as many local spaces as possible to plant trees and capture carbon. The billions poured into fossil-fuel subsidies could be diverted into cleaner energy and technology. Maybe we need to transition away from air travel, or offer incentives to develop a more ecological way to fly. But I would be hesitant to say, let's pick three solutions, because we definitely need more than that! The experts have a lot of solutions, but we need to forge a strategy from them in a democratic way, taking care of the needs of the most vulnerable. That's where the Citizens' Assembly comes in.

Plus, our first demand – tell the truth – gives people a platform to take their own demands forward. For instance, it has taken a lot of work to ensure that our XR Farmers group and Animal Rebellion are cooperating and not antagonizing each other. Even in the energy sector, it's quite a minefield. If you look at the IPCC report, its models for bringing down carbon emissions to a net total of zero by 2050 rely on the use of nuclear power and negative-emission technologies, many of which are untested: where will the captured carbon be stored, and what effect will it have on those habitats? The truth is simple: there's an emergency, that's just a fact. The solutions and social implications, they're complex.

People who've got involved in the Rebellions, often first-time young activists, speak very highly of the welcome and induction techniques that XR provides. Could you tell us about them?

We call it the XR DNA. It was developed by Robin Boardman and the Communities team, and it goes through the values and principles of XR, what got us here, how we operate, how to join in – the three DNA building blocks are story, strategy, structure. We run it at festivals or you can do it online. You can just click on a Zoom call and have a welcome and an introduction. The idea is that the DNA transmits the information that allows the movement to develop and lays a solid foundation for its culture. The training is also really good in helping people find where they can fit in. We have what we call XR butterflies who float around from team to team – I was a butterfly when I joined, because there's always so much that needs doing in each team, and there's no leader allocating people to different types of work. You have to find your own place individually and work out what you're good at, which can take time.

Your mode of drawing people into civil disobedience – the process of education, of people being able to take their own decisions about how they want to be involved – is a striking contrast to the vanguardist approach of a tradition like the Black Bloc. Could you talk us through a few concrete examples of how decisions are made?

Generally our model is: if you want to take an action, and it's non-violent, you can. You don't have to get permission from anyone; you don't have to go through some body that assesses it. But sometimes there are really strong disagreements. Before the 2019 October

Rebellion, Roger Hallam and some others in the Action circle proposed using drones to disrupt Heathrow Airport. Quite a few of us saw the proposal coming up on WhatsApp groups and went, 'Actually, maybe we're not happy with that.' There was a lot of discussion, with some arguing that it wasn't non-violent – because drones are used as weapons – and that our priority should be mass civil disobedience in the capital, rather than a small-group action out at Heathrow. It went back and forth, but most people weren't comfortable with the action, and eventually we said that it shouldn't be an XR action. So they organized as a separate group, the Heathrow Pause, which had thirty or forty people in it, many of whom weren't in XR anyway. So we decided that using a kind of consensus.

It's not a perfect system. It didn't work in the case of the Canning Town Station action this October, when a small group of protesters climbed on the roof of a train, stopping it from moving, and angry passengers dragged them off. Someone set up a poll the night before which found that over 70 per cent of XR people didn't want it to go ahead – and then it did. If we'd had more time, we could have followed the same process as with Heathrow. But that can be quite slow: you get the coordinators talking to their teams and then feeding back to the other coordinators, usually over Zoom or WhatsApp – there are too many WhatsApp chats. And most of us were on the ground in Trafalgar Square at the time, so there was no opportunity to discuss it. But so many people were upset by it that we're now talking about streamlining the process, so that key people in each team can come together and take decisions quickly. Something like this will probably happen again, because we're such a big movement, growing so quickly.

The Action circle is always quite strategic and careful about ensuring that roadblocks don't prevent people from getting to a hospital, for example. We chose those five bridges to block in November 2018 because they're always shutdown for the London Marathon, so there's obviously a plan in place to keep emergency services clear. There was total support for most of the actions this October: the mothers and babies' nurse-in outside the Google office; the Youth group climbing up the YouTube building; the huge wooden pyramid at Oxford Circus; the National Portrait Gallery protest against BP sponsorship. Then there are always smaller ongoing actions carried out by local groups. 'Clean up Barclays' was taken up by lots of groups – activists with mops and buckets, swabbing down the bank branches, calling on them to disinvest from fossil fuels. The regional groups are completely autonomous.

Have Extinction Rebellion groups been established in any other countries?

Yes. After the November 2018 Rebellion, XR groups were springing up everywhere – we counted six hundred fifty-five local groups in fifty-six countries. This October there was a major action in New York in Times Square, and another in Madrid. There were lots of small-scale actions, where the groups are smaller or where protest is more dangerous. In each country, members decide what is appropriate for them and adapt the model – and, of course, they work alongside existing environmental organizations, as we do. There's an XR campaign to challenge Bolsonaro's government in Brazil on state-sanctioned violence and ecocide by landowners and miners, in solidarity with indigenous groups. This August, Brazilian embassies in eleven countries were sprayed with blood-red paint and slogans like *Sangue Indígena, Nenhuma Gota a Mais* – indigenous blood, not one drop more. But there, for example, the XR coordinator couldn't do a magazine interview because it would have put their life at risk – especially on issues around deforestation. The Brazilian group has added a new first demand, about ecology and justice for indigenous people's rights. The situation is just as bad in Colombia, and much less reported. Five indigenous leaders were assassinated there recently, and seven hundred have been killed since 2016. Indigenous peoples are the best caretakers of their land, but instead of being given stewardship of it, they're being murdered on a horrendous scale.

How would you assess Extinction Rebellion's achievements to date?

Our first demand – for the government to tell the truth – hasn't exactly been met. Corbyn moved for the British parliament to declare a climate emergency, which was passed, but the Johnson government didn't budge. During the October Rebellion, Johnson himself called us 'uncooperative crusties', though a minion came to collect one of the trees XR was distributing in Parliament Square. They're still subsidizing the fossil-fuel industry, still talking about expanding Heathrow Airport – so our second demand has not been met either. Strangely enough the call for a Citizens' Assembly, which I always thought was our most radical demand, has been the most successful. Climate Assembly UK will take place at the start of 2020, over four weekends, with one hundred ten members drawn from thirty thousand households. The House of Commons set it up through several of its Select Committees.

The Scottish government will also be creating an assembly to make recommendations on how to reach net-zero emissions. A couple of smaller assemblies have already taken place in Camden and Oxford, and several other local councils – Devon, Leeds, Sheffield – are planning to follow suit. Even though Johnson has ignored our demands, over half the local governments in the UK have now got their own figures for reducing emissions between 2025 and 2050, and some of them are quite ambitious. Regional XR groups are lobbying their municipalities for measures like free public transport; they're looking at issues like clean air around schools. There was even a police station in Surrey that declared a climate emergency.

As it has been taken up more widely, our first demand has also been broadened out, from 'Tell the truth' to 'What's your truth?' – what should your community, your industry, be doing about the crisis? We now have a Media Tell the Truth team that focuses on trying to get the press to report on the climate. There's Culture Declares, for artists to get involved, and also Writers Rebel. During the October Rebellion there was an action to shut down London Fashion Week, to get the fashion industry to tell the truth about their water wastage and emissions. And what will it take to make the aviation sector bring down emissions? What does society look like if we tell the truth about the emergency we're in – and in which directions should it move?

9

Environment and Well-Being

A Perspective from the Global South

SHARACHCHANDRA LELE

2020

I write this from Bengaluru, during the 2020 lockdown imposed by the Modi government to tackle the Covid-19 pandemic. The lockdown has triggered two contrasting streams on social media. On the one hand, images of a cleaner Yamuna River, of the Himalayas newly visible from the hitherto polluted industrial towns in Punjab, and even of Mount Everest, which can now be seen from villages on the Gangetic plain, elicit comments like 'Mother Earth is healing' and 'How can we retain the green dividend of Covid-19?' On the other, the footage of hundreds of thousands of now-jobless migrant workers, confined in transit camps or desperately setting out to walk hundreds of miles to their villages, reveals the seamy underbelly of capitalist economic growth and the discrimination that runs deep in our society. In this context, with economies shattered and a global depression looming, the ongoing 'green strategy' debate in NLR may seem irrelevant. But I will argue that it is only if we engage in this debate, while using a broader, integrated socio-environmental perspective, that we can understand why 'Mother Earth' cannot heal herself as things stand, and why retaining the 'green dividend' of Covid-19 is intertwined with the fate of workers.

So far, the discussion has largely been restricted to the question of whether the 'egalitarian green growth' or 'green new deal' proposed by Robert Pollin should provide the road map for environmental strategy, or whether the steady-state economy propounded by Herman Daly or in fact degrowth are essential. In the process, some confusion has arisen about what we mean by 'growth'. More importantly, the debate has skirted the vital questions of what we really want – human well-being and social justice, as well as saving the planet – and how these three societal goals are interconnected. Though written from the perspective of the Global South, I believe the arguments that follow have a general application.

I. PROBLEMS OF GROWTH

What exactly do we mean by terms like 'growth' and 'steady state'? For Daly, the economy is an expanding subsystem, functioning within a finite eco-sphere; the economy's growth entails increasing 'biophysical throughputs', which threatens the operation of the overall earth system. Daly calls for limits both to population growth and to the depletion of natural resources (fossil fuels, minerals; potentially water, air and soil pollution) to maintain the economic subsystem in a 'steady state'. Since biophysical throughput is 'coupled' with GDP, these limits to quantitative expansion would involve a moratorium on GDP growth, although he argues that this need not jeopardize our quest for well-being, which could come from qualitative development.

For Pollin, on the other hand, rising GDP – that is, an increase in economic activity – is inherently desirable because it is causally linked to job creation and higher incomes, and thus, implicitly, to overall well-being. Solely focused on 'stabilizing' the climate, he proposes an environmental strategy – trillion-dollar global investment in clean-energy sectors and a dramatic contraction in fossil-fuel use – that would reduce carbon emissions by 80 per cent over the next thirty years, as mandated by the IPCC, without reducing aggregate income; indeed Pollin argues clean-energy investment at this scale (1.5 to 2 per cent of GDP) will lead to significant job creation. He opposes degrowth, which he understands as a contraction of GDP, because he believes this will lead to a deep recession, precipitating mass unemployment, falling living standards and a consequent decrease in well-being. Aside from these calamitous social consequences, Pollin also argues degrowth would be ineffectual from the point of view of the climate: a GDP contraction of 10 per cent, far deeper than the 2008–09 recession, would, *ceteris paribus*, only reduce carbon emissions by a tenth, not the 80 per cent by 2050 required by the IPCC. The lynchpin of Pollin's agenda is the rapid decoupling of growth from emissions – the plausibility of which advocates of degrowth reject.

As with Daly, the main concern of degrowthers Mark Burton and Peter Somerville is material throughput. Growth for them means relentless resource extraction, consuming not only fossil fuels but water, air, forests, croplands and fishing grounds. They argue that the material footprint of aggregate human activity is currently 1.7 times the earth's biocapacity. Hence, rather than more growth, or even Daly's steady state, they want to see economic activity shrink through drastic cuts to industrial production, construction, agriculture (fossil-fuel-dependent monocultures) and distribution (sea, air and road transportation systems). Their explicit target is the Global North, where consumption levels would need to be limited. The contraction of GDP is a necessary consequence of degrowth, but they hope it can be managed equitably: 'in theory', such contraction might be limited to the rich, since 'high emissions are strongly correlated with concentrations of wealth and income.' Moreover, if consumption is to be reduced, who needs the higher income? Like Daly, they assume that well-being can be decoupled from income and material consumption, especially in the high-income countries of the Global North.

Examined from a Southern perspective, the relative limitations of each approach become clear. First, as Pollin acknowledges, 'development' cannot be reduced to GDP growth, even in developing countries. Furthermore, as many of us have long argued, GDP growth in itself is neither sufficient nor necessary to ensure true development.[1] Since GDP is an average measure that ignores inequality, it can increase while the poor remain poor – as in Brazil, for example – or be stagnant while the well-being of the poorest rises dramatically, as the Kerala model in India has shown. The goal therefore must always be the enhancement of individual and community well-being, measured by actual physical and social outcomes across the socioeconomic spectrum, and not by using average income as a proxy. The moment when well-being decoupled from income has long passed in the Global North, which is clearly mal-developed and overgrown.

The real question from a developing-country perspective is whether Daly's goal of a steady-state economy with no growth in material throughput would constrain development too much. The answer is probably: yes, it would. However 'soft' or non-material one's developmental strategy, it is difficult to visualize how the vast population of poor people in the Global South can achieve a modicum of development without some increase in the use of material resources for cooking, housing (including some protection from the heat) and clothing, not to mention education and travel. The environmental impact of the 2 or 3 billion global poor moving out of poverty and

---

1   See Sharachchandra Lele, 'Sustainable Development: A Critical Review', *World Development*, vol. 19, no. 6, 1991, pp. 607–21; Jeroen van den Bergh and Giorgos Kallis, 'Growth, A-Growth or Degrowth to Stay within Planetary Boundaries?', *Journal of Economic Issues*, vol. 46, no. 4, 2014, pp. 909–20.

achieving a 'decent living standard' will be small compared to the damage wreaked by present levels of (over)consumption in the Global North.[2] A strategy based on a steady state in material throughput is therefore not appropriate at this stage for developing nations.

At the same time, a steady state in throughput in the rich world is not going far enough; there, degrowth – reducing material consumption – is the only tenable approach. The typical middle-class citizen in the Global North is consuming at completely unsustainable levels, on multiple fronts: carbon footprint, water use, land despoliation, destruction of biodiversity and so forth. Beyond environmental considerations, many in high-income countries suffer from the physical and psychological maladies of over-development. The focus everywhere must be on multi-dimensional well-being and environmental sustainability. The South must concentrate not on economic growth but on development to raise its level of well-being, while minimizing its environmental impact. The North must work out what's needed for it to transition to enhance genuine well-being without further economic growth, while decisively reducing its material throughput.

2. DEFINITIONS OF WELL-BEING

The idea of a steady-state economy puts constraints on material throughput, but does not tell us much about what life in such an economy would be like. Daly touches on this when he says that 'life ought to have some purpose beyond economic growth', and draws a distinction between 'quantitative' growth and 'qualitative' development: something can get better without getting bigger (and vice versa). But his approach to measuring well-being remains largely economistic: the Index of Sustainable Economic Welfare (ISEW) that he and John Cobb put forward in 1989 proposed to correct GDP by including unpaid domestic work and deducting 'defensive' expenditure and the depreciation of natural capital caused by environmental harm.[3]

The idea of well-being has come a long way since Daly's ISEW, or its still-economistic successor, the Genuine Progress Indicator. Much of the initial thinking came from the development debates in the

---

2   Narasimha Rao and Paul Baer, '"Decent Living" Emissions: A Conceptual Framework', *Sustainability*, vol. 4, no. 4, 2012, pp. 656–81.

3   See Herman Daly and John Cobb, *For the Common Good: Redirecting the Economy toward Community, the Environment and a Sustainable Future*, Boston, MA, 1989.

context of the Global South. At a conceptual level, Manfred Max-Neef's nine fundamental human needs were followed by Amartya Sen's notion of 'development as freedom'.[4] In terms of metrics, the simplistic Human Development Index – life expectancy, literacy, income – has given way to more complex, multi-dimensional measures, no longer limited to the Global South: the Gross National Happiness Index, the OECD's Better Life Index, the World Happiness Report and the Social Progress Indicator (SPI), which includes basic human needs (nutrition, water, sanitation, shelter, personal safety), foundations of well-being (access to knowledge, information, health, environmental quality) and opportunity (individual rights, personal freedom, inclusiveness, access to advanced education). Degrowthers have also embraced the idea that well-being is not about consumption but about enhancing the quality of life through tranquillity, conviviality and rich experience.

A detailed discussion of well-being theory is beyond the scope of this article, but it may be useful to start from the position that a 'good society' has three distinct goals. The first is individual well-being, which has both material and non-material aspects, and is measured in terms of their level of satisfaction in the present. The second is equity, which speaks to intra-generational justice of all kinds. The third is sustainability, which addresses the temporal dimension – the desire to have non-declining well-being, both for oneself and for future generations.[5] A 'good society' will aim to ensure all three. However, recognizing that ideas about individual well-being, equity and sustainability will differ among individuals, communities and cultures, we also need to specify what processes will be followed in reconciling different values and interests. Ideas of democratic decision-making, procedural justice and rights of recognition need to be foregrounded as an additional concern.

---

4   Manfred Max-Neef, Antonio Elizalde and Martin Hopenhayn, 'Development and Human Needs', in Ekins and Max-Neef, eds, *Real-Life Economics: Understanding Wealth Creation*, London 1992, pp. 197–213; Amartya Sen, *Development as Freedom*, New York, 1999.

5   See Lele et al., 'Framing the Environment', in Lele et al., eds, *Rethinking Environmentalism: Linking Justice, Sustainability and Diversity*, Cambridge, MA, 2018, pp. 1–22.

3. BEYOND SUSTAINABILITY

What is the relationship between the environment and this three-pronged idea of a 'good society'? The discussion so far seems to treat environmental concerns as largely synonymous with sustainability – that is: our ability to continue to do in future what we are doing today. This reduction of 'environmentalism' to 'sustainability-ism' is not new. Originating in renewable-resource management – the ability of a resource to remain as productive in the future as it is today – the term has become a green buzzword, so that 'being sustainable' means 'saving the planet' in some generalized sense, while 'unsustainable' means doing something today that is harming tomorrow. But framing all environmental problems as sustainability issues can sideline other ethical concerns that have been central to environmental thinking and that are quite distinct from concern for one's future. Two additional dimensions we need to consider are equity or justice, and conservation.

Environmental justice

Concern for justice has been central to environmentalism. Many environmental conflicts are rooted in the fact that one person's actions – setting up a factory, building a dam – adversely affect someone else's well-being (health, livelihood) through inter-linked environmental processes: industrial effluents blowing downwind, or flowing downstream; village lands submerged for a dam. If the villagers, or the people living downwind from the factory, have rights to life, livelihood and a clean environment, anything that impinges upon these rights constitutes an environmental or biophysical injustice. If you ask someone why having to breathe toxic fumes spewed by someone else is wrong, they will likely say, 'Because it's unfair' – not, 'Because it's unsustainable.'

Similarly, because natural resources are limited – environmentalism's core assumption – their distribution is a zero-sum game, which means their misallocation can be a source of injustice. If the water transported from the dam to an agricultural community is then allocated in proportion to land ownership, ignoring the rights of the landless, or if city water boards supply fee-paying households but exclude slum-dwellers, or for cultural or historical reasons supply water to one town at the expense of another, this constitutes an issue of resource inequity, or environmental injustice. Note that in these cases, the injustice – whether purely environmental or also social – is occurring here and now, not over a future timeframe: it is an intra-generational issue. Note, too, that the scale on which this injustice occurs is often quite localized. Notwithstanding the tendency to cast *all* environmental problems in global terms,[6] many are actually sub-global in both their proximate causes and their impact.

I use the term 'environmental injustice' here in a somewhat different sense to that popularized by Robert Bullard's *Dumping in Dixie*. What I am calling environmental or biophysical injustice refers simply to the unfair impacts of an environmental process, without reference to the social status of the polluter, or pollutee. Bullard's pioneering work pointed out that there is almost always an additional layer of unfairness in cases of environmental injustice – what I would call 'social injustice' – in that pollutees tend to be socially marginalized communities. Without denying that social justice often correlates with biophysical injustice, I suggest it is more useful to keep the two analytically distinct, so as to clarify the source of the inequity.[7]

Of course, many environmental problems have both spatial and temporal dimensions. Climate change is a classic example. Although typically framed in Garrett Hardin's terms as a tragedy of the commons – or, more precisely, of open access to the global commons – climate change involves serious temporal and spatial asymmetries. The temporal question is well recognized – today's emissions affect the climate over hundreds of years – hence the prevailing framing of climate change as a global sustainability problem. But, as Anil Agarwal and Sunita Narain pointed out, there are multiple spatial asymmetries as well.[8] The CO_2 that has accumulated in the global atmosphere so far has been largely the product of post-1850 emissions by the North – emissions that underpinned the prosperity it currently enjoys.[9] Moreover, per capita emissions in the North are still five to ten times higher than those in the Global South. Even holding the South solely responsible for its population growth and so discounting

---

6   See, for instance, Johan Rockström et al., 'A Safe Operating Space for Human-ity', *Nature*, vol. 461, 2009, pp. 472–5.

7   Robert Bullard, *Dumping in Dixie: Race, Class and Environmental Quality*, Boulder, CO, 1990; and Lele, 'Sustainable Development Goal 6: Watering Down Justice Concerns', *WIREs Water*, vol. 4, no. 4, 2017.

8   Anil Agarwal and Sunita Narain, 'Global Warming in an Unequal World: A Case of Environmental Colonialism', Centre for Science and Environment, New Delhi, 1991.

9   Even today, a large fraction of China's emissions should arguably be 'debited to' the Global North, because China is producing goods for satiating the appetites of Northern consumers.

this growth from per capita statistics – by using, say, 1990 population figures in the denominator – does not significantly change this inequity. Finally, the impacts of global warming are going to be felt more in the South, starting with the island states and monsoonal sub-tropics, than in many temperate countries; tundra-bound Canada or Russia may even welcome rising temperatures. Add to this the social (in)justice component – that the capacity to take adaptive action is severely limited in poor countries – and one can see why most in the South talk of climate as a justice issue. Stepping back from parochial positions, North or South, one could say that climate change is simultaneously an environmental-sustainability and an environmental-justice question.[10]

This points again to the problems of the 'equitable green growth' position, which models aggregate emissions and aims for an 'under 2°C world' without foregrounding the distribution of benefits and costs. Global models of energy use and climate change typically 'grandfather in' the existing, asymmetrical pattern of energy use and emissions, and then speak of aggregate reductions towards some climate-stabilization goal. The 2015 Paris Accord effectively ratified this highly inequitable approach by leaving it to each country to set its own mitigation targets; the US aggravated the injustice by pulling out of even this under Donald Trump. At the end of his piece, Pollin acknowledges that even the transition to clean energy that he proposes will end with the average US citizen emitting five times more carbon than their counterpart in India, and recognizes the gross injustice of this. But he rejects any practical possibility of equalizing emissions globally, and argues that the only feasible way of introducing an element of fairness would be to require the US to provide large-scale financial assistance to poorer countries to effect their own transition to clean energy. The willingness to sacrifice concern for justice on the altar of 'global climate sustainability' has been a hallmark of green growth thinking; what is more surprising from a Southern perspective is that Pollin calls his strategy 'egalitarian green growth'.

A tunnel-vision approach in which CO_2 becomes the only focus also risks imposing other environmental injustices.[11] For instance, Pollin talks of supplementing solar and wind energy with

10   John Byrne, Young-Doo Wang, Hoesung Lee and Jong-dall Kim, 'An Equity-and Sustainability-Based Policy Response to Global Climate Change', *Energy Policy*, vol. 26, no. 4, 1998, pp. 335–43.

11   Navroz Dubash, 'Environmentalism in the Age of Climate Change', *Seminar*, vol. 601, 2009, pp. 63–6.

hydropower, despite the World Commission on Dams Report (2000) exposing the devastating socio-environmental impact of dams, especially in the Global South. Indeed, the Indian government has seized on the opportunity presented by climate change to justify its incredibly destructive and risky large dams in the north-east in the name of 'clean energy'. In its extreme form, carbon-centric environmentalism also offers *carte blanche* to the nuclear-energy industry.[12]

A similar tunnel vision afflicts calls to solve the climate problem through large-scale reforestation, as Vettese proposes, which can impose high costs on forest- and grassland-dependent communities in the densely populated and not-yet-industrialized South. Our analysis shows that the Modi government's Paris Accord commitment to sequester 2.5 to 3 billion tonnes of CO_2eq in India's forests can only be achieved by reversing the recent achievements in decentralized governance, restoring power to the neo-colonial forest departments and significantly damaging livelihoods.[13] Vettese uncritically supports a particularly egregious afforestation-based solution, E. O. Wilson's 'half earthing', which attempts to address climate and biodiversity concerns simultaneously. Unsurprisingly, the 'half' of the earth to be put under 'protection' happens to be largely in the Global South, which has led to heavy criticism of the proposal as both unjust and ineffective.[14]

The ends of conservation

When Rachel Carson's *Silent Spring* (1962) drew attention to the connection between DDT and the decline of the bald eagle, was she thinking about the future of humankind or that of these iconic birds? What motivates campaigns to save the tiger, the whale or the butterfly? At root, the desire to preserve beautiful biota seems to stem from a spiritual or aesthetic concern (biodiversity campaigners typically do not fight for the preservation of rare pathogens or endangered viruses).[15] Some argue that human beings have an inherent 'biophilia',

---

12   M. V. Ramana, 'Second Life or Half-Life? The Contested Future of Nuclear Power', in Thijs van de Graaf et al., eds, *The Palgrave Handbook of the International Political Economy of Energy*, London, 2016, pp. 363–96.

13   Navroz Dubash, Radhika Khosla, Ulka Kelkar and Lele, 'India and Climate Change: Evolving Ideas and Increasing Policy Engagement', *Annual Review of Environment and Resources*, vol. 43, no. 1, 2018, pp. 395–424.

14   See Bram Büscher et al., 'Half-Earth or Whole Earth? Radical Ideas for Conservation and Their Implications', *Oryx*, vol. 51, no. 3, 2016, pp. 407–10.

15   The concept of 'ecosystem services' focuses on the material benefits, direct and indirect, resulting from the conservation of natural ecosystems. Its critics charge it

others that biota confer a sense of 'place' or 'relational value'; a more radical position accords nature the 'right' to exist independently of human well-being.[16] Animal-rights campaigners have raised the question of inter-species justice – the ethical imperative that we treat all sentient beings with respect.

Conservation, then, may involve a combination of (spiritual) well-being and justice. Even the notion of preserving wildlife for future generations to enjoy is only meaningful if we care about these living things ourselves. Yet as with sustainability, an exclusive focus on biodiversity can obscure questions of human, intra-generational justice.[17] The half-earth example illustrates this tension. By contending that biodiversity loss has reached a 'global tipping point', half-earth ecologists obscure the fact that the greatest loss of wild habitats has been in the developed North; moreover, framing biodiversity loss as a 'global' phenomenon, akin to climate change, is misleading since loss of biota in one place may not materially affect people elsewhere.

In short, environmentalism speaks to all dimensions of well-being: material and spiritual, individual and distributive, present and future. The environmental aspect has to do with the role of biophysical processes, whether in providing materials for food, shelter and clothing, or in furnishing the conditions for non-material well-being, such as green surroundings or wildlife; or in linking upstream polluters with downstream pollutees in a river basin, or connecting current generations to future ones through climate change or resource depletion. 'Sustainability' does not capture these diverse concerns, while calling them 'extra-ecological', as Lola Seaton does, is part of a long history of misleading compartmentalization: 'sustainability' or 'conservation' as the environmental question; 'justice' as the social question; and 'productivity' or 'efficiency' as the developmental

---

with aiming at a 'commodification of nature'. See Kathleen McAfee, 'Selling Nature to Save It? Biodiversity and Green Developmentalism', *Environment and Planning D: Society and Space*, vol. 17, no. 2, 1999, pp. 133–54.

16   Stephen R. Kellert and E. O. Wilson, *The Biophilia Hypothesis,* Washington, DC, 1995; Madhav Gadgil, 'Why Conserve Living Diversity?', *The Hindu*, 29 March 1998, pp. 6–7; Kai M. A. Chan et al., 'Why Protect Nature? Rethinking Values and the Environment', *Proceedings of the National Academy of Sciences*, vol. 113, no. 6, 2016, pp. 1,462–5. For a critique, see Hayward, *Political Theory and Ecological Values*, New York, 1998.

17   See Ramachandra Guha, 'Radical American Environmentalism and Wilderness Preservation: A Third World Critique', *Environmental Ethics*, vol. 11, no. 1, 1989, pp. 71–83, for an early critique of uni-dimensional 'deep ecology' thinking.

question. We need to frame the definition of a good, environmentally sound society in more inclusive and interconnected terms.

Not climate alone

Mis-framing the climate crisis as solely a matter of global sustainability is one part of the problem; conceiving of it as the 'only' environmental crisis, or as the 'mother' of all ecological problems, is the other part. Many environmental problems pre-date the climate crisis and continue to threaten current and future well-being across the world, especially in the South. Water scarcity, for example, is arguably a more urgent problem in India and many other countries in the South than the risks posed by climate change.[18] Indiscriminate groundwater pumping has already exhausted aquifers in peninsular India and some of its northern regions, while the ill-considered construction of dams and promotion of surface irrigation has resulted in declining river flows – especially baseflows, which are critical to aquatic life – and aggravated upstream-downstream conflicts. Lack of clean drinking water and sanitation is a major driver of ill-health in the subcontinent. Yet the link between the water crisis and climate change is tenuous, while water pollution has more to do with sewage management and lax enforcement than with rising global temperatures.[19]

Countries in the Global North have 'solved' many of their local environmental problems, partly by exporting their production to China and their waste to Africa, but partly also by building strong environmental movements in the 1970s. For many in the North, climate change – which seemed to come out of nowhere, laying bare their continuing vulnerability – became *the* environmental crisis. But many communities in the South are already 'vulnered': freed only a few generations ago from colonial exploitation, they are struggling with the double blow of crushing poverty and regional environmental problems. Maybe climate change will aggravate these, but given their small carbon footprint *vis-à-vis* the North, what sense does it make for them to engage in discussions about reducing their emissions, or indeed their 'material throughput' as a whole to achieve a steady-state

---

18 Veena Srinivasan et al., 'The Nature and Causes of the Global Water Crisis: Syndromes from a Meta-Analysis of Coupled Human-Water Studies', *Water Resources Research*, vol. 48, no. 10, 2012.

19 Lele et al., 'Why Is the Arkavathy River Drying? A Multiple-Hypothesis Approach in a Data-Scarce Region', *Hydrology and Earth System Sciences*, vol. 19, no. 4, 2015, pp. 1905–17.

economy? And what sense does it make to focus exclusively on climate-change adaptation when farmers are committing suicide by the thousands, a million deaths per year are attributed to air pollution, millions of families spend arduous hours each day collecting water for their domestic needs, and many more lose their livelihoods as their land is taken by mining, dams and other 'development' projects?

From where I sit, we cannot think of 'unsustainability' as the only problem, climate change as its only cause – and renewables as the only solution. We need consistently to frame the problem as an integrated, multi-dimensional environment-cum-development crisis. Climate mitigation and adaptation must come as a 'co-benefit' of policies that promote locally and regionally sustainable and equitable development.[20]

4. IDENTIFYING THE PROBLEM

To develop strategies to tackle this environment–development crisis, we must first examine the causes of under-development in the South and mal-development in the North – characterized by low levels of well-being and high levels of inequality and environmental injustice, undermining our collective future. The answers are of course complex, and there is space here to discuss only a few of the aspects raised in the debate so far: capitalism, power relations, technology, fossil fuels – and values.

First, it's worth recalling the other contributors' responses to the question of what is causing climate change, and how it might be mitigated: they focused on population growth (Daly) and consumption (Daly, Vettese, Mark Burton and Peter Somerville) as the proximate drivers of climate change, and technology, deployed through massive public investment (Pollin) or lifestyle changes (Vettese) as possible solutions. This is reminiscent of the Ehrlichs's formula from the 1970s, which sees environmental impact (i) as the product of population (p), affluence/consumption (a) and technology/efficiency (t) – summarized as 'i=pat'.[21] Part of the problem with this equation is that it suggests that population, affluence and technology

---

20 Navroz Dubash, D. Raghunandan, Girish Sant and Ashok Sreenivas, 'Indian Climate Change Policy: Exploring a Co-Benefits Based Approach', *Economic and Political Weekly*, 1 June 2013.

21 See Paul R. Ehrlich, Anne H. Ehrlich and John P. Holdren, *Ecoscience: Population, Resources, Environment*, San Francisco, 1977.

are causal variables, each capable of driving environmental impact. For those located in the Global North, it may appear that 'the decision about how many children to have' is being taken by individuals. In the Global South, however, the vast majority have no such agency; high fertility rates are closely linked to poverty, gender discrimination and poor provision of healthcare, education and social welfare.[22] Population growth is best understood not simply as a cause of environmental damage, but as a symptom of deeper societal pressures. We therefore need to examine the ultimate drivers of poverty, overconsumption and resource depletion.

Capitalism is clearly one of the ultimate drivers. Capitalism not only allows for profit to accrue through private ownership of capital, but obliges owners of capital to actively pursue returns in competition with each other. As others in the series have pointed out, this imperative requires the economy to be constantly growing, meaning consumption must continually increase too, even – or perhaps especially – in countries that are already affluent. Previous contributors have examined the role played by capitalism 'writ large' – 'financialized monopoly capitalism, geared towards continuous growth and concentration of income', as Daly put it. To this I would add that as a form of social relationship, the capitalist system is based, *inter alia*, on legitimizing the conversion of 'savings' – accumulated labour value – into 'capital' on which one expects to earn returns. This makes all of us who have money in the bank (which is being lent out to earn interest) and who invest in mutual funds (which invest in companies to earn returns) complicit in capitalism. To dismantle this system, we will for starters have to give up any expectation of 'earnings' from our savings, and ask all bankers to do the same. This tiny step would itself require a revolution in our way of thinking.

But capitalism is not the only explanation; other 'semi-independent' factors are at work.[23] Looming large from a Global South perspective is colonialism's role in enabling accumulation in the North and perpetuating poverty in the South; neo-colonialism, in the form of disadvantageous terms of trade, continues today. Moreover, many post-colonial states have oscillated between outright dictatorships and pseudo-democracies (as recent events show, the Global North

---

22   See, for example, Lourdes Arizpe, M. Priscilla Stone and David C. Major, eds, *Population and Environment: Rethinking the Debate*, New York, 2019.

23   I use the term 'semi-independent' to acknowledge the significant interplay and often mutual reinforcement between different 'ultimate' factors. See Lele, 'Rethinking Sustainable Development', *Current History*, vol. 112, no. 757, 2013, pp. 311–16.

may be heading in the same direction). The 'state' in most Southern countries is looked upon with deep suspicion, as more likely to perpetuate colonial injustices and indulge in crony capitalism than ameliorate the lot of the poor. This combination of colonialism, neo-colonialism and internal colonialism needs to be kept in mind as semi-independent from capitalism. Likewise, there are other oppressive social structures that cause inequalities of power – racism, caste-ism, patriarchy – which often lead to environmental injustice. While colonialism can be seen as an extension of capitalism, and racism has clearly been intertwined with both at various points, forms of discrimination based on race, caste and gender existed long before modern-day capitalism took shape and must as such be recognized as semi-independent factors.

The only way to counter these systems is by deepening both the idea and the structures of democracy. But as the case of India shows, the scale of the task should not be underestimated. Even as India proudly proclaims itself the world's most populous democracy, the quality of the inherited 'Westminster model' leaves much to be desired and is eroding further as we speak. Nor can undemocratic practices be attributed simply to capitalist manipulation. India's power structures retain many vestiges of colonial rule which strengthen the power of the state against the common citizen. For a country more than twice as populous as Europe, and four times more so than the US, there are effectively no tiers of reliably democratic government below the level of the provinces, which in many cases are the size of a large European nation. Undemocratic decision-making is not just the product of capitalism but is rooted in other histories and practices – the traditions of social discrimination mentioned above, but also the absence of a deep-rooted belief in the democratic process (beyond elections) and in the ideas of transparency and accountability that go with it. Undemocratic government therefore needs to be addressed semi-independently of capitalism.

Third, (reductionist) science and (inappropriate) technology are further drivers of environmental degradation that need to be seen as semi-independent factors. The industrial revolution marked a sea change in our understanding of nature – and in our ability to manipulate it. For the first time, we were able to convert fossil energy into mechanical, and later electrical, power. Subsequently, there were revolutions in chemistry (including the development of DDT), microbiology (including antibiotics), nuclear power and, most recently, information technology and genetics. This dramatic expansion in our capacity to manipulate nature has not been matched by an expanded understanding of the 'external' effects of such manipulation: how DDT might accumulate in the food web, for example, or the waste-management risks associated with nuclear energy. In some instances, prescient warnings were ignored: the Swedish climate scientist Svante Arrhenius predicted in 1896 that the burning of fossil fuels would cause the earth's temperature to rise. In most other cases, the environmental and health effects of our inventions were discovered long after the fact. Carson's work on DDT, for example, points to the absence of any preliminary testing for the ecological consequences of introducing such a powerful chemical into the environment – thoughtlessness that stemmed in part from a reductionist postwar technological triumphalism. Though the corporate manufacturers of DDT naturally spent large sums trying to discredit Carson's revelations, the problem cannot be said to have originated in capitalism.

Nuclear power provides a comparable case. In India, as in many other countries, the nuclear-energy sector is completely state-owned. Its champions have been scientists, motivated by fame or national pride, and driven by their faith in technological solutions and their arrogant conviction that they are above rigorous public scrutiny of their budgets or of the harm that uranium mining is doing to indigenous communities in India's hinterland. Once formed in this mode of thinking, no amount of data on birth defects or the costs of radioactive-waste disposal will shake their faith in nuclear technology. The role of private capital in this story is minimal.

Or again, take the exploitation of water. Until the 1970s, groundwater in India was basically open-well water, consumed largely for domestic use. The advent of borewell-drilling technology led to a 'revolution', and India is today by far the world's largest consumer of groundwater, mostly for irrigation. Consequently, large parts of the country are now seeing declining water tables. Almost all the innovation and scientific research has concentrated on 'developing' this resource – new means for detecting groundwater reserves, estimating (immediate) yields and pumping from greater depths. Very little attention, either in India or globally, has been paid to understanding where it comes from – crudely speaking: is it fossil groundwater, or annually recharged? – and where it goes – how much actually flows into rivers or oceans? – or to how we can measure its movement, monitor its consumption and so on.

But the blame for this lopsided scientific development can hardly be laid solely at the door of capitalism. Most of the initial prospecting and drilling was publicly funded, and though the drill and pump manufacturers are capitalist firms with vested interests, the impetus to drill and pump ultimately comes from individual farmers trying to grow a more profitable crop or households trying to secure their water supply – under market conditions, of course; but the market economy in food existed long before industrial capitalism came into being. There is an interesting parallel between the over-exploitation of fossil fuels and that of groundwater in India: groundwater began to be exploited because a technology was developed that gave us access not only to its renewable, but its non-renewable (fossil) component. As with fossil fuel, the immediate gains far outweighed the long-term costs, and as a society, we were not able to put institutional arrangements in place rapidly enough to prevent us from undermining our future.

There is indeed a fundamental relationship between technological change and industrial capitalism. All economic systems are about who controls the surplus value left over from the production process once the elementary needs of the labourers have been met. Fossil energy dramatically increased the quantum of surplus. Once unleashed by technologies of conversion into mechanical and electrical power, this concentrated energy source was so cheap that one could scale up production without significantly increasing labour input – shifting from hand looms to power looms, in the classic example. As the technological revolution penetrated beyond energy generation and thermodynamics into the fields discussed above (metallurgy, biochemistry, microbiology, genetics, IT), it generated an ever-greater surplus, creating in the process an illusion of unlimited technological possibilism. Of course, social relations of production had to legitimize the appropriation of this surplus by the owners of the means of production rather than, say, by the whole community. But the availability of cheap fossil energy is what made it possible.[24]

Few societies could anticipate the implications of this huge surplus and establish institutional arrangements to distribute it more equitably. For most, the upshot was – Marx would say, inevitably – industrial capitalism. But nobody, capitalist or communist, paid much attention until about the 1970s to whether the fossil resource that was powering much of this technological revolution would run out, or – Arrhenius notwithstanding – to whether its use might adversely affect the environment. One cannot blame capitalism for what appears to be a

---

24 For a detailed, if perhaps exaggerated, argument about the energy-economy linkage, see Mansoor Khan, *The Third Curve: The End of Growth as We Know It*, Mumbai, 2013.

'normal' human response – refusing to look a technological gift horse in its mouth.

It may be more accurate to say that industrial capitalism co-evolved with fossil fuel and other technologies: while the initial surplus came from coal, capitalism drove innovation towards harnessing other fuels – liquification of natural gas, off-shore oil rigs, fracking – and 'post-industrial' technologies; in the process, capitalism itself has changed, as the IT revolution allows finance to move at speeds unimaginable a couple of decades ago.[25] This co-evolution means that we need to address, not capitalism alone, but the nature of the surplus that fossil fuels help to generate and how best to use and distribute it. Should we splurge it all now, on the assumption that we will always find another source of cheap energy somewhere, or use it sparingly in the North, to enable the South to raise its standard of living, while also preserving most of it as a buffer for future generations? We need to engage in a similar fashion with the other mixed blessings unleashed by modern technologies – biological, nuclear, IT: insisting upon much greater democratic control over the innovation process than capitalism and technological hubris has hitherto allowed.

As well as dismantling structural forces such as capitalism and colonialism, the multi-dimensional crisis we face demands that we attend to the question of values – seeking to transform them on multiple fronts: our ideas of well-being (unlimited material wealth or subsistence, affection and freedom?), of fairness, and how we view and value nature or non-human life-forms. We also need an ethics of 'process' to govern the inevitable trade-offs between stakeholders with different values and interests. Moreover, many of the 'solutions' to the crisis are plagued with uncertainty, so decision-making needs to be open and accountable. But how to set about changing values, if we are largely socialized into them? Constantly bombarded by messages glorifying consumerism, violence and competition, how do we embrace frugality, peace and cooperation without changing the structures responsible for the bombardment? Many educationists have argued that change begins with the individual and then adds up to the aggregate. Historically, transformations in values were often brought about by charismatic religious leaders. Today, the change must come about in a more horizontal, dispersed fashion, and

---

25 For a different take on the relationship between industrial capitalism and the adoption of fossil fuel, beginning with coal in Britain, see Andreas Malm, *Fossil Capital: The Rise of Steam Power and the Roots of Global Warming*, London, 2016.

education offers one important possible route.[26] Other approaches – persuasion through public debate, learning by doing or practical action – need to be explored as well. As critics of the voluntary simplicity movement have argued, the point is not to stop at individual change but to begin there and then organize 'outwards'.[27] Structural change will not follow automatically; it will have to be fought for. The point is to keep alive the process of constant reflection on one's own values in the course of struggle and organization, to see how they are influenced by our actions and by the new structures we create. In Gandhi's words, 'there cannot be a system so good that the individuals in it need not be good'.

5. UTOPIAS, NOT PRAGMATICS

What then of strategies? I do not propose any panaceas here. Looking for pragmatic solutions, as Pollin does, forces us into a narrowed framing of the problem: one value (sustaining future generations), one problem (climate change), one goal (reduce carbon emissions) and one solution (renewables).[28] Once we open out the debate to include not only sustainability but justice, well-being, conservation and democratic processes, it becomes impossible to think in terms of simple strategies or single-technology solutions. We need to think of strategies that are not pragmatic but utopian – because the pragmatic is a seductive pathway to the status quo.

First, we need a shift in our thinking. We have to counter the hold on our collective minds of economic growth-ism, technological hubris and Adam Smith's idea of individual self-interest automatically leading to societal good. We must reject established hierarchies of thinking, in which economists and engineers rule the roost, social scientists are in a sorry second place, and the humanities are nowhere in the picture.[29] We must reopen the question of values, asking what

---

26 'The goal of education is not mastery of subject matter, but of one's person': David Orr, 'What Is Education For?', *In Context*, vol. 27, 1991, pp. 52–5.

27 See Ken Conca, Thomas Princen and Michael Maniates, eds, *Confronting Consumption*, Cambridge, MA, 2002, especially the chapter by Maniates.

28 Doubts have also been raised about the technical feasibility of the type of energy transition Pollin proposes. See, for example, Ted Trainer, 'Can Renewables Meet Total Australian Energy Demand? A "Disaggregated" Approach', *Energy Policy*, vol. 109, 2017; and Vaclav Smil, 'A Global Transition to Renewable Energy Will Take Many Decades', *Scientific American*, vol. 310, no. 1, January 2014.

29 Manfred Max-Neef's pyramid of disciplines is illuminating in this regard: Max-Neef, 'Foundations of Transdisciplinarity', *Ecological Economics*, vol. 53, no. 1, 2005.

we mean by a good society and making the case for why we should care about our fellow humans, future generations and the natural world. Our analyses must be equally multi-dimensional, avoiding the trap of mono-causality, or trying to explain everything through Marxism, feminism, or some other system. It is vital to bridge the structure–agency divide, to explore how our actions in production, consumption and the deployment of our 'savings' implicate us in the very system we are struggling against.

Second, we need concrete structural changes. On the economic front, while universal basic income may be a starting point, the end-goal must be transferring ownership of productive assets. There are real opportunities for this in the Global South, not least in devolving control of state-owned forests to local communities – Nepal took a big leap in the early 1990s, and India is moving in the same direction through its landmark Forest Rights Act.[30] These shifts combine a transfer of control over the means of production with a democratiz-ation of environmental decision-making, as local communities get a say on development projects such as mines and dams. This could be made into a stepping-stone towards co-design and co-ownership of those projects. Simultaneously, Covid-19 has reopened the discussion on progressive taxation, if only to generate resources to fight the pandemic. Instead of falling prey to the rhetoric of needing 'financial packages to restart the economy', we should be asking, 'how can we shape a different economy?'

On the political front, the battle is clearly to create deeper demo-cratic processes and to align them with environmental problems. Fully participatory democracy may be a far cry, but the principle of envi-ronmental and social subsidiarity – that is, to federate upwards only those functions that cannot be discharged at a lower level – could help to strengthen transparency and accountability. Democratization must include public oversight of science and technology, but we also need to educate our scientists and engineers in ethics and sociology, to help them understand the challenges we face on the socio-environmental front and to hold them accountable for their actions.

Education will be essential to all the proposals discussed above. The purpose of education is not an instrumentalist 'skilling' to produce biddable masses for current economic and political systems to exploit. Its purpose is transformative: to imbue everyone with broad human values and critical thinking abilities. Only then can we

---

30 See the special section on the Forest Rights Act in *Economic and Political Weekly*, 24 June 2017.

overcome the confines of race, caste, gender and other prejudices, reconnect with our environments and become politically aware and active citizens. The glimpse of Mount Everest from Bihar is likely to be ephemeral, as the power plants in the region resume full operations after lockdown, burning coal mined by backbreaking labour, in pits that ravage the surrounding forests of indigenous peoples in order to feed the appetites of consumers in the urban centres of India and the world. But with new thinking on the environment–development conundrum, with concepts like *buen vivir* and *vikalp sangam* on which to ground new coalitions, we can hope to glimpse a better future for humanity and nature alike.[31]

---

31 See Ashish Kothari on 'Radical Ecological Democracy' and other essays in Julien-Francois Gerber and Rajeswari Raina, eds, *Post-Growth Thinking in India: Towards Sustainable Egalitarian Alternatives*, New Delhi, 2018.

10

Climates of Capital

For a Trans-Environmental Eco-Socialism

NANCY FRASER

2021

Climate politics has moved to centre stage.[1] Even as pockets of denialism persist, political actors of multiple hues are turning green. A new generation of activist youth is insisting that we cease to evade the mortal threat posed by global warming. Chastising elders for stealing their future, these militants claim the right and responsibility to take all necessary steps to save the planet. At the same time, movements for degrowth are gaining strength. Convinced that consumerist lifestyles are driving us into the abyss, they seek a transformation of ways of living. Likewise, indigenous communities, North and South, have been winning wider support for struggles only lately recognized as ecological. Long engaged in defending their habitats and livelihoods from colonial invasion and corporate extractivism, they find new allies today among those seeking non-instrumental ways of relating to nature. Feminists, too, are infusing new urgency into long held ecological concerns. Positing psycho-historical links between gynophobia and contempt for the earth, they mobilize for forms of life that sustain reproduction – both social and natural. Meanwhile, a new wave of anti-racist activism includes environmental injustice among its targets. Adopting an expansive view of what it means to 'defund the police', the Movement for Black Lives demands a massive redirection of resources to communities of colour, in part to clean up toxic deposits that ravage health.

Even social democrats, lately complicit with or demoralized by neoliberalism, are finding new life in climate politics. Reinventing

---

1 A version of this essay appears in Nancy Fraser, *Cannibal Capitalism: How Our System Is Devouring Democracy, Care, and the Planet – and What We Can Do About It*, London and New York, 2022.

themselves as proponents of a Green New Deal, they aim to recoup lost working-class support by linking the shift to renewable energy with high-paying union jobs. Not to be left out, strands of right-wing populism are also greening. Embracing eco-national-chauvinism, they propose to preserve 'their own' green spaces and natural resources by excluding (racialized) 'others'. Forces in the Global South are also engaged on several fronts. While some claim a 'right to development', insisting that the burden of mitigation should fall on northern powers that have been spewing greenhouse gases for two hundred years, others advocate 'commoning' or a 'solidary and social economy'; while still others, donning the environmentalist mantle, utilize neo-liberal carbon-offset schemes to enclose lands, dispossess those who live from them and capture new forms of monopoly rent. Finally, corporate and financial interests have skin in the game. Profiting handsomely from booming speculation in eco-commodities, they are invested not just economically but also politically in ensuring the global climate regime remains market-centred and capital-friendly.

Eco-politics, in a word, has become ubiquitous. No longer the exclusive property of stand-alone environmental movements, climate change now appears as a pressing matter on which *every* political actor must take a stand. Incorporated into a slew of competing agendas, the issue is variously inflected according to the differing commitments with which it keeps company. The result, beneath a superficial consensus, is a roiling dissensus. On the one hand, growing numbers of people now view global warming as a threat to life as we know it on Planet Earth. On the other hand, they do not share a common view of the societal forces that drive that process – nor of the societal changes required to stop it. They agree (more or less) on the science but disagree (more than less) on the politics.

Yet the terms 'agree' and 'disagree' are too pallid to capture the situation. Present-day eco-politics unfolds within, and is marked by, an epochal crisis. A crisis of ecology, to be sure, but also one of economy, society, politics and public health – that is, a *general crisis* whose effects metastasize everywhere, shaking confidence in established worldviews and ruling elites. The result is a crisis of hegemony – and a 'wilding' of public space. No longer tamed by a ruling commonsense that forecloses out-of-the-box options, the political sphere is now the site of a frantic search not just for better policies, but for new political projects and ways of living. Gathering well before the Covid outbreak, but greatly intensified by it, this 'unsettled atmosphere' permeates eco-politics, which perforce unfolds within it. Climate dissensus is fraught, accordingly, not 'only' because the fate of the earth hangs in the balance, nor 'only' because time is short, but also because the *political climate*, too, is wracked by turbulence.

In this situation, safeguarding the planet requires building a counter-hegemony. What is needed is to resolve the present cacophony of opinion into an eco-political commonsense that can orient a broadly shared project of transformation. Certainly, such a commonsense must cut through the mass of conflicting views and identify exactly what in society must be changed to stop global warming – effectively linking the authoritative findings of climate science to an equally authoritative account of the socio-historical drivers of climate change. To become counter-hegemonic, however, a new commonsense must transcend the 'merely environmental'. Addressing the full extent of our general crisis, it must connect its ecological diagnosis to other vital concerns – including livelihood insecurity and denial of labour rights; public disinvestment from social reproduction and chronic undervaluation of care work; ethno-racial-imperial oppression and gender and sex domination; dispossession, expulsion and exclusion of migrants; militarization, political authoritarianism and police brutality. These concerns are intertwined with and exacerbated by climate change, to be sure. But the new commonsense must avoid reductive 'ecologism'. Far from treating global warming as a trump card that overrides everything else, it must trace that threat to underlying societal dynamics that also drive other strands of the present crisis. Only by addressing *all* major facets of this crisis, 'environmental' and 'non-environmental', and by disclosing the connections among them, can we begin to build a counter-hegemonic bloc that backs a common project and possesses the political heft to pursue it effectively.

This is a tall order. But what brings it within the realm of the possible is a 'happy coincidence': all roads lead to one idea – namely, capitalism. Capitalism, in the sense I shall define below, represents the socio-historical driver of climate change, and the core institutionalized dynamic that must be dismantled in order to stop it. But capitalism, so defined, is also deeply implicated in seemingly non-ecological forms of social injustice – from class exploitation to racial-imperial oppression and gender and sexual domination. And capitalism figures centrally, too, in seemingly non-ecological societal impasses – in crises of care and social reproduction; of finance, supply chains, wages and work; of governance and de-democratization. Anti-capitalism, therefore, could – indeed, *should* – become the central organizing motif of a new commonsense. Disclosing the links among multiple strands of injustice and irrationality, it represents the

key to developing a powerful counter-hegemonic project of eco-
societal transformation.

That, at any rate, is the thesis I shall argue here. In what follows, I
unfold it on three different levels, which complement and reinforce one
another. Making the case, first, on the structural level, I contend that
capitalism, rightly understood, harbours a deep-seated ecological contradiction, which inclines it non-accidentally to environmental crisis.
But far from standing alone, I claim, this contradiction is entwined
with several others, equally endemic to capitalism, and cannot be
adequately addressed in abstraction from them. Shifting, next, to the
historical register, I chart the specific forms that capitalism's ecological
contradiction has assumed in the various phases of the system's development, up to and including the present. Contra single-issue ecologism,
this history discloses the pervasive entanglement of eco-crisis and
eco-struggle with other strands of crisis and struggle, from which they
have never been fully separable in capitalist societies. Turning, finally,
to the political level, I contend that eco-politics today must transcend
the 'merely environmental' by becoming anti-systemic across the board.
Foregrounding global warming's entwinement with other pressing
facets of our general crisis, I claim that green movements should turn
trans-environmental, positioning themselves as participants in an
emerging counter-hegemonic bloc, centred on anti-capitalism, which
could, at least in principle, save the planet.

I. CAPITALISM'S ECOLOGICAL CONTRADICTION

What does it mean to say that capitalism is the principal socio-historical
driver of global warming? At one level, this claim is empirical, a
statement of cause and effect. Against the usual vague references to
'anthropogenic climate change', it pins the rap not on 'humanity' in
general, but on the class of profit-driven entrepreneurs who engineered the fossil-fuelled system of production and transportation that
released a flood of greenhouse gases into the atmosphere. That's a
claim I shall defend empirically later on, in the historical portion of
my argument. But there is more at work here than historical causality.
Capitalism, as I understand it, drives global warming non-accidentally,
by virtue of its very structure. It is this strong, systematic claim, and
not its weaker empirical cousin, that I unpack now.

I begin by preempting a possible misunderstanding. To say that capitalism drives climate change non-accidentally is *not* to say that
ecological crises occur only in capitalist societies. On the contrary,
many precapitalist societies have perished as a result of environmental

impasses, including some of their own making – as when ancient empires ruined the farmlands on which they depended through deforestation or failure to rotate crops. Likewise, some self-proclaimed postcapitalist societies generated severe environmental damage, through relentless quotidian coal-burning and spectacular one-off disasters such as Chernobyl. Such cases show that ecological devastation is not unique to capitalism.

What *is* unique, however, is the structural character of the link between ecological crisis and capitalist society. Precapitalist eco-crises occurred in spite of 'nature-friendly' worldviews and largely thanks to ignorance – for example, through failure to anticipate the consequences of deforestation or overplanting. They could have been prevented – and sometimes were – by social learning that prompted shifts in social practice. Nothing in the inherent dynamics of these societies required the practices that spawned the damages. The same is true for self-proclaimed postcapitalist societies. 'Really existing socialisms' practiced unsustainable agricultural and industrial regimens, poisoning the land with chemical fertilizers and fouling the air with CO_2. Unlike their precapitalist predecessors, of course, their practices aligned with worldviews that were not at all 'nature-friendly', and their actions were shaped by ideological pressures enjoining 'the development of the productive forces'.

What is crucial, however, is that neither the worldviews nor the pressures arose from dynamics *internal* to socialism. Their roots lay, rather, in the geopolitical soil in which these socialisms germinated – in a world-system structured by competition with capitalist societies, by the 'catch-up' extractivist mindset which that environment fostered, and by the fossil-fuelled models of mega-industrialization favoured by it. To say this is not to let the rulers of these societies off the hook; they will remain forever culpable for disastrous decisions made in bureaucratic–authoritarian milieus saturated with fear and obsessed with secrecy, qualities they deliberately cultivated. The point is rather that nothing in the nature of socialist society requires such milieus or such decisions. Absent the prevailing external constraints and internal deformations, such societies could in principle develop sustainable patterns of interaction with nonhuman nature.

The same cannot be said for capitalist societies. They are unique among known social systems in entrenching a deep-seated tendency to ecological crisis at their very core. As I shall explain, a systemic 'ecological contradiction' is inscribed in the DNA of capitalist society, anchored in its signature institutional structure and developmental dynamics. As a result, capitalist societies are primed to generate recurrent environmental crises throughout their history. Unlike those of other societies, their ecological impasses cannot be resolved by increased knowledge or green bona fides. What is required, in addition, is deep-structural transformation.

Economic and non-economic

To see why, we must revisit the concept of capitalism. Contrary to the usual view, capitalism is not an economic system but something bigger. More than a way of organizing economic production and exchange, it is also a way of organizing the relation of production and exchange to their *non-economic conditions of possibility*. It is well understood in many quarters that capitalist societies institutionalize a dedicated 'economic' realm – the realm of a peculiar abstraction known as 'value' – where commodities are produced through privately owned means of production by exploited wage labourers and sold on price-setting markets by private firms, all with the aim of generating profits and accumulating capital. What is often overlooked, however, is that this realm is constitutively dependent – one could say, parasitic – on a host of social activities, political capacities, and natural processes that are defined in capitalist societies as non-economic. Accorded no 'value' and positioned outside it, these constitute the economy's indispensable presuppositions. Certainly, commodity production is inconceivable without the unwaged activities of social reproduction that form and sustain the human beings who perform wage labour. Nor could such production exist apart from the natural processes that assure availability of vital inputs, including raw materials and sources of energy. Neither, finally, would profit or capital be possible without the legal orders, repressive forces and public goods that underpin private property and contractual exchange. Essential conditions for a capitalist economy, these non-economic instances are not external to capitalism, but integral elements of it. Conceptions of capitalism that omit them are ideological. To equate capitalism with its economy is to parrot the system's own economistic self-understanding – and thus to miss the chance to interrogate it critically. To gain a critical perspective, we must understand capitalism broadly – as an institutionalized social order that encompasses not only the economy but also those activities, relations and processes, defined as 'non-economic', that make 'the economy' possible.[2]

---

2   Nancy Fraser, 'Behind Marx's Hidden Abode: For an Expanded Conception of Capitalism', NLR 86, Mar–Apr 2014, pp. 55–72.

What is gained from this revision is the ability to examine something crucial: *the relation established in capitalist societies between the economy and its 'others'* – including that vital other known as nature. At its core, this relation *is contradictory and crisis-prone*. On the one hand, the system's economy is constitutively dependent on nature, both as a tap for production's inputs and as a sink for disposing its waste. At the same time, capitalist society institutes a stark division between the two 'realms' – constructing the economy as a field of creative human action that generates value while positioning 'nature' as a realm of stuff, devoid of value, but infinitely self-replenishing and generally available to be processed in commodity production.

This ontological gulf becomes a raging inferno when capital enters the mix. A monetized abstraction engineered to self-expand, capital commands accumulation without end. The effect is to incentivize owners bent on maximizing profits to commandeer nature's gifts as cheaply as possible, while also absolving them of any obligation to replenish what they take and repair what they damage. The damages are the flip-side of the profits. With their ecological-reproduction costs discounted, all the major inputs to capitalist production and circulation are vastly cheapened – not 'just' raw materials, energy and transport, but also labour, as wages fall with the cost of living when capital wrests food from nature on the cheap. In every case, capitalists appropriate the savings from cheap inputs in the form of profit, while passing the environmental costs to those who must live with – and die from – the fallout, including future generations.

More than a relation to labour, then, *capital is also a relation to nature* – a predatory, extractive relation, which consumes ever more biophysical wealth in order to pile up ever more 'value', while disavowing ecological 'externalities'. What also piles up, not accidentally, is an ever-growing mountain of eco-wreckage: an atmosphere flooded by carbon emissions; climbing temperatures, crumbling polar ice shelves, rising seas clogged with islands of plastic; mass extinctions, declining biodiversity, climate-driven migration of organisms and pathogens, increased zoonotic spillovers of deadly viruses; super-storms, megadroughts, giant locust swarms, jumbo wildfires, titanic flooding; dead zones, poisoned lands, unbreathable air. Systemically primed to free-ride on a nature that cannot really self-replenish without limit, capitalism's economy is always on the verge of destabilizing its own ecological conditions of possibility.

The D-words

Here, in effect, is an ecological contradiction lodged at the heart of capitalist society – the relation this society establishes between economy and nature. Grounded deep in the system's structure, this contradiction is encapsulated in four D-words: *dependence, division, disavowal* and *destabilization*. In a nutshell: capitalist society makes 'economy' *depend* on 'nature', while *dividing* them ontologically. Enjoining endless accumulation of value, while defining nature as not partaking of it, this arrangement programmes economy to *disavow* the ecological reproduction costs it generates. The effect, as those costs mount exponentially, is to *destabilize* ecosystems – and, periodically, to disrupt the entire jerry-rigged edifice of capitalist society. Simultaneously needing and rubbishing nature, capitalism is a cannibal that devours its own vital organs, like a serpent that eats its own tail.[3]

The contradiction can also be formulated in terms of class power. By definition, capitalist societies devolve the task of organizing production to capital, or rather, to those dedicated to its accumulation. It is the class of capitalists whom this system licenses to extract raw materials, generate energy, determine land use, engineer food systems, bio-prospect medicinals and dispose of waste – effectively ceding to them the lion's share of control over air and water, soil and minerals, flora and fauna, forests and oceans, atmosphere and climate, which is to say, over all the basic conditions that sustain life on Earth. Capitalist society thus vests a class that is strongly motivated to trash nature with the power to manage our relations with it.

Granted, governments sometimes intervene *post hoc* to mitigate the damages – but always reactively, in the mode of catch-up, and without disturbing the owners' prerogatives. Because they are always a step behind the emitters of greenhouse gases, environmental regulations are easily subverted by corporate workarounds. And because

---

3 My account of capitalism's ecological contradiction is indebted to James O'Connor's ground-breaking theorization of 'the second contradiction of capitalism'. He paved the way by drawing on the thought of Karl Polanyi to conceptualize the 'conditions of production' and the tendency of capital to undermine them. See 'The Second Contradiction of Capitalism, with an Addendum on the Two Contradictions of Capitalism', in James O'Connor, *Natural Causes: Essays in Ecological Marxism*, New York, 1998, pp. 158–77. John Bellamy Foster correctly notes some reductionist aspects of O'Connor's account in 'Capitalism and Ecology: The Nature of the Contradiction', *Monthly Review*, vol. 54, no. 4, 2002, pp. 6–16. But O'Connor remains a major touchstone.

they leave intact the structural divisions that license private firms to organize production, they do not alter the fundamental fact: the system gives capitalists motive, means and opportunity to savage the planet. It is they, and not humans in general, who have brought us global warming – but not by chance or simple greed. Rather, the dynamic that has governed their actions and led to that outcome is baked into the very structure of capitalist society.

Whichever formulation we start with, the conclusion we reach is the same: capitalistically organized societies carry an ecological contradiction in their DNA. They are primed to precipitate 'natural catastrophes', which occur periodically but not accidentally throughout their history. Thus, these societies harbour a built-in tendency to ecological crisis. They generate ecosystemic vulnerabilities on an ongoing basis, as part and parcel of their *modus operandi*. Although not always acute or even apparent, the vulnerabilities pile up over time, until a tipping point is reached and the damage bursts forth into view. I shall consider some historical examples in the following section.

Here, however, I have been stressing the structural character of this tendency. The point is all-important, not least for its practical entailments. To say that capitalism's ecological problem is structural is to say that we cannot save the planet without disabling some core, defining features of our social order. What is needed, first and foremost, is to wrest the power to dictate our relation to nature away from the class that currently monopolizes it, so that we can begin to reinvent that relation from the ground up. But that requires dismantling the system that underpins their power: the military forces and property forms, the pernicious ontology of 'value' and the relentless dynamic of accumulation, all of which work together to drive global warming. Eco-politics must, in sum, be anti-capitalist.

Mutually constitutive domains

That conclusion is conceptually powerful as it stands. But it doesn't yet tell the whole story. To complete the picture, we need to consider some additional structural features of capitalist society that also impact nature and the struggles surrounding it. What is crucial here is a point I alluded to earlier: nature is neither the only non-economic background condition for a capitalist economy nor the only site of crisis in capitalist society. Rather, as already noted, capitalist production also relies on social-reproductive and political prerequisites. And these arrangements, too, are contradictory – no less than the arrangements surrounding nature, with which they interact in ways that we ignore at our peril. These relations, too, must be included in an eco-critical theory of capitalist society.

Consider the social-reproductive conditions for a capitalist society. Here, too, capitalism organizes more than just production. It also structures the relations between production and the multiple forms of carework performed by communities and families – chiefly, but not only, by women. Sustaining the human beings who constitute 'labour' and forging the social bonds that enable cooperation, carework is indispensable to any system of social provisioning. But capitalism's distinctive way of organizing care is as contradictory as its way of organizing nature. Here, too, the system works through splitting – in this case, splitting production off from reproduction and treating the first alone as a locus of value. The effect is to license the economy to free-ride on society, to appropriate carework without replenishment, to deplete the energies needed to provide it – and thus to jeopardize an essential condition of its own possibility. A tendency to social-reproductive crisis is lodged at the core of capitalist society.[4]

An analogous contradiction dogs the relation in capitalist society between 'the economic' and 'the political'. On the one hand, a capitalist economy necessarily relies on a host of political supports: repressive security forces that contain dissent and enforce order; legal systems that guarantee private property and authorize accumulation; multiple public goods that enable private firms to operate profitably. Absent these political conditions, a capitalist economy could not exist. But capitalism's way of relating economy to polity is also destabilizing. Splitting off the private power of capital from the public power of states, this arrangement incentivizes the first to hollow out the second. Firms whose *raison d'être* is endless accumulation have every reason to evade taxes, weaken regulation, privatize public goods, offshore their operations – and thus to undermine the political prerequisites for their own existence. With the cannibal again primed to devour its own preconditions, a tendency to political crisis is installed at the very heart of capitalist society.[5]

Here, then, are two further contradictions of capital, which also follow the 4–D logic of division, dependence, disavowal and destabilization. Considered in this light, as analytical abstractions, they

---

4 Nancy Fraser, 'Contradictions of Capital and Care', NLR 100, July–August 2016, pp. 99–117.

5 Nancy Fraser, 'Legitimation Crisis? On the Political Contradictions of Financialized Capitalism', *Critical Historical Studies*, vol. 2, no. 2, 2015, pp. 1–33.

closely parallel the ecological contradiction dissected here. But that formulation misleads. The three contradictions do not in fact operate in parallel but, rather, *interact* with one another – and with the economic contradictions diagnosed by Marx. In fact, the interactions between them are so intimate and mutually constitutive that none of them can be fully understood in isolation from the others.

Consider that the work of social reproduction is deeply concerned with matters of life and death. Care of children encompasses not only socialization, education and emotional nurturance but also gestation, birthing, postnatal tending to bodies and ongoing physical protection. Likewise, care for the sick and dying is focused on healing bodies and easing pain as well as on providing solace and assuring dignity. And everyone – young or old, sick or well – depends on carework to maintain shelter, nutrition and sanitation for both physical well-being and social connection. In general, then, social-reproductive work aims to sustain beings who are simultaneously natural and cultural. Confounding that distinction, it manages the interface of sociality and biology, community and habitat.

Social reproduction is thus intimately entwined with ecological reproduction, which is why so many crises of the first are also crises of the second – and why so many struggles over nature are also struggles over ways of life. When capital destabilizes the ecosystems that support human habitats, it jeopardizes caregiving as well as the livelihoods and social relations that sustain it. Conversely, when people fight back, it is often to defend the entire eco-social nexus at a single stroke, as if to defy the authority of capitalism's divisions. Eco-critical theorists should follow their example. We cannot adequately understand capitalism's ecological contradiction unless we think the latter together with its social-reproductive contradiction. Although the system works to separate both nature and care from the economy, it simultaneously sets in motion extensive interactions among them. These interactions deserve a prominent place in the eco-critical theory of capitalist society.

The same point holds for the ecological and the political, which are also intimately linked in capitalist society. It is public powers, usually states, which supply the legal and military framework which enables capital to expropriate natural wealth *gratis* or on the cheap. And it is to public powers that people turn when ecological damages become so immediately threatening that they can no longer be ignored. It is states, in other words, that capitalist societies task with policing the boundary between economy and nature: with promoting or restraining 'development', with regulating or deregulating emissions, with

deciding where to site toxic-waste dumps, whether and how to mitigate their effects, whom to protect and whom to place in harm's way.

Struggles over the relation between economy and nature are thus
unavoidably political – in more than one sense. Typically focused on
the concrete policies that states should pursue in order to protect
nature from economy, they often turn into conflicts over the limits of
public power, its right and capacity to rein in private (corporate)
power. Also at stake in such struggles is jurisdiction: the proper scale
and agency for intervention in matters, such as global warming, that
are by definition trans-territorial. Likewise at issue is the grammar of
nature: the social meanings attributed to it, our place within it and
relation to it. Finally, what looms behind every eco-contest is the
all-important meta-political question: who exactly in society should
determine those matters? At every level, therefore, the nature-econ-
omy nexus is political. We cannot understand the ecological dimension
of capitalism's current crisis unless we grasp its interactions with the
political strand. Nor can we hope to resolve the first without also
resolving the second.

The ecological is also entangled, finally, with capitalism's constitutive division between exploitation and expropriation. Corresponding
roughly to the global colour line, that division marks off populations
whose social-reproduction costs capital absorbs, through the payment
of wages, from those whose labour and wealth it simply seizes,
without compensation. Whereas the first are positioned as free
rights-bearing citizens, able to access (at least some level of) political
protection, the second are constituted as dependent or unfree subjects, enslaved or colonized, unable to call on state protection and
stripped of every means of self-defence. This distinction has always
been central to capitalist development, from the era of New World
racialized chattel slavery to that of direct-rule colonialism, to post-
colonial neo-imperialism and financialization. In each case, the
expropriation of some has served as a disavowed enabling condition
for the profitable exploitation of others.[6]

But expropriation has also served as a method by which capital
accesses energy and raw materials very cheaply, if not for free. The
system develops in part by annexing chunks of nature for whose
reproduction costs it does not pay. In appropriating nature, however,
capital simultaneously expropriates human communities, for whom

---

6   Nancy Fraser, 'Is Capitalism Necessarily Racist?', Presidential Address, 2018
Eastern Division, *Proceedings and Addresses of the American Philosophical Association*, vol. 92, 2018, pp. 21–42.

the confiscated material and befouled surrounds constituted a habitat, their means of livelihood and the material basis for their social reproduction. These communities thus bear a hugely disproportionate share of the global-environmental load; their expropriation affords other (whiter) communities the chance to be sheltered, at least for a while, from the worst effects of capital's cannibalization of nature. The system's built-in tendency to ecological crisis is therefore tightly linked to its built-in tendency to create racially marked populations for expropriation. In this case too, eco-critical theory cannot adequately understand the first apart from the second.

All told, capitalism's ecological contradiction cannot be neatly separated from the system's other constitutive irrationalities and injustices. To ignore the latter by adopting the reductive ecologistic perspective of single-issue environmentalism is to miss the distinctive institutional structure of capitalist society. Dividing economy not only from nature but also from state, care and racial/imperial expropriation, this society institutes a tangle of mutually interacting contradictions, which critical theory must track together, in a single frame. As we shall see, that conclusion gains additional support when we shift our focus to history.

Nature: A terminological excursus

First, however, a word about 'nature'. Widely recognized as slippery, that term has appeared in the preceding pages in two different senses, which I now propose to disaggregate, before introducing a third. In speaking of global warming as a brute reality, I have assumed a conception of nature as the object studied by climate science: a nature that 'bites back' when carbon sinks are flooded, operating via biophysical processes that proceed behind our backs, independently of whether or not we understand them. That scientific-realist conception – call it Nature I – is at odds with another meaning I invoked to explain capitalism's ecological contradiction. 'Nature' there was referenced from capital's viewpoint, as the ontological other of 'Humanity': a collection of stuff, devoid of value, but self-replenishing and appropriable as a means to the systemic end of value expansion. That conception – call it Nature II – is a construct of capitalism, historically specific to it, but by no means a simple fiction or mere idea. Operationalized in the dynamic of capital accumulation – which also proceeds systemically, independently of our understanding – it has become a potent force with momentous practical consequences for Nature I. Much of my argument to this point has sought to illuminate the catastrophic hijacking of Nature I by Nature II in capitalist society.

Now, however, as we turn to history, we are poised to meet yet another conception of nature. This one, Nature III, is the object studied by historical materialism: concrete and historically changing, always already marked by prior metabolic interactions among its human and nonhuman elements. This is nature entangled with human history, shaped by and shaping the latter. We see it in the transformation of biodiverse prairies into monocultural farm lands; in the replacement of old-growth forests by tree plantations; in the destruction of rainforests to make way for mining and cattle ranching; in the preservation of 'wilderness areas' and the reclamation of wetlands; in farmed animals and genetically modified seeds; in climate- or 'development'-induced species migrations that trigger zoonotic spillovers of viruses – to cite examples from the (relatively short) capitalist phase of the earth's history. Jason Moore evokes the idea of Nature III when he proposes to replace the uppercase singular 'Nature' with the lowercase plural 'historical natures' in his groundbreaking *Capitalism in the Web of Life*.[7] I shall use Moore's expression in what follows, along with the adjective 'socio-ecological', to portray the society–nature interface as an interactive historical nexus – a nexus that capital has tried to control and now threatens to obliterate.

This third conception of nature, as inextricably entangled with human history, will be front and centre in the following step of my argument, which situates capitalism's ecological contradiction historically. But that focus by no means excludes or invalidates Nature I or Nature II. Contra Moore, both of those conceptions are legitimate – and compatible with Nature III.[8] And both will find a place in my

---

7   Jason Moore, *Capitalism in the Web of Life: Ecology and the Accumulation of Capital*, London, 2015. Unfortunately, Moore appears to assume that Nature III can simply replace Nature I, which he proceeds to dismiss as 'Cartesian'. That assumption is politically disabling, as it effectively invalidates climate science. It is also conceptually confused. As I explain below, those conceptions of nature are not in fact incompatible and can be deployed in concert. For more on my differences with Moore, see Nancy Fraser and Rahel Jaeggi, *Capitalism: A Conversation in Critical Theory*, Brian Milstein, Cambridge, 2018, pp. 94–6.

8   One should make use of all three conceptions of Nature. Each pertains to a different level of analysis and genre of inquiry: Nature I to biophysical science; Nature II to structural analysis of capitalist society; Nature III to historical materialism. Properly understood, they do not contradict one another. The appearance of contradiction arises only when one fails to distinguish the levels and confounds the conceptions. Thus, the current debate between critical realists and social constructivists (or 'anti-Cartesians') is largely misplaced. Each side fastens on one conception,

story – whether as 'objective' historical forces that operate behind our backs or as (inter)'subjective' beliefs that motivate our actions. We'll see, too, that the beliefs collide with one another – and with other, subaltern understandings of nature, yet to be identified, but also possessing the capacity to 'bite back' – in this case, through social struggle and political action. In sum, we need all three conceptions of nature working in concert to chart the historical career of capitalism's ecological contradiction.

2. SOCIO-ECOLOGICAL REGIMES OF ACCUMULATION

To this point, I have elaborated capitalism's tendency to ecological crisis in structural terms, as if it existed outside of time. In reality, however, this tendency finds expression only in historically specific forms or, as I shall call them, 'socio-ecological regimes of accumulation'. I use that phrase to designate the various phases whose succession forms capitalism's history. Each regime represents a distinctive way of organizing the economy–nature relation. Each features characteristic methods of generating energy, extracting resources and disposing of waste. Likewise, regimes exhibit distinctive trajectories of expansion – ways of annexing previously external chunks of nature through historically specific mixes of conquest, theft, commodification, nationalization and financialization. Finally, regimes develop characteristic strategies for externalizing and managing nature: methods of offloading damages onto families and communities that lack political clout or are deemed disposable; and schemes for distributing responsibility for mitigation among states, intergovernmental organizations and markets. What makes a regime distinctive, then, is where it draws the line between economy and nature and how it operationalizes that division. Equally important, as we shall see, are the concrete meanings a regime ascribes to nature – in theory and practice.

None of these matters is given once and for all with the advent of capitalism. Rather, they shift historically, often in times of crisis. Those are times when the long-brewing effects of capitalism's ecological contradiction become so apparent, so insistent, that they can no longer be finessed or ignored. When that happens, the established organization of the econom–nature relation appears dysfunctional, unjust,

---

which it illegitimately totalizes, while wrongfully excluding the others. See also Andreas Malm, *The Progress of This Storm: Nature and Society in a Warming World*, London, 2018.

unprofitable or unsustainable and becomes subject to contestation. The effect is to incite broad struggles among rival political blocs with competing projects for defending or transforming that relation. When they do not end in stalemate, such struggles may install a new socio-ecological regime. Once in place, the new regime provides pro-visional relief, overcoming at least some of its predecessor's impasses, while incubating new ones of its own, whose effects will become apparent later, as it matures. That outcome is guaranteed, insofar as the new regime fails to overcome capitalism's built-in tendency to ecological crisis, but merely defuses or displaces it, however creatively.

That, at any rate, is the scenario that has prevailed to date. As a result, capitalism's history can now be viewed as a sequence of socio-ecological regimes of accumulation, punctuated by regime-specific 'developmental' crises, each of which is resolved provisionally by the successor regime, which in due course generates a develop-mental crisis of its own.[9] Later, we shall consider whether this sequence may now be coming to an end, thanks to a deeper dynamic that subtends it: namely, the epochal trans-regime progression of global warming – cumulatively escalating, seemingly implacable, and threat-ening to stop the whole show. Whatever we say about that, there is no denying that the economy–nature division has mutated several times in the course of capitalism's history, as has the organization of nature. My principal aim in this section is to chart these shifts – and the crisis dynamics that drive them.

The historical career of capitalism's ecological contradiction spans four regimes of accumulation: the mercantile-capitalist phase of the sixteenth through eighteenth centuries; the liberal-colonial regime of the nineteenth and early twentieth; the state-managed phase of the second third of the twentieth century; and the current regime of financialized capitalism. In each of these phases, the economy–nature relation has assumed a different guise, as have the crisis phenomena generated by it. Each regime, too, has precipitated distinctive types of struggles over nature. Yet one thing has remained constant through-out. In each case, eco-crisis and eco-struggle have been deeply entwined with other strands of crisis and struggle, also grounded in structural contradictions of capitalist society.

---

9   I owe the terms 'developmental' and 'epochal' crises, as well as the distinction between them, to Jason Moore, who has adapted them for eco-critical theory from Immanuel Wallerstein and Giovanni Arrighi. See Moore's essay, 'The Modern World System as Environmental History? Ecology and the Rise of Capitalism', *Theory and Society*, vol. 32, no. 3, 2003.

Animal muscle

I begin with mercantile capitalism – and with the question of energy. In that phase, agriculture and manufacturing ran almost entirely on animal muscle, both human and otherwise (oxen, horses, etc.), plus some wind and water, just as they had for millennia. Continuous in this respect with precapitalist societies, mercantile capitalism was what J. R. McNeill calls a 'somatic' regime: the conversion of chemical into mechanical energy occurred inside the bodies of living beings as they digested food, which originated from biomass.[10] This meant that, as in earlier eras, the only way to augment available energy was through conquest. Only by annexing land and commandeering additional supplies of labour could mercantile-capitalist powers increase their forces of production. In the event, they made ample use of those time-tested methods, but on a vastly expanded scale that encompassed the 'New World' as well as the 'Old'.

In the periphery, then, mercantile-capitalist agents installed brutal systems of socio-ecological extractivism. From the silver mines of Potosí to the slave plantations of Saint-Domingue, they worked land and labour to the point of exhaustion, making no effort to replenish what they expended.[11] Electing instead to devour new human and nonhuman 'inputs' forcibly incorporated from 'the outside', they left trails of environmental and social wreckage across whole continents. Those on the receiving end fought back with varying degrees of success. Aimed at countering wholesale assaults on habitats, communities and livelihoods, their resistance was necessarily integrative. Whether communalist, counter-imperial or republican, it combined what we would now call 'environmental' struggles with struggles over labour, social reproduction and political power.

In the metropole, meanwhile, capital scaled up by other means. Forcible land enclosures in England facilitated the conversion of farmland to sheep pasture, enabling expanded manufacture of textiles even in the absence of mechanization. That shift in land use and property regime converged with a major round of administrative state-building in the sixteenth century – and with a world-changing scientific revolution in the seventeenth. The latter gave us the

---

10   For the distinction between 'somatic' and 'exosomatic' energy regimes, see J. R. McNeill, *Something New Under the Sun: An Environmental History of the 20th Century*, London, 2000, especially pp. 10–16.

11   Jason Moore, 'Potosí and the Political Ecology of Underdevelopment, 1545–1800', *Journal of Philosophical Economics*, vol. 4, no. 1, 2010, pp. 58–103.

mechanical view of nature, an early version of Nature I that was instrumental in the creation of Nature II. Hardening distinctions inherited from Greek philosophy and Christianity, the mechanical view expelled nature from the cosmos of meaning, effectively replacing suppositions of socio-natural proximity with a deep ontological chasm. Objectified and externalized, Nature now appeared as Humanity's antithesis – a view that seemed to some to license its 'rape'.[12] As it turned out, philosophical ideas of this sort proved inessential to modern science and were eventually dropped from later versions of Nature I. But they found a second life in capital's metaphysic, which posited Nature II as inert and there for the taking.

In general, then, mercantile capitalism articulated conquest and extractivism in the periphery with dispossession and modern science in the core. We could say, with the benefit of hindsight, that in this era capital was amassing biotic and epistemic forces whose larger productive potential would only become apparent later, with the advent of a new socio-ecological regime of accumulation.

King Coal

That regime began to take shape in early nineteenth century England, which pioneered the world-historic shift to fossil energy. Watt's coal-fired steam engine opened the way to the world's first 'exosomatic' regime: the first to take carbonized solar energy from beneath the crust of the earth and convert it to mechanical energy *outside of living bodies*. Tied only indirectly to biomass, the liberal-colonial regime appeared to liberate the forces of production from the constraints of land and labour. At the same time, it called into being a new historical nature. Coal, previously of interest only locally, as a substance to burn for heat, now became an internationally traded commodity. Extracted from confiscated lands and transported in bulk across long distances, energy deposits formed over hundreds of million years were consumed in the blink of an eye in order to power mechanized industry – without regard for replenishment or pollution. Equally important, fossilized energy provided capitalists with a means to reshape the relations of production to their advantage. In the 1820s and '30s, British textile manufacturers, reeling from strikes in the

---

12   There are good accounts of all this in Philippe Descola's brilliant book, *Beyond Nature and Culture,* trans. Janet Lloyd, Chicago, 2014; and in Carolyn Merchant's classic, *The Death of Nature: Women, Ecology and the Scientific Revolution,* San Francisco, 1990 [1980].

mills, shifted the bulk of their operations from place-bound hydro-power to mobile steam – which also meant from country to city. In that way, they were able to tap concentrated supplies of proletarian-ized labour – workers with less access to means of subsistence and more tolerance for factory discipline than their rural counterparts.[13] Apparently, the cost of coal (which, unlike water, had to be bought) was outweighed by gains from intensified exploitation.

If coal-fired steam powered the industrial revolution in production, it also revolutionized transport. Railroads and steamships compressed space and quickened time, speeding the movement of raw materials and manufactures across great distances, thus accelerating capital's turnover and swelling profits. The effects on agriculture were also profound. With hungry proletarians massed in the cities, there was money to be made from unsustainable, profit-driven farming in the countryside. But that arrangement greatly exacerbated the metabolic rift between town and country. Nutrients plundered from rural soil were not returned at the point of extraction but discharged into urban waterways as organic waste. Thus, the liberal-colonial regime exhausted farmlands and polluted cities in a single stroke.[14]

This massive disruption of the soil-nutrient cycle epitomized capi-talism's ecological contradiction in its liberal-colonial phase. Equally emblematic was the response, as fixes purporting to solve Europe's soil-depletion crisis served only to displace or exacerbate it. One improbable but profitable undertaking centred on guano. A new his-torical nature becomes a world commodity: that substance was scraped from steep rocky crags off the coast of Peru by semi-enslaved Chinese workers and shipped to Europe for sale as fertilizer – all to the principal benefit of English investors. One result was a series of anti- and inter-imperial wars for control of the trade.[15] Another, as deposits built up over centuries began to dwindle within a few decades, was the motive to invent and deploy chemical fertilizers, whose downstream effects include soil acidification, groundwater pollution, ocean dead zones and rising levels of nitrous oxide in the atmos-phere – all deeply inimical to humans and other animals.

---

13   Andreas Malm, 'The Origins of Fossil Capital: From Water to Steam in the British Cotton Industry', *Historical Materialism,* vol. 21, no. 1, 2013, pp. 15–68.

14   The expression 'metabolic rift' comes from Marx via John Bellamy Foster, as does this account of the disruption on the soil-nutrient cycle. See Foster, 'Marx's Theory of Metabolic Rift: Classical Foundations for Environmental Sociology', *American Journal of Sociology,* vol. 105, no. 2, 1999, pp. 366–405.

15   John Bellamy Foster, Brett Clark and Richard York, *The Ecological Rift: Capitalism's War on the Earth,* New York, 2011.

There is also a further irony. Fossil-fuelled production in the capitalist core expanded throughout the liberal-colonial era. But as the guano gambit showed, the appearance of liberation from land and animal muscle was an illusion. Exosomatic industrialization in Europe, North America and Japan rested on a hidden abode of somatic-based extractivism in the periphery. What made Manchester's factories hum was the massive import of 'cheap natures' wrested from colonized lands by masses of unfree and dependent labour: cheap cotton to feed the mills; cheap sugar, tobacco, coffee and tea to stimulate the 'hands'; cheap bird shit to feed the soil that fed the workers.[16] Thus, the apparent savings of labour and land was actually a form of 'environmental load displacement' – a shift in the demands placed on biomass from core to periphery.[17] Colonial powers ramped up the process by calculated efforts to wipe out manufacturing in their colonies. Deliberately destroying textile production in Egypt and India, Britain reduced those lands to suppliers of cotton for its mills and captive markets for its products.[18]

Theorists and historians of eco-imperialism are only now reckoning the full extent of this cost shifting,[19] while also revealing the close connection of anti-colonialism with proto-environmentalism. Rural struggles against liberal-colonial predation were also 'environmentalisms of the poor', struggles for environmental justice *avant la lettre*.[20] They were struggles, too, over the meaning and worth of nature, as European imperialists raised on distanced scientific conceptions sought to subjugate communities that did not distinguish sharply between nature and culture.

16   This expression comes from Jason Moore, 'The Rise of Cheap Nature', in Moore, ed., *Anthropocene or Capitalocene? Nature, History and the Crisis of Capitalism,* Oakland, CA, 2016, pp. 78–115.

17   Alf Hornborg, 'Footprints in the Cotton Fields: The Industrial Revolution as Time-Space Appropriation and Environmental Load Displacement', *Ecological Economics,* vol. 59, no. 1, 2006, pp. 74–81.

18   Aaron Jakes, *Egypt's Occupation: Colonial Economism and the Crises of Capitalism,* Stanford, 2020.

19   For example: Mike Davis, 'The Origins of the Third World', *Antipode,* vol. 32, no. 1, 2000, pp. 48–89; Alf Hornborg, 'The Thermodynamics of Imperialism: Toward an Ecological Theory of Unequal Exchange', in Hornborg, *The Power of the Machine: Global Inequalities of Economy, Technology, and Environment,* Lanham, 2001, pp. 35–48; Joan Martinez-Alier, 'The Ecological Debt', *Kurswechsel,* vol. 4, 2002, pp. 5–16; John Bellamy Foster, Brett Clark and Richard York, 'Imperialism and Ecological Metabolism', in Foster et al., *The Ecological Rift,* pp. 345–74.

20   Joan Martinez-Alier, *The Environmentalism of the Poor: A Study of Ecological Conflicts and Valuation,* Northampton, MA, 2003.

In the capitalist core, where people *did* make that distinction, (proto-)environmentalism looked rather different. The most celebrated version conjured a 'Nature' viewed, like the one fantasized by capital, as Humanity's Other, but figured as sublime and beyond price – hence as demanding reverence and protection. The flip side of Nature II, this Nature was equally ideological. But far from licensing extractivism, it fed Romantic-conservative critiques of industrial society. Originally pastoralist and backward-looking, the natural sublime infused stand-alone 'environmentalisms of the rich',[21] which focused on wilderness preservation. Often thought to exhaust the whole of (proto)environmentalism in this era, it coexisted in reality with another perspective, which linked capital's assault on nature with class injustice. Key proponents of that perspective were William Morris, whose eco-socialism included a powerful aesthetic dimension, and Friedrich Engels, whose social environmentalism focused initially on industrialism's deleterious impact on urban working-class health and later on 'the dialectics of nature' – or what we would now call co-evolutionism and biological emergentism. Both thinkers seeded rich traditions of socialist ecology, subsequently obscured by narrow single-issue understandings of environmentalism, but now being recovered and extended.[22]

Age of the car

Liberal-colonial capitalism's chief legacy was not environmentalism, however, but the fateful world-changing shift to exosomatic energy, which 'liberated' fossilized stores of carbon that had been safely sequestered beneath the earth's crust for many millennia. That legacy, which brought us global warming, was embraced and extended in the following era of state-managed capitalism, as a new global hegemon orchestrated a vast expansion in greenhouse gas emissions. The United States, having supplanted Britain, built a novel exosomatic-industrial complex around the internal-combustion engine and refined oil. The result was the age of the automobile: icon of consumerist freedom, catalyst of highway construction, enabler of suburbanization,

---

21   To invert Joan Martinez-Alier's expression.

22   For a masterful reconstruction of nineteenth- and twentieth-century socialist environmentalism in England, see John Bellamy Foster, *The Return of Nature: Socialism and Ecology,* New York, 2020. Among the many recent extensions of this tradition, see Murray Bookchin, *Social Ecology and Communalism,* Chico, CA, 2005, and Michael Löwy, *Ecosocialism: A Radical Alternative to Capitalist Catastrophe,* London, 2015.

spewer of carbon dioxide and reshaper of geopolitics. Thus, coal-fired 'carbon democracy' gave way to an oil-fuelled variant, courtesy of the United States.[23]

Refined oil also powered social democracy. Profits from auto and related manufactures supplied a sizeable chunk of the tax revenues that financed postwar social provision in wealthy countries. The irony went largely unnoticed: what underwrote increased public spending on social welfare in the Global North was intensified private plunder of nature in the Global South. Apparently, capital would foot the bill for some social-reproduction costs here only if permitted to dodge a much larger bill for natural-reproduction costs there.[24] The linchpin of the arrangement was oil, without which the whole operation would have ground to a halt. To guarantee supplies and control, the US sponsored a raft of *coups d'état* in the Persian Gulf and Latin America, securing the profits and position of Big Oil and Big Fruit. The latter, like Big Food more generally, capitalized on the evolving technology of oil-guzzling, ozone-depleting refrigerated transport to regionalize an unsustainable industrialized food system, while further contaminating the atmosphere.[25] All told, oil-fuelled social democracy at home rested on militarily imposed oligarchy abroad.[26]

At the same time, the US also begat a powerful environmental movement. One current, descended from the nature-romanticism of the previous regime and originating in the nineteenth century, centred on wilderness protection through the creation of reserves and national parks, often by means of indigenous displacement.[27] 'Progressive', as opposed to backward-looking, this environmentalism of the rich was compensatory: it aimed at enabling (some) Americans to escape industrial civilization temporarily; it neither confronted the latter nor sought to transform it. As state-managed capitalism developed, however, it hatched another environmentalism, which targeted the industrial nucleus of the regime. Galvanized by Rachel Carson's *Silent Spring*, this current pushed for state action to curtail corporate pollution. The result was the Environmental Protection Agency, a parallel of sorts to the New Deal

---

23   Timothy Mitchell, 'Carbon Democracy', *Economy and Society*, vol. 38, no. 3, 2009, pp. 399–432.

24   Alyssa Battistoni, 'Free Gifts: Nature, Households and the Politics of Capitalism', PhD thesis, Yale University, 2019.

25   Susanne Freidberg, *Fresh: A Perishable History*, Cambridge, MA, 2010.

26   Mitchell, 'Carbon Democracy'.

27   Karl Jacoby, *Crimes Against Nature: Squatters, Poachers, Thieves and the Hidden History of Conservation*, Oakland, CA, 2014.

agencies that supported social reproduction. Founded in 1970, at the tail end of the state-managed era, the EPA was the regime's last major effort to defuse systemic crisis by 'internalizing externalities' as objects of state regulation. The jewel in its crown was the Super-fund, tasked with cleaning up toxic-waste sites on US territory on capital's dime. Financed chiefly by taxes on the petroleum and chemical industries, the Fund realized the principle of 'polluter pays' through the coercive agency of the capitalist state – in contrast to current carbon-trading schemes, which substitute the carrot for the stick and work through markets.

However progressive in that respect, state-capitalist regulation of nature – like that of social reproduction – was built on disavowed cost-shifting. The regime unloaded eco-'externalities' disproportion-ately onto poor communities, especially communities of colour, in the core, while ramping up extractivism and environmental-load displace-ment in the periphery. Moreover, US environmentalism's industrial wing misframed its central issue of corporate pollution. Positing the national-territorial state as the relevant unit for eco-policy, it failed to reckon with the inherently transborder character of industrial emis-sions.[28] That 'oversight' would prove especially fateful with respect to greenhouse gases, whose effects are by definition planetary. Although the process was not fully understood at the time, the detonation of that ticking timebomb was hugely hastened, as the regime relentlessly cranked out CO_2 throughout its lifespan.

Globalized bads

All of these 'bads' continue on steroids today, in the era of financial-ized capitalism – but on an altered basis. Relocation of manufacturing to the Global South has scrambled the previous energic geography. Somatic and exosomatic formations now coexist side-by-side through-out Asia, Latin America and some regions of Africa. The Global North, meanwhile, increasingly specializes in the 'post-material' triad of IT, services and finance – AKA Google, Amazon and Goldman Sachs. But once again, the appearance of liberation from nature is misleading. Northern 'post-materialism' rests upon southern materi-alism – mining, agriculture, manufacturing – as well as on fracking and offshore drilling in its own backyard. Equally important, con-sumption in the Global North is ever more carbon intensive – witness

---

28 For 'misframing', see Nancy Fraser, 'Reframing Justice in a Globalizing World', NLR 36, November–December 2005, pp. 69–88.

steep rises in air travel, meat-eating, cement-making and overall material throughput.

Meanwhile, capital continues to generate new historical natures at a rapid pace. These include new must-have minerals, such as lithium and coltan – the latter an essential ingredient of mobile phones, Central African *casus belli* and super-profitable commodity mined in some instances by enslaved Congolese children. Other neoliberal natures are familiar objects newly enclosed, such as water, whose privatization is fiercely resisted by populations intent on safeguarding not only their 'material interests' but also 'the source of life' and related subaltern views of the nature–community nexus.[29]

Although enclosures have been integral to every phase of capitalism, they assume some ingenious-insidious new forms under the current regime, as cutting-edge bio-tech joins with state-of-the-art intellectual-property law to engineer new types of monopoly rent. In some cases, Big Pharma claims ownership of indigenous plant-based medicinals, such as those derived from the Indian neem tree whose genome they lately decoded, despite the fact that the curative properties in question have been known and used for centuries throughout South Asia; similarly, Big Agra seeks to patent crop strains, such as Basmati rice, on the basis of notional genetic 'improvements' in order to dispossess the farming communities that developed them. In other cases, by contrast, the expropriators bioengineer new historical natures that do not occur 'in nature'. A notorious example is Monsanto's Terminator seeds, deliberately designed to be sterile so that farmers must purchase them every year. Here, a multinational intentionally snuffs out the natural life-renewing process by which seeds are reproduced in order to engorge the artificial life-extinguishing process by which capital reproduces itself.[30] Effectively turning its own conception of Nature II upside down, capital now denies to others the use of that 'free gift' on which it has always relied: nature's capacity to self-replenish. The result is a tangle of super-profits and multiple miseries, in which the environmental entwines with the social. Sharply rising peasant debt leads to waves of peasant suicides, further impoverishing regions already saddled with a growing share of the global environmental load: extreme pollution in cities,

---

29   Adrian Parr, *The Wrath of Capital: Neoliberalism and Climate Change Politics*, New York, 2013.

30   The best account of dispossession through this marriage of bio-tech and intellectual property remains Vandana Shiva's 'Life Inc.: Biology and the Expansion of Capitalist Markets', *Sostenible?*, vol. 2, 2000, pp. 79–92.

hyper-extractivism in the countryside and disproportionate vulner-ability to the increasingly lethal impacts of global warming.

These asymmetries are compounded by new, financialized modes of regulation, premised on new, neoliberal conceptions of Nature II. With the delegitimation of public power comes the new-old idea that the market can serve as the principal mechanism of effective govern-ance, now tasked with saving the planet by curtailing greenhouse-gas emissions. But carbon-trading schemes only draw capital away from the sort of massive coordinated investment needed to de-fossilize the world's economy and transform its energic basis. Money flows instead into speculative trade in emissions permits, ecosystem services, carbon offsets and environmental derivatives. What enables such 'regulation', and is also fostered by it, is a new green-capitalist imaginary, which subjects the whole of nature to an abstract economizing logic, even when it does not directly commodify it. The idea that a coal-belching factory here can be 'offset' by a tree plantation there assumes a nature composed of fungible, commensurable units, whose place-specificity, qualitative traits and experiential meanings can be disregarded.[31]

The same is true for the hypothetical auction scenarios, beloved of environmental economists, that purport to assign value to a 'natural asset' according to how much various actors would pay to realize their competing 'preferences' regarding it: are indigenous communities sufficiently 'invested' in preserving their local fishing stocks to outbid the corporate fleets that threaten to deplete them? If not, the rational use of the 'asset' is to allow its commercial exploitation.[32] These green-capitalist scenarios represent a sophist-icated new way of internalizing nature, which cranks epistemic abstraction up a notch, to the meta-level. But some things never change. Like its predecessor variants of Nature II, financialized nature, too, is a vehicle of expropriation.

Under these conditions, the grammar of eco-politics is shifting. As global warming has displaced chemical pollution as the central issue, so markets in emissions permits have supplanted coercive state power as the go-to regulatory mechanism, and the international has replaced the national as the favoured arena of eco-governance. Environmental

---

31 Larry Lohmann, 'Financialization, Commodification and Carbon: The Contradictions of Neoliberal Climate Policy', *Socialist Register*, vol. 48, 2012, pp. 85–107.

32 Martin O'Connor, 'On the Misadventures of Capitalist Nature', in Martin O'Connor, ed., *Is Capitalism Sustainable? Political Economy and the Politics of Ecology*, New York, 1994, pp. 125–51; Martinez-Alier, *The Environmentalism of the Poor*.

activism has altered accordingly. The wilderness-protection current has weakened and split, with one branch gravitating to the green-capitalist power centre, the other to increasingly assertive movements for environmental justice. The latter rubric now encompasses a broad range of subaltern actors, from southern environmentalisms of the poor resisting enclosures and land grabs, to northern anti-racists targeting disparities in exposure to toxins, indigenous movements fighting pipelines and eco-feminists battling deforestation – many of which overlap and link to one another in transnational networks.

At the same time, state-focused projects, lately sidelined, are now re-emerging with new vigour. As populist revolts, both left and right, have shattered belief in the magical properties of 'free markets', some are returning to the view that national-state power can serve as the principal vehicle of eco-societal reform – witness nationalists like Marine Le Pen's 'New Ecology', on the one hand, and Green New Dealers, on the other. So, too, labour unions, long committed to defending the occupational health and safety of their members but wary of curbs on 'development', now look to green infrastructure projects to create jobs. Finally, at the other end of the spectrum, degrowth currents find new recruits among youth attracted by their bold civilizational critique of spiralling material throughput and consumer lifestyles – and by the promise of *buen vivir* through veganism, commoning or a social and solidary economy.

3. FOR A NEW ECO-POLITICS

To this point, I've offered structural arguments and historical reflections in support of two propositions: first, that capitalism harbours a deep-seated ecological contradiction that inclines it non-accidentally to environmental crisis; and second, that those dynamics are inextricably entwined with other, 'non-environmental' crisis tendencies and cannot be resolved in isolation from them. The political implications are conceptually simple if practically challenging: an eco-politics capable of saving the planet must be *anti-capitalist* and *trans-environmental*.

The historical reflections offered here deepen those propositions. What I first presented as an abstract 4–D logic, wherein capital is programmed to destabilize the natural conditions on which it depends, now appears as a concrete process, unfolding in space and time. Its trajectory looks roughly like this: a socio-ecological impasse originating in the core prompts a round of plunder in the periphery (including the periphery within the core), which targets the natural wealth of populations deprived of the political means of self-defence. In each case, too, the 'fix' involves the conjure and appropriation of a new historical nature, previously dross, but suddenly gold, a must-have world-commodity, conveniently viewed as unowned and there for the taking. What follows in each case, finally, are uncontrolled down-stream effects, which spark new socio-ecological impasses, prompting further iterations of the cycle. Reiterated in each regime, this process unfolds expansively, on a world scale. Churning through sugar and silver, coal and guano, refined oil and chemical fertilizers, coltan and GMO seeds, it proceeds in stages from conquest to colonization, neo-imperialism to financialization. The result is an evolving core-periphery geography, in which the boundary between those two co-constituted spaces shifts periodically, as does the boundary between economy and nature. The process that produces those shifts generates the distinctive spatiality of capitalist development.

That process also fashions capitalism's historical temporality. Each impasse is born from the collision of our three Natures, which operate on different time scales. In each episode, capital, in thrall to its fantasy of an eternally giving Nature II, able to self-replenish without end, re-engineers Nature III to its own specifications, which dictate minimal outlays for eco-reproduction and maximal speed up of turnover time; Nature I, meanwhile, proceeding on a time scale 'of its own', registers the effects biophysically and 'bites back'. In time, the ensuing eco-damages converge with other 'non-environmental' harms, rooted in other 'non-environmental' contradictions of capitalist society. At that point, the regime in question enters its developmental crisis, leading to efforts to fashion a successor. Once installed, the latter reorganizes the nature–economy nexus in a way that dissolves the specific block-age but preserves the law of value, which commands maximum expansion of capital at maximum speed. Far from being overcome, then, capitalism's ecological contradiction is repeatedly displaced – in time as well as in space. The costs are offloaded not only onto existing populations that 'do not count' but also onto future generations. The lives of the latter, too, are discounted so that capital may live unen-cumbered and without end.

That last formulation suggests that the temporality of capitalism's ecological contradiction may not be 'merely' developmental. Beneath the system's tendency to precipitate an unending string of regime-specific crises lies something deeper and more ominous: the prospect of an *epochal crisis*, rooted in centuries of escalating greenhouse-gas emissions, whose volume now exceeds the earth's capacities for sequestration. The trans-regime progression of global warming portends a crisis of a different order. Implacably cumulating across the entire sequence of regimes and historical natures, climate change provides the perverse continuity of a ticking timebomb, which could bring the capitalist phase of human history – if not human history *tout court* – to an ignoble end.

A *trans-environmental project*

To speak of an epochal crisis is *not*, however, to proclaim imminent breakdown. Nor does it rule out the advent of a new regime of accumulation that could provisionally manage or temporarily defer the current crisis. The truth is that we can't know for sure whether capitalism has any more tricks up its enormously inventive sleeve that could stave off global warming, at least for a while, nor if so, for how long. Nor do we know whether the system's partisans could invent, sell and implement those tricks quickly enough, given that they, and we, are in a race for time with Nature I. But this much is clear: anything more than a *pro tem* stopgap would require a deep reordering of the economy–nature nexus, severely constraining, if not wholly abolishing, the prerogatives of capital.

That conclusion vindicates my principal thesis: an eco-politics aimed at preventing catastrophe must be anti-capitalist and trans-environmental. If the rationale for the first of those adjectives is already clear, the justification for the second lies in the close connection between ecological depredation and other forms of dysfunction-cum-domination inherent in capitalist society. Consider, first, the internal links between natural despoliation and racial/imperial expropriation. Claims of *terra nullius* to the contrary, the chunks of nature that capital appropriates are virtually always the life-conditions of some human group – their habitat and meaning-laden place of social interaction; their means of livelihood and material basis of social reproduction. Moreover, the human groups in question are virtually always those that have been stripped of the power to defend themselves, and often those relegated to the wrong side of the global colour line. This point was evidenced again and again throughout the sequence of regimes. It shows that ecological questions cannot be separated from questions of political power, on the one hand, nor from those of racial oppression, imperial domination and indigenous dispossession and genocide, on the other.

A similar proposition holds for social reproduction, which is closely imbricated with natural reproduction. For most people, most of the time, ecosystemic damages add heavy stresses to the business of caregiving, social provision and the tending of bodies and psyches – occasionally stretching social bonds to the breaking point. In most cases, too, the stresses bear down hardest on women, who shoulder primary responsibility for the well-being of families and communities. But there are exceptions that prove the rule. These arise when power asymmetries enable some groups to offload the 'externalities' onto others – as in the era of state-managed capitalism, when wealthy northern welfare states financed (more or less) generous social supports in the homeland by intensifying offshore extractivism. In that case, a political dynamic linking domestic social democracy to foreign domination enabled a racialized, gendered tradeoff of social reproduction for eco-depredation – a bargain that capital's partisans later rescinded by designing a new, financialized regime that allowed them to have it both ways.

No wonder, then, that struggles over nature have been deeply entangled with struggles over labour, care and political power in every phase of capitalist development. Nor that single-issue environmentalism is historically exceptional – and politically problematic. Recall the shifting forms and definitions of environmental struggle in the sequence of socio-ecological regimes. In the mercantile era, extractivist mining poisoned Peruvian lands and rivers, while land enclosures destroyed English woodlands, prompting considerable pushback in both cases. But participants in these struggles did not separate protection of nature or habitat from defence of livelihoods, political autonomy or the social reproduction of their communities. They fought rather for all those elements together – and for the forms of life in which they were integrated. When 'nature defence' *did* appear as a free-standing cause, in the liberal-colonial era, it was among those whose livelihoods, communities and political rights were *not* existentially threatened. Unencumbered by those other concerns, their stand-alone environmentalism was – necessarily – an environmentalism of the rich.[33]

As such, it contrasted starkly with contemporaneous social environmentalisms in the core and anti-colonial environmentalisms in the periphery, both of which targeted intertwined harms to nature and humans, anticipating present-day struggles for eco-socialism and

---

33 The point parallels one that Black- and socialist-feminists have repeatedly made about single-issue feminism, which purports to isolate 'genuine' gender issues from 'extraneous' concerns and thereby ends up with a 'bourgeois' or corporate feminism tailored to the situation of professional-managerial women, for whom alone those concerns are extraneous.

environmental justice. But those movements were expunged from environmentalism's official history, which canonized the single-issue definition. This broadened somewhat in the following era of state-managed capitalism, as wilderness protectionists were joined by activists urging deployment of capitalist-state power against corporate polluters. What eco-successes this regime achieved were due to its use of that power, while its failures stemmed from the refusal to reckon seriously with trans-environmental entanglements – with the inherently trans-territorial character of emissions; with the force of home-grown environmental racism; with the power of capital to subvert regulation by lobbying, workarounds and regulatory capture; and with the limitations intrinsic to a focus on eco-abuses as opposed to the normal, lawful workings of a fossil-fuelled consumerist economy. All those evasions are alive, well and still wreaking havoc today, in the era of financialized capitalism. Especially problematic, then and now, is the guiding premise that 'the environment' can be adequately protected without disturbing the institutional framework and structural dynamics of capitalist society.

The path ahead

Will these failures be repeated today? Will our chances to save the planet be squandered by our failure to build an eco-politics that is trans-environmental and anti-capitalist? Many essential building blocks for such a politics already exist in one form or another. Environmental-justice movements are already in principle trans-environmental, targeting entwinements of eco-damage with one or more axes of domination, especially gender, race, ethnicity and nationality; and some of them are explicitly anti-capitalist. Likewise, labour movements, Green New Dealers and some eco-populists grasp (some of) the class prerequisites for fighting global warming, especially the need to link the transition to renewable energy to pro-working-class policies on incomes and jobs, and the need to strengthen the power of states against corporations. Finally, decolonial and indigenous movements plumb the entwinement of extractivism and imperialism. Along with degrowth currents, they press for a deep rethink of our relation to nature and ways of living. Each of these eco-political perspectives harbours some genuine insights.

Nevertheless, the current state of these movements is not (yet) adequate to the task at hand – whether viewed individually or as an ensemble. Insofar as environmental-justice movements remain focused overwhelmingly on the disparate impact of eco-threats on subaltern populations, they fail to pay sufficient heed to the underlying structural dynamics of a social system that produces not only disparities in outcomes but a *general crisis* that threatens the well-being of all, not to mention the planet. Thus, their anti-capitalism is not yet sufficiently substantive, their trans-environmentalism not yet sufficiently deep.

Something similar is true of state-focused movements, especially (reactionary) eco-populists, but also (progressive) Green New Dealers and labour unions. Insofar as these actors privilege the frame of the national-territorial state and job creation through green-infrastructure projects, they presume an insufficiently broad and variegated view of 'the working class', which in reality includes not just construction workers, but also service workers; not only those who work for a wage, but also those whose work is unpaid; not just those who work 'in the homeland', but also those who work offshore; not only those who are exploited, but also those who are expropriated. Nor do state-focused currents adequately reckon with the position and power of that class's opposite number, insofar as they retain the classic social-democratic premise that the state can serve two masters – that it can save the planet by taming capital and needn't abolish it. Thus, they, too, are insufficiently anti-capitalist and trans-environmental – at least at present.

Finally, degrowth activists tend to muddy the political waters by conflating what *must* grow in capitalism – namely, 'value' – with what *should grow but can't* within capitalism – namely, goods, relations and activities that can satisfy the vast expanse of unmet human needs across the globe. A genuinely anti-capitalist eco-politics must dismantle the hard-wired imperative to grow the first, while treating the question of how sustainably to grow the second as a political matter, to be decided by democratic deliberation and social planning. Equally, orientations associated with degrowth, such as lifestyle environmentalism, on the one hand, and prefigurative experiments in commoning, on the other, tend to avoid the necessity of confronting capitalist power.

Taken together, moreover, the genuine insights of these movements do not yet add up to a new eco-political commonsense. Nor do they yet converge on a counter-hegemonic project for eco-societal transformation that could, at least in principle, save the planet. Essential trans-environmental elements – labour rights, feminism, anti-racism, anti-imperialism, class consciousness, pro-democracy, anti-consumerism, anti-extractivism – are present, to be sure. But they are not yet integrated in a robust diagnosis of the structural-cum-historical roots of the present crisis. What is missing to date is a clear and convincing perspective that connects all of our present woes, ecological and otherwise, to one and the same social system – and through that to one another.

I have insisted here that that system has a name: capitalist society, conceived expansively to include all the necessary background conditions for a capitalist economy – nonhuman nature and public power, expropriable populations and social reproduction – all non-accidentally subject to cannibalization by capital, all now under the wrecking ball and reeling from it. To name that system, and conceive it broadly, is to supply another piece of the counter-hegemonic puzzle we need to solve. This piece can help us to align the others, to disclose their likely tensions and potential synergies, to clarify where they have come from and where they might go together. Anti-capitalism is the piece that gives political direction and critical force to trans-environmentalism. If the latter opens eco-politics to the larger world, the former trains its focus on the main enemy.

Anti-capitalism is thus what draws the line, necessary to every historical bloc, between 'us' and 'them'. Unmasking carbon trading as the scam that it is, it pushes every potentially emancipatory current of eco-politics to publicly disaffiliate from 'green capitalism'. It pushes each current, too, to pay heed to its own Achilles heel, its inclination to avoid confronting capital, whether by pursuing (illusory) delinking or (lopsided) class compromise or (tragic) parity in extreme vulnerability. By insisting on their common enemy, moreover, the anti-capitalism piece of the puzzle indicates a path that partisans of degrowth, environmental justice and a Green New Deal can travel together, even if they can't now envision, let alone agree on its precise destination.

It remains to be seen, of course, whether any destination will actually be reached – or whether the earth will continue to heat to boiling point. But our best hope for avoiding the latter fate is to build a counter-hegemonic bloc that is trans-environmental and anti-capitalist. Where exactly such a bloc would take us were it to succeed also remains obscure. But if I had to give the goal a name, I'd opt for 'eco-socialism'.[34]

---

34 The content of a viable, twenty-first-century eco-socialism remains to be invented. For some preliminary reflections, see Nancy Fraser, 'What Should Socialism Mean in the Twenty-First Century?', *Socialist Register*, vol. 56, 2020, pp. 282–94.

Naive Questions on Degrowth

KENTA TSUDA

2021

Recent discussions of environmental strategy, including in these pages, have tended to polarize around two positions, crisply summarized by Robert Pollin as 'Degrowth versus a Green New Deal'.[1] The opposition presupposes stable and coherent sets of proposals on each side. Some have raised doubts about whether the presupposition is sound as concerns degrowth. Although sympathetic to the project, for example, ecological economist Herman Daly characterizes the degrowth movement as sloganeering in search of a programme. True enough, there are no white papers identifying institutions to manage a deliberate economic contraction, nor the legal changes they would make. Programmes, however, can be proposed at different levels of analysis. The American Green New Deal, for example, is presently articulated in a 14-page resolution presaging a series of yet-unwritten laws.[2] Degrowth proposals tend to be pitched at a similarly general level. An influential paper calls for 'an equitable downscaling of production and consumption that increases human wellbeing and enhances ecological conditions at the local and global level, in the short and long term'.[3] Broadly speaking, degrowth proponents start

---

1 These positions do not exhaust contributions to NLR's series on environmental strategy. For example, Sharachchandra Lele focuses on how both the Green New Deal and degrowth paths prioritize climate action, at the expense of concerns more urgent for societies of the Global South. Nancy Fraser argues for a project of social transformation beyond the 'merely environmental', broader than both Green New Deal and degrowth. Thanks to Dan Luban and Freya McCaie for thoughts on an earlier draft of this essay, which expresses only my individual views.

2 House Resolution no. 109, 7 February 2019.

3 Francois Schneider, Giorgos Kallis and Joan Martinez-Alier, 'Crisis or Opportunity? Economic Degrowth for Social Equity and Ecological Sustainability', *Journal of Cleaner Production*, vol. 18, no. 6, 2010, p. 512. In their defence of degrowth in these pages, Mark Burton and Peter Somerville concede: 'How degrowth might happen, we don't know'. See 'Degrowth: A Defence', above, p. 97.

from the proposition that the scale of world economic activity already exceeds the planet's capacity to sustain it, and call for a managed contraction of economic life.

What follows poses a series of questions about degrowth theory, 'naive' in the sense that they are preliminary. Degrowth literature is maturing, its academic community consolidating.[4] The points raised here are not intended to foreclose the possibility that its advocates may develop adequate answers further down the line. The aim is to bring a beginner's eye to degrowthers' central categories – decoupling, material throughput, managed economic contraction – and to press the theory on questions of coherence and administrative viability. The essay examines first methodological, then practical issues posed by degrowth, before going on to probe the nature of the problem for which degrowth is the purported remedy and the nature of alternative solutions. To start with, however, we need to examine some of the assumptions underlying concepts of 'growth' and 'consumption'.

Growth as such

Degrowthers tend to elide the colloquial meaning of consumption, as something like discretionary 'retail therapy', with the term's economic definition: the final use of a resource as a good or service. The latter sense encompasses not only the ostensibly superfluous resource uses that degrowthers would reduce or ban, but also unambiguously essential ones: nutritious food, commodious shelter, healthcare and childcare.[5] As a rule, the capacity for more consumption is socially desirable, even if every individual instance of consumption is not. Some increases in consumption can be enabled by redistribution of existing wealth. But there will always be something whose growth would be, as Daly puts it, both desirable and possible, and reallocation is unlikely to exhaust this.[6] To illustrate, imagine that a technological breakthrough yields 'Leviathan', a maximally egalitarian artificial intelligence. Using its awesome superintelligence and

4   Martin Weiss and Claudio Cattaneo, 'Degrowth: Taking Stock and Reviewing an Emerging Academic Paradigm', Ecological *Economics*, vol. 137, July 2017.

5   As Lele comments, 'It is difficult to visualize how the vast population of poor people in the Global South can achieve a modicum of development without some increase in the use of material resources for cooking, housing (including some protection from the heat) and clothing, not to mention education and travel'. See above, p. 140.

6   Herman Daly, 'A Further Critique of Growth Economics', *Ecological Economics*, vol. 88, 2013, p. 21.

capacity, Leviathan unifies the globe and enacts perfect egalitarianism. Avoiding economic distortions and administrative troubles in ineffable AI ways, Leviathan distributes the world's net wealth of $360 trillion among the world's 7.8 billion people – roughly $46,000 per person, slightly lower than the wealth of a median adult in Portugal. Leviathan also distributes net global income, allocating each person roughly $18,000 per annum, the median income in some European countries.[7] Leviathan has yielded an arguably decent level of wealth and income to all.

Would populations support affirmative measures to forego all future growth, in favour of statically maintaining the wealth levels provided by Leviathan? I think not. The benefits of additional wealth need to be considered at the margin: even at a decent standard of living, growth can enable more flourishing – a marginal year of healthspan, a decision to have an additional child – and a more secure future for existing levels of flourishing: extra resources for R&D on the frontiers of biomedical research or basic science; more investment in state capacity and the processes of need-fulfillment. In principle, there could be a time when every human being is sated on every margin, and growth is no longer desirable. But to assert that that moment has arrived is to close one's eyes to reality.

In conventional terminology, economic growth is a Kaldor–Hicks efficient transaction, in that it generates sufficient benefits for transactional winners to compensate transactional losers, thus potentially leaving no one worse off and some better off.[8] That does not make GDP growth necessarily desirable, for two reasons. First, not all economic effects are legible, and GDP data may misrepresent economic reality. Degrowthers are not alone in pointing out the deficiencies of such indices. The formulae for national reporting have been determined by sometimes arbitrary methodological choices, making GDP too narrow to capture all economic activity that is legible. More importantly, GDP figures necessarily exclude economic effects that remain unquantifiable, either because they are not accounted for in human knowledge or because they elude measurement and neat articulation. Transactions are embedded in a web of

---

7   Credit Suisse Research Institute, 'Global Wealth Databook 2019', p. 2, table 3.1. Global GDP (PPP) is approximately $139 trillion: IMF Datamapper, 'GDP, Current Prices'.

8   Allan Feldman, 'Kaldor–Hicks Compensation', in Peter Newman, ed., *The New Palgrave Dictionary of Economics and the Law*, London, 1998, pp. 417–21; see also Gordon Tullock, 'Two Kinds of Legal Efficiency', *Hofstra Law Review*, vol. 8, no. 3, 1980, pp. 663–4.

complex socioeconomic relations – they can be exploitative, harmful and, importantly for this discussion, have detrimental ecological effects. Many of these innumerable externalities – positive and negative – are not understood, or even apprehended, and so cannot be captured in GDP.

Second, the desirability of growth is a political and thus a historical question. Discussion of growth's desirability is meaningless if unmoored from the distribution of political power. The welfarist justification for growth is that the bigger pie can be distributed in socially desirable ways. Actual division, however, is decided politically – in the last instance, by coercion. When an oligarchy offers welfarist theory as an *ex ante* justification for pro-growth policy, one should anticipate 'time inconsistency' – re-division of the enlarged pie may be endlessly deferred. However, if the balance of political forces is sufficient to bring about redistribution, everyone can agree to a Kaldor–Hicks efficient transaction. In a sense, this is a central wager of revolutionary thinking: capitalist development of the productive forces is Kaldor–Hicks efficient, and so is desirable if one is confident that it is maturing a future power available to redistribute the bigger pie. Any categorical – that is, ahistorical – statement about the societal impact and hence desirability of growth is necessarily an over-generalization. Growth can only be evaluated 'as applied'.

Degrowth theory generally locates its critique of economic expansion in the environmental crisis of the twenty-first century. However, extra-ecological rationales are invoked in passing. So far, attempts to articulate a moral theory of anti-consumption have largely served to illustrate the difficulties of the project. For example, degrowther Giorgos Kallis advocates a 'culture of limits', which he derives from Aristotle and the city states of Classical Greece. Kallis proposes a collective life organized around an ethics of 'limitarian' freedom, in which humans flourish to the extent that they discipline their desires and confine their actions to fulfilling 'real' needs, as opposed to illusory ones generated by hubris.[9] As a personal perspective, this sounds interesting, perhaps compelling. But degrowth is necessarily a collective undertaking; it occurs at the societal, likely global, level or not at all.

Therefore, any case for degrowth must justify not only private preferences, but also public choices. It is one thing to choose to live by limitarian ethics, another to legislate it. Kallis envisages his limitarian

---

9   Giorgos Kallis, *Limits: Why Malthus Was Wrong and Why Environmentalists Should Care*, Stanford, 2019.

philosophy being 'autonomously' imposed by the demos upon itself; if this is a prediction, it seems like a bad one. Even if one is inclined to some version of the austere life he describes, it is a leap to proclaim its universal applicability and to welcome its imposition by the state. Degrowthers may have a more persuasive moral theory in the pipeline. Until they provide one, a social strategy based on the extra-ecological case for degrowth would be fundamentally arbitrary, requiring a high degree of coercion.

Degrow what – and how much?

The notion that there is a limit to growth has a basic plausibility. Degrowth arguments often start from a kind of cosmic perspective, invoking ecological economists' emphasis on terrestrial finitude. 'The economy is a sub-system of a larger system, the ecosphere, which is finite, non-expanding, materially closed', as Daly puts it. No amount of ingenuity, entrepreneurial tinkering or government investment can overcome the constraints of physical reality – the stock of accessible materials, the flow of solar radiation. At some point, growth must end. The time horizon is relevant, however. Independent of any anthropogenic action, the sun will one day transition to a red-giant state and Earth will become uninhabitable. These eventualities are not relevant for present practical-political purposes. The burden, therefore, is on degrowth proponents to rationalize degrowth now.

The necessary premise of the degrowth thesis is that life on Earth is threatened by the scale of contemporary 'material throughput', that is, the rate of 'extraction of raw materials from nature and their return to nature as waste'. In this view, 'economic growth unavoidably increases throughput'. Degrowthers see no escape through cleaner energy or more efficient resource use, due to the dynamic known as the 'Jevons rebound'.[10] In 1865, the English economist William Stanley Jevons showed that improved efficiency in the combustion of coal counterintuitively resulted in accelerated depletion of coal supplies: the efficiency improvement initially reduced demand for coal – less coal needed per unit of mechanical work. But due to the resulting change in price, consumers responded by demanding more mechanical work (new steam engines became cost-effective for a wider range

---

10   See respectively: Joshua Farley, 'Steady State Economics', Giorgos Kallis, 'Introduction', Blake Alcott, 'Jevons' Paradox (Rebound Effect)' and the editors' contribution, 'From Austerity to Dépense', in Giacomo D'Alisa, Federico Demaria and Giorgos Kallis, eds, *Degrowth: A Vocabulary for a New Era*, New York, 2014.

of applications) and thus more coal. Degrowthers generalize the Jevons-rebound effect from the nineteenth-century coal market to the civilizational use of physical materials considered in aggregate.[11] Technological progress may render resource use more efficient – the same work or consumption can be generated from fewer resources – but, degrowthers posit, all efficiency gains are offset by expansions in scale. The macro-level rebound effect, they claim, quashes hopes of technological advances that would reduce material throughput to a sustainable level without a policy of downsizing.

The macroeconomic rebound effect is an axiom of degrowth theory, not a finding, and there is reason to doubt it. Whether the rebound effect applies to a given efficiency gain is an empirical question: apparently it applied to nineteenth-century improvements in coal combustion, at least for a time. There is no reason to believe that it necessarily transfers to all situations, however. Efficiency gains will not yield a rebound effect, for example, where they generate an entirely distinct substitute good. Increased use of petroleum-fuelled engines that were more efficient than coal-fired engines brought no rebound effect in coal consumption, at least not by the mechanism Jevons described; rather it expanded the use of a distinct resource, petroleum.[12] Degrowthers side-step this by emphasizing the commensurability of all terrestrial resources – with the above example, of coal and petroleum. 'Material throughput', encompassing all resources and sinks, is capacious enough to make substitution impossible: one cannot substitute away from physical reality. But is it a helpful category or merely a placeholder term?

In the abstract, one can posit a civilizational metabolism or production function with physical inputs (natural resources) and outputs (goods, services, wastes) that has existed since at least the beginning of human history. Relative to today, inputs in 1900 included

---

11   The Jevons paradox 'permeates market societies and beyond', asserts degrowth advocate Samuel Alexander. 'The implication of this is that technology and efficiency improvements are not going to solve the ecological crisis': Samuel Alexander, 'Planned Economic Contraction: The Emerging Case for Degrowth', *Environmental Politics*, vol. 21, no. 3, 2012, p. 356; 'The more efficiently we use resources, the lower they cost, and the more of them we end up using. This is, in essence, growth': Giorgos Kallis, et al., 'Research on Degrowth', *Annual Review of Environment and Resources*, vol. 43, 2018, p. 296. Heterodox theorists who are otherwise critical of degrowth theory also embrace this position: see John Bellamy Foster, Brett Clark and Richard York, *The Ecological Rift: Capitalism's War on the Earth*, New York, 2010, p. 179, characterizing a macro-level rebound effect as a necessary feature of technological development under capitalism.

12   Foster et al., *The Ecological Rift*, p. 170.

proportionately more horses, coal and firewood, and less silicon and fewer carbon-fibre precursors; by 2100 there may be fewer horses, less coal and more silicon and carbon fibre, in addition to other materials barely used today. In other words, the composition of this metabolism or production function is highly variable and unstable. On the basis of what unit do degrowthers render disparate inputs and outputs commensurable across human-technological history?

Degrowthers do not specify a reliable measure of resource use to anchor 'material throughput'.[13] To the extent that they confront the measurement problem, they refer to proxies. Some discuss consumption mass as a proxy for material throughput – the aggregated weight of the physical materials consumed over time, already estimated at national level as domestic material consumption. They concede the measure is crude as a proxy for throughput, as the mass involved in an activity does not express its ecological impact.[14] As a proxy, it fails to register the differential ecological harms of materials, for example, that of a mercury-infused coal ash pile and an equal mass of food scraps in a compost bin. Furthermore, it is premised upon the capacity of statisticians to capture all sources and sinks touched by anthropogenic activity and render the effects on them legible as mass quantities – a daunting and, as far as I know, incomplete task. The alternative proxy is GDP growth itself, according to Daly 'the best index we have of total resource throughput'.[15] But this introduces a fatal ambiguity when degrowthers make claims about a 'coupling' between GDP growth and throughput: which proxy are they using for the latter? If the proxy is mass, the relationship has an unreliable empirical basis. If the proxy is GDP growth itself, the statement is tautological.

In addition to these methodological problems of legibility, degrowthers have to confront questions of magnitude. They advocate

---

13   It seems like the ideal unit would need to be defined relative to total civilizational time, e.g., the ecological burden of a tank of petroleum would be accounted for in terms of its depletion of civilizational time. Creating such a unit of measurement would require two things that humanity currently lacks: some rough projection of the course of the civilizational future and a detailed understanding of how different sources/sinks dynamically interact with and factor into that history as technology changes.

14   See Jason Hickel and Giorgos Kallis, 'Is Green Growth Possible?', *New Political Economy*, vol. 25, no. 4, 2020, p. 3; Giorgos Kallis, *Degrowth: The Economy, Key Ideas*, Newcastle, 2018, p. 109.

15   Daly, 'A Further Critique of Growth Economics', p. 21. 'Whatever it is that GDP measures, this is strongly correlated with environmental damage': Kallis, 'Introduction', *Degrowth*, p. 9.

shrinking GDP to slow material throughput. But addressing heterogeneous forms of damage – say, pollock overfishing in the Gulf of
Alaska, deforestation in the Amazon – is unlikely to require the same
reduction in throughput. The degrowth regime would need to be
cautious, reducing throughput to the threshold necessary to safeguard
the most sensitive natural systems. What is that threshold, and what
GDP reduction do we need in order to achieve it? Does the answer to
these questions change, depending on when we start degrowing? What
is the slope at our current point on the growth-throughput curve?

The answers to these questions are vitally important, because any
calibration error will have grave consequences. Undershoot, and
humanity experiences the strife of contraction but still ends up with
an uninhabitable, wasteland Earth. Overshoot and Earth remains
habitable, but with a 'deadweight loss' paid in unnecessary human
suffering, mostly by the poor, and a foregone alternative future of
social investment and scientific developments. In other words, accept-
ing for the sake of argument degrowthers' axiom that it is necessary
to reduce throughput to save civilization, the degree of reduction
matters – a lot.

Degrowthers hope that an empowered democratic state will shoulder the social costs of feeding, sheltering, educating, investing and
innovating, boosting its capacities through redistribution, expropriation of private wealth or by monetary policy. But even these efforts
would require resources that a state cannot substitute away from, like
the coercive apparatus itself and the personnel to wield it. In a contracting economy, the state would inevitably command a shrunken tax
base, an emptier treasury and tighter constraints on public financing.
All else being equal, its capacity to act would be weaker with each
year of deepening contraction. There is no political means of escape
from the importance of magnitudes.

Ultimately, while 'material throughput' may be a fruitful category
for thought experiments, it is deeply flawed as a basis for effective
environmental policymaking. Throughput is not directly accessible,
and available proxies appear so inadequate as to render meaningful
empirical treatment impossible. Degrowth theory is thin on questions
of magnitude, both for throughput thresholds and degrowth targets.
In these circumstances, while degrowthers are free to elaborate upon
the concept, others may justly respond with the Latin adage *quod
gratis asseritur, gratis negatur*: what is freely asserted – without sub-
stantiating grounds – may be freely denied.

Implementation?

But let us set aside methodological difficulties and extend the thought experiment. Imagine that a degrowth regime has developed the means of accurately measuring material throughput and reliably modelling its relationship with GDP. It has set out a well-defined throughput target and calculated the GDP reduction necessary to achieve it. The regime now needs to implement the plan. What does the administration of a planned contraction look like?

To mitigate the suffering, degrowthers universally insist on a policy of 'controlled' or 'managed' contraction. With economic reduction carefully engineered, the degrowther regime would coordinate public remediation of unemployment, homelessness, hunger and other privations, as society shifted down to the optimal level of material throughput. Central to the plan would be an industrial policy of sectoral – or perhaps, inter-firm – discrimination. Socially beneficial (and thus environmentally tolerable) enterprises would be allowed to expand, while detrimental ones might be targeted for direct shut-down. The result would be localized pockets of growth – providing jobs, tax revenue, innovation – within a contracting aggregate economy. Without any clear administrative proposals from degrowthers to go on, let us imagine that the regime might use the tax code: start with a rebuttable presumption of harm and impose tax penalties if a firm reports net growth. Firms that can prove their contribution to the public interest would qualify for a licence to grow, or exemption from the tax penalties. Alternatively, the regime could authorize a government agency to identify socially undesirable firms and place them into something like a receivership for orderly wind-down.

To prevent firms from undermining the broader degrowth policy, the regime would have to account for all major enterprises. Each firm would need to be categorized as either operating in the public interest and thus allowed to continue business as usual, or socially undesirable and therefore subject to wind-down. Some candidates for localized shutdown are already easy to identify: degrowthers mention coal-fired power generation. Likewise, there are obvious candidates for localized growth: breakthrough medical technology, new sources of energy, toxic-waste clean-up services, perhaps degrowth research itself. Other cases would be harder. For example, Mark Burton and Peter Somerville suggest that steel and cement production for the construction industry could be phased out; but a policy of wind-down here might face resistance from low-income housing organizations and workers priced out of greener eco-houses. Such tradeoffs would be common when categorizing so many industries and firms. Along the way, officials will make mistakes, terminating beneficial enterprises, coddling destructive ones.

Degrowthers claim that desirable economic activity can be defined as fulfilling human needs.[16] Since needs are finite, they argue, the economic activity required to meet them is finite too. The task of government is to foster need-satisfying activities and eliminate superfluous ones. But degrowthers provide no conclusive list of human needs – likely because such an account is not possible. Need is not a freestanding category; it is dependent upon other conditions of ethical or social flourishing. Some needs, under that label or another, are uncontroversial: everyone can agree that a human being should have food, shelter, healthcare, a baseline education, association with amiable fellow humans. One can broaden out from this – freedom of conscience, capacity for self-expression, privacy, a qualified freedom of expression. But a needs-based theory is not doing much work in defining these entitlements, and effectively every universalist political theory is agreed on them.

It is in drawing borders that a theory proves its worth, and here the degrowthers' theory of need falls short. For every disagreement about the growth justified by need-fulfillment, we would have cascading disagreements about the boundary of the category 'need'. One degrowther, for example, suggests state organization of 'conviviality' in the form of public feasts and philosophizing, presumably rationalized, as with all social provision, as need fulfillment.[17] But the author of this contribution would deny the universality of the 'convivial need' so defined, and would take affirmative measures to avoid such large-group socializing and indoctrination. One person's need is another person's chore. Some theorists propose to resolve the indeterminacy problem by labelling needs at a high level of generality, for example, confining basic needs to physical survival, health and personal autonomy, because these must be satisfied before actors can achieve 'any other valued goal'.[18] But this formulation too is what lawyers would call 'void for vagueness', and even these theorists

---

16   Kallis, *Limits: Why Malthus Was Wrong*, passim; Burton and Somerville, 'Degrowth: A Defence', above, p. 96.

17   Kallis, *Limits*, p. 116; Kallis draws upon contributions of researcher Aaron Vansintjan. Kallis, 'Introduction', *Degrowth*, p. 11.

18   Ian Gough, 'Climate Change and Sustainable Welfare: The Centrality of Human Needs', *Cambridge Journal of Economics*, vol. 39, no. 5, Sept 2015, p. 1197.

concede that what health and autonomy entail is contestable and in-determinate.[19] A policy of degrowth cannot proceed logically from a stable category of needs because no such category exists.

Degrowthers' procedural argument is no stronger. They insist that managed contraction will be administered democratically, with the demos imposing limits to consumption upon itself. Anyone who has cracked a book on democratic theory will notice the incompleteness of these pronouncements. What arrangements do degrowthers envis-age for their democracy and how would they achieve them? What institutions do they think will yield policies in the public interest? Administrative juries? Plebiscitary democracy? Democratic central-ism? In the absence of even a mention of institutions, the invocation of democracy rings hollow. In short, degrowthers fail to describe how they will administer the managed economic contraction. The process could be messy.

Domestic policy is only the start. Degrowthers do not directly address the issue of international coordination, but presumably all large economies would need to contract in order to achieve the required material-throughput reductions. Degrowth in one country is a non-starter. International coordination of degrowth, however, threatens to reproduce the domestic coordination problem within the anarchic dynamics of inter-state politics, where economic magnitude comes armed with military power. It seems likely that every state will aim to maximize its relative position in a degrowth world – that is, to degrow the least relative to other nations. Recognizing this problem, powerful states will then aim to establish an international agree-ment – a Global Degrowth Pact, say – to constrain each other. The Pact would include mechanisms to monitor and punish defection. Pact members would settle on metrics against which national contrac-tion could be measured. Where national statistics failed to conform to the degrowth schedule, punishment would kick in – escalating economic sanctions, for example.

So much for the Pact on paper. What about in practice? The Pact would need to define criteria for degrowth to be applied to widely varying economies, with each government wanting the discretion to define these for itself. Most would no doubt argue that their propor-tion of degrowth should be reduced, invoking the degrowth principle of 'localized growth in the public interest', or other specific national

19   Of course defining health and illness is not easy: some claim that conceptions of health are always internal to cultural systems of thought and thus inherently contestable': Gough, 'Climate Change and Sustainable Welfare', p. 1197.

circumstances. In the absence of determinate public-interest criteria, each government's claims would be hard to contest. How much contraction is demanded of each nation is likely to take on an arbitrary character, accommodating the will of the powerful rather than optimizing for achievement of ecological targets.

Enforcement would remain a work in progress: states routinely distort national macroeconomic indicators, but under the Pact, the incentives to do so would be magnified. Ministries might send promising junior officials to prestigious universities to sharpen their facility in cooking the books. Governments will deploy this expertise both to dissemble their own numbers and to scrutinize those of other nations. The Pact could also face a further problem endemic to group coordination: defection. Though degrowthers hope to see substantial international redistribution, this might fall short, leaving poorer countries with a still-smaller tax base to alleviate unemployment, homelessness, disease and famine. Their suffering populations might turn to revolution. Responding to popular demands, the new government would modify the *ancien régime*'s degrowth commitments, or even repudiate the Pact altogether. The larger Pact members might ignore the withdrawal of a microstate, but would be unlikely to countenance the defection of a major power. The response of the 'international degrowth community' would be swift and furious: a punitive, exogenously imposed degrowth.

Climate first

These hypotheticals merely illustrate that a global degrowth policy would require significant resources to administer, and even with them might fall into a spiral of bureaucratic mismanagement and international conflict. But methodological questions aside, even the administrative problems of degrowth, domestic and international, are not necessarily disqualifying if the strategy is absolutely essential for civilizational survival. Is that the case?

Advocates take it as axiomatic that degrowth is necessary for human activity to stay within Earth's carrying capacity, or 'planetary boundaries'. These usually refer to the limits for each of the nine earth-system processes set out by Johan Rockström and Mattias Klum, beyond which there is a high risk of the Earth tipping from the stable 'Holocene-like' conditions of the last 10,000 years into a biophysical state that may no longer support modern human societies. Where possible, Rockström and Klum suggest specific metrics for the boundaries and current status of each earth-system process – climate change, biosphere integrity (i.e., extinctions), stratospheric ozone depletion, ocean acidification, nitrogen and phosphorous pollution, forest cover, freshwater use, atmospheric aerosol loading and 'novel entities', still to be defined.[20]

According to Rockström and Klum, human activity is not yet pressing against all nine boundaries. Two of the processes – extinctions and phosphorous/nitrogen pollution – are in the high-risk zone, beyond safe 'planetary-boundary' limits. Climate change and de-forestation are at the stage of increased risk, pressing against their boundaries.[21] Of the remaining five systems, four have not yet transgressed their planetary boundaries, and one remains undefined. There are valid criticisms to be made of this methodology. Some of the 'global average' metrics are of questionable value, as it is not clear that Rockström and Klum are addressing systems that exist as global commons.[22] Nevertheless, the point to be made here is the relevance of degrowth strategies for these earth-system processes. Degrowthers usually imply that their prescriptions would protect them all. However, the only planetary boundary they expressly address is the atmosphere's capacity to act as a greenhouse-gas sink. Their proposition is that, compared to all alternative strategies, it is only through degrowth that human civilization can avert catastrophic anthropogenic climate change. In other words, the ecological rationale for degrowth boils down to necessary climate action.

If we accept the urgency of climate change as the most pressing environmental issue, it is worth asking, first, what would be the

---

20   Johan Rockström and Mattias Klum, *Big World, Small Planet*, New Haven, CT, 2014, pp. 59–79.

21   For climate change, in 2014 Rockström and Klum gave a current measurement of 396.5 ppm atmospheric CO_2, with a planetary boundary of 350–450 ppm; they take a tougher line than the IPCC, which sets 430 ppm as the level for a temperature increase of less than 1.5°C relative to pre-industrial levels. Deforestation presently leaves 62 per cent of original forest cover, with a planetary boundary of 54–75 per cent. See *Big World, Small Planet*, pp. 67–9.

22   For example, freshwater availability is a localized phenomenon. Conserving water in Juneau, Alaska, in a large temperate rainforest, may have no direct impact on water availability in, say, a village in Northern India that experiences devastating groundwater depletion. There could be indirect connections between the two – for example, relative changes in water pricing could ripple from Juneau across the world economy – but the 'commons' in question is not a shared freshwater source. Averaging sustainable water-usage rates, or defining one global freshwater-usage threshold that levels the differences between them, is practically useless. For a similar criticism see David Molden, 'Planetary Boundaries: The Devil is in the Detail', *Nature Climate Change*, vol. 1, 2009, pp. 116–17.

swiftest and most practical way to address it, using the tools we have to hand and our available knowledge? And second, the political question: what are the obstacles to implementing this minimal programme? As far as tools are concerned, a regime of legal constraints that implicitly limits growth, without precluding it, is perhaps so familiar that it eludes notice. Liberal regimes' civil and political rights already set limits on social activity, including the transactions that collectively generate economic growth. In some jurisdictions, rights extend into the environmental sphere, often defined by statute rather than by constitution. For example, in the US, laws passed in the early 1970s invest individuals with rights against harm from certain forms of water and air pollution, even against harms they may suffer from the 'taking' of endangered species. Actually existing rights regimes are severely limited, both in terms of their *de jure* reach and their realization in practice. But these examples demonstrate that a legal regime of ecological constraints to control emissions is conceivable; and in contrast to the to-be-defined arrangements of a degrowth regime, they do have the merit that they actually exist.

As for a minimalist climate-action programme, many environmentalists would agree that the major emitter states would need to adopt the following measures:

1. Compel emissions reductions, with a phase-out of widespread fossil-fuel use and other major sources of greenhouse-gas pollution, through some combination of emissions pricing – for example, a carbon tax – and direct regulation: stricter emission and efficiency standards, moratoria on extractive use of public lands. Political-economy considerations suggest that, efficiency notwithstanding, the mix of these policies would ultimately lean heavily on an array of sector-specific decarbonization laws – that is, industrial policy.[23]
2. Elimination of atmospheric stocks of legacy emissions, for example by large-scale expansion of public-land conservation, soil-conservation laws and investment in sequestration research and innovation.
3. Redistributive policy to, at the least, offset the dislocations of emission-reduction efforts.
4. International coordination. Under present conditions, this would most likely take the form of treaties linking trade policy to emissions reductions, eliminating the possibility of climate-action arbitrage. Any international redistribution from rich industrialized societies to the

---

23 Danny Cullenward and David Victor, *Making Climate Policy Work*, Cambridge, 2020.

Global South would likely occur in some inadequate form within such treaties. Though highly imperfect, this would be preferable to the other realistic alternative: emissions reductions under the imperial boot through manipulation of the SWIFT system, economic sanctions and military intervention.[24]

Together with increased public investment in basic scientific research, these would be the elements of a minimalist climate programme. They are necessary, but potentially insufficient (for example, if pursued too late). They are climate action's low-hanging fruit.

Degrowth prescriptions have no necessary relationship to climate action. Without doubt, there is a realistic possibility of recession as an outcome of decarbonization, before a new equilibrium could emerge. But to tack on degrowth prescriptions too would be courting economic disaster. Considerations of egalitarianism or social solidarity need not militate against a minimalist climate-action programme. 'Carbon taxes are not socialist', necessarily.[25] Nor is there a necessary relationship between land conservation and distributive justice. But minimalist climate action is a better fit for a programme of social transformation than the recessionary trauma of degrowth.

As proponents of the American Green New Deal suggest, climate action can be embedded in a transformative social policy. Indeed, the Green New Deal proposal may be both under-ambitious and administratively over-confident. The Green New Deal focuses on off-setting the predicted social costs of climate action. In American society, however, the need for deepened redistribution reaches far beyond the imperative to compensate for decarbonization. To render redistribution most efficient, social policy should take the broadest, most universal form, as opposed to piecemeal add-ons to disparate laws.[26] This applies equally to social policy in a decarbonizing society: the best approach is to extend public benefits by some general criterion – rate schedules in the tax code – or as a universal benefit like socialized

---

24   Noting the fate of successive UN climate talks, Lola Seaton argues that a global inter-governmental body with genuine legislative capabilities and practical powers of implementation is an essential component of a viable green strategy; a weakness of many environmentalist proposals is that they assume such an agent exists, or could easily be created. See above, p. 111.

25   Scott Edwards, 'No, Carbon Taxes Are Not Socialist', *Jacobin*, 10 October 2010.

26   Louis Kaplow and Steven Shavell, 'Why the Legal System Is Less Efficient than the Income Tax in Redistributing Income', *Journal of Legal Studies*, vol. 23, no. 2, 1994.

healthcare. In other words, there are efficiency reasons to unbundle social policy and environmental protection.

The Green New Deal assumes that legislators – or the bureaucrats to whom legislators would defer the detailed policymaking – will be able to anticipate the consequences of decarbonization and devise appropriate offsetting redistributive changes, monetary or in-kind. There is little reason to believe that forecasting of that sort can be accurate, and prediction failures could be devastating to many. In contrast to broad universal programmes, redistributive add-ons to environmental protections probably risk distorting climate action at the margin of its ecological impact: every redistributive add-on will require 'pork' to buy off resistant legislators, dissipating resources otherwise available for deepening the ecological impact.

Re-politicization?

While climate action could be embedded in any number of potential broader social changes – transition to socialism, ascent of a degrowth technocracy, triumphant Catholic integralism – climate action *qua* climate action does not require totalizing regime change. Its minimalist version should in principle be possible under any rational capitalist regime. Further, one would expect any such regime to pursue this course. The most important political fact for the formation of any green strategy is that the actually existing capitalist regime has declined this obvious – and, thirty years ago, relatively unburdensome – climate action. What explanation do degrowthers offer for this? According to its proponents, degrowth explicitly sets out to 're-politicize environmentalism'.[27] Yet, such as it is, degrowthers' political analysis is ideational, fixating on collective understandings – the 'development consensus', the 'growth imaginary'. Degrowthers in fact rarely discuss political power or those who wield it. Writing in the imperative, their prescriptions urge 'us' to wiser, more responsible ways of living. But this raises the puzzle of the status quo: who imposes climate crisis on whom?

There's little mystery about the 'whom'. The young – generations Z and Alpha – will enter adulthood as climate change and associated political chaos intensify. The outcomes – famine, disease, displacement, upheaval and political violence – will fall disproportionately among the poor and the Global South. On top of these are the negative opportunity costs. The irrational delay in mitigating climate crisis

27   Kallis, 'Introduction', *Degrowth*, pp. 8, 9.

has already deprived future humanity of resources that would otherwise have been at its disposal. 'Future humanity' itself is a category shaped by the crisis: taking untold lives and destroying social wealth, climate change will deprive humanity of all the knowledge and experiences that would have come to fruition in an alternate universe where countermeasures were initiated in good time.

How about the 'who', the agents of this disorder? In March 1982, NASA scientist James Hansen told the House of Representatives that 'substantial climate change' was likely during the next decades, 'if man continues to modify the atmospheric composition at present rates'. Climate models indicated 'a large climate impact for increased carbon dioxide and trace gases'.[28] The Federal government may have known about the greenhouse effect earlier – the oil majors have been aware of it since at least the late 1960s – but Hansen's testimony can be used as a conservative estimate of when Washington was served notice of the climate crisis. A minimalist climate-action programme was already conceivable: officials within the Nixon Administration had proposed the general notion of Pigouvian 'effluent charges' and MIT engineer David Wilson approached legislators proposing a tax to limit CO_2 emissions in particular as early as 1974.[29]

With the exception of a few policy changes at the end of the Obama Administration – promptly reversed by the Trump Administration – the Federal government has systematically moved in the opposite direction. Since 1990, the United States has emitted over 200 billion metric tons of CO_2 equivalent GHGs. The Federal government's own role as a direct source of emissions is considerable. The US military uses more oil than any other institution in the world: between 2001 and 2017, it emitted 1.2 billion metric tons of carbon dioxide equivalent.[30] Unlike emissions from frequently criticized sources like pickup trucks or the beef industry, military emissions account for, to say the least, unproductive 'negative utility' activities, squandering trillions of taxpayer dollars to devastate (in many cases, violently end) the lives of innumerable civilians with whom ordinary Americans have no grievances.

28   US House of Representatives Committee on Science and Technology, 'Carbon Dioxide and Climate: The Greenhouse Effect', no. 115, 25 March 1982, p. 40.

29   Chris Berdik, 'The Unsung Investor of the Carbon Tax', *Boston Globe*, 10 August 2014.

30   Neta Crawford, 'Pentagon Fuel Use, Climate Change and the Costs of War', Brown University, Costs of War Project, 12 June 2019.

The state's deepening of the climate crisis is underpinned by the control of this policy domain by fossil-fuel corporations and their trade association, the American Petroleum Institute. Big Oil has tapped the Federal government for billions of dollars in direct subsidies annually. These amounts are dwarfed, however, by a hidden subsidy in the form of what the government is *not* doing – its deferral of climate action, which according to a recent IMF paper is worth $649 billion to fossil-fuel companies every year – second only to China's corresponding subsidies, at $1.4 trillion.[31] Oil and gas interests spent over $200 million on electioneering and federal lobbying in 2020. This dominance and subversion of state power is not a realization of the *laissez-faire* ideal; it is corporatism, the interpenetration of state and big capital.

Many powerful interests stand to lose from climate chaos, which has already arrived in the US in the form of unprecedented storms, wildfires and floods. Why has corporate America allowed Big Oil to subvert the state's climate-change policy for so long? Surely, Mancur Olson's so-called logic of collective action is at play: concentrated interests – fossil-fuel corporations – face fewer obstacles in organizing and coopting the relevant instrumentalities of the state, compared to the diffuse majorities of the public or corporate America writ large.

But to grasp the situation, we also need to historicize it. Contemporary environmental backlash in America dates to the late 1970s, when Congress resisted environmental legislation proposed by the Carter Administration in the context of the international oil crisis, and attacks on environmentalism began to appear in print. According to Philip Shabecoff's history, the Reagan presidency, particularly the first term, was 'perceived by business leaders as a chance to go on the offensive'. Reagan staffed the environmental bureaucracy with businessmen and pro-business ideologues. For example, Anne Gorsuch, mother of Trump's recently confirmed Supreme Court appointment, was placed at the Environmental Protection Agency on the recommendation of industrialist Joseph Coors along with an Aerojet PR executive and in-house lawyers from Exxon, General Motors and Coors itself. Reagan appointees succeeded in weakening

---

31 David Coady et al., 'Global Fossil Fuel Subsidies Remain Large: An Update Based on Country-Level Estimates', IMF Working Paper 19/89, May 2019, Appendix 5. Direct US government subsidies to fossil-fuel companies are estimated at $4.9 billion per annum: Joseph Aldy, 'Money for Nothing: The Case for Eliminating Us Fossil Fuel Subsidies', *Resources*, no. 184, 2014, pp. 35–6.

environmental agencies and braking the energetic Federal environmental protection of the late sixties.[32]

In other domains, too, the period since the 1970s – variously described as the 'long downturn' or 'great stagnation' – has been characterized by the turn of big business to politics and rent-seeking, to avert a future in which they could be otherwise eliminated as uncompetitive. Reagan's Sagebrush Rebellion, Big Oil's knowing climate-change obfuscation and other fronts of the environmental backlash conform to this pattern. The climate crisis can be viewed as the social toll of Big Oil resorting to political means to perpetuate its free access to the skies as a pollution sink. In this process, it has been abetted by the rest of big capital, in tacit agreement that one sector of American big business will not mobilize against another, each safely retaining its place at the governmental trough.

If this hypothesis is correct, degrowthers have it backwards: the specific character of the environmental crisis and climate change arises not from out-of-control economic dynamism but its opposite: the politics of stagnation. Where degrowthers posit crazed economic expansion, one looks in vain at the data for evidence of that runaway dynamism and cornucopian excess. It may be that degrowth theory is another case of overstatement from misdiagnosis, analogous to the hyperbolic automation discourse that Aaron Benanav has criticized.[33] If this is correct, the struggle to avert ecological catastrophe and irreparable damage to the future of human civilization arises not from substantive differences over the remedial policy package, but as part of a generalized political crisis that transcends the ecological domain. There will be contestation of the details of climate action, of course, as with any large-scale public policy. But its broad contours are undisputed. Grand questions remain only in the political domain: how will humanity change who wields political power, displacing the forces that veer towards civilizational destruction?

---

32   Philip Shabecoff, *A Fierce Green Fire: The American Environmental Movement*, Washington, DC, 1993, pp. 226, 210–11. Shabecoff writes, 'To some it seemed that Carter's retreat on many issues, including stiffer air pollution regulations, signalled the beginning of the end for the era of environmental activism that launched on Earth Day': p. 203.

33   See Aaron Benanav, 'Automation and the Future of Work I', NLR 119, September–October 2019.

12

Energy Dilemma

CÉDRIC DURAND

2021

The ecological bifurcation is not a gala dinner. After a summer of extreme climatic events and a new IPCC report confirming its most worrying forecasts, large parts of the world are now roiled by an energy crisis that prefigures further economic troubles down the road. This conjuncture has buried the dream of a harmonious transition to a post-carbon world, bringing the question of capitalism's ecological crisis to the fore. At COP26, the dominant tone is one of powerlessness, where impending miseries have left humanity cornered between the immediate demands of systemic reproduction and the acceleration of climate disorders.

Prima facie, one might think that steps are being taken to address this cataclysm. More than fifty countries – plus the entire European Union – have pledged to meet net-zero emissions targets that would see global energy-related CO_2 emissions fall by 40 per cent between now and 2050. Yet a sober reading of the scientific data shows that the green transition is off track. Falling short of global net zero means that temperatures will continue to rise, pushing the world well above 2°C by 2100. According to the UN Environment Programme, nationally determined contributions, which countries were requested to submit in advance of COP26, would reduce 2030 emissions by 7.5 per cent. Yet a 30 per cent drop is needed to limit warming to 2°C, while 55 per cent would be required for 1.5°C.[1]

As a recent *Nature* editorial warned, many of these countries have made net-zero pledges without a concrete plan to get there.[2] Which gases will be targeted? To what extent does net zero rely on effective

---

1   United Nations Environment Programme, *Emissions Gap Report 2021*, 26 October 2021.

2   Editorial, 'Net-Zero Carbon Pledges Must Be Meaningful to Avert Climate Disaster', *Nature*, 31 March 2021.

reduction rather than offsetting schemes? The latter have become particularly attractive for rich countries and polluting corporations, since they do not directly diminish emissions and involve transferring the burden of carbon-cutting to low- and medium-income nations (which will be most severely affected by climate breakdown). On these crucial issues, reliable information and transparent commitments are nowhere to be found, jeopardizing the possibility of credible international scientific monitoring. The bottom line: based on the current global climate policies – those implemented and those proposed – the world is on track for a devastating increase in emissions during the next decade.

In spite of this, capitalism has already experienced the first major economic shock related to the transition beyond carbon. The surge in energy prices is due to several factors, including a disorderly rebound from the pandemic, poorly designed energy markets in the UK and EU which exacerbate price volatility, and Russia's readiness to secure its long-term energy incomes.[3] However, at a more structural level, the impact of the first efforts to restrict the use of fossil fuels cannot be overlooked. Due to government limits on coal burning, plus shareholders' growing reluctance to commit to projects that could be largely obsolete in thirty years, investment in fossil fuel has been falling. Although this contraction of supply is not enough to save the climate, it is still proving too much for capitalist growth.

Putting together several recent events gives a taste of things to come. In the Punjab region of India, severe shortages of coal have caused unscheduled power blackouts.[4] In China, more than half the provincial jurisdictions have imposed strict power-rationing measures. Several companies, including key Apple suppliers, have recently been forced to halt or reduce operations at facilities in Jiangsu province, after local governments restricted the supply of electricity.[5] Those restrictions were an attempt to comply with national emissions targets by restricting coal-fired power generation, which still accounts for about two-thirds of China's electricity. To contain the spill over of these disruptions, Chinese authorities have put a temporary brake on their climate ambitions, ordering 72 coal mines to increase their

---

3 David Sheppard, 'Gas Shortages: What Is Driving Europe's Energy Crisis?', *Financial Times*, 10 October 2021.

4 'Cuts Spell Dark Days for Punjab Inc: Industrialists', *Times of India*, 12 October 2021.

5 Cheng Ting-Fang and Lauly Li, 'Apple Suppliers Warn that China Energy Disruption Threatens Supply Chain', *Financial Times*, 5 October 2021.

supply and relaunching imports of Australian coal that were halted for months in the midst of diplomatic tensions between the two countries.[6]

In Europe, it was the surge in gas prices that triggered the current crisis. Haunted by the memory of the *gilets jaunes* uprising against Macron's carbon tax, governments have intervened with energy subsidies for the popular classes. More unexpectedly, though, gas price increases have precipitated chain reactions in the manufacturing sector. The case of fertilizers is telling. A US group, CF Industries, decided to shut down production of its UK fertilizer plants, which had become unprofitable due to price increases. As a by-product of its operations, the firm previously supplied 45 per cent of the UK's food-grade CO_2 – whose loss unleashed weeks of chaos for the industry, affecting various sectors from beer and soft drinks to food packaging and meat. Globally, the surge in gas prices is affecting the farming sector via the increase in fertilizer prices. In Thailand, the cost of fertilizers is on track to double from 2020, raising costs for many rice producers and putting the planting season at risk.[7] If this continues, governments may have to step in to ensure essential food supplies.

The global and widespread repercussions of energy shortages and price increases underscore the complex fallout involved in the structural transformation necessary to eliminate carbon emissions. While a reduction is underway in the supply of hydrocarbon, increases in sustainable energy sources are not sufficient to meet growing demand. This leaves an energy mismatch that could derail the transition altogether. In this context, countries can either return to the most readily available energy source – coal – or succumb to an economic contraction driven by the surge in costs and their effects on profitability, consumption prices and the stability of the financial system. In the short term, then, there is a trade-off between ecological objectives and the requirement to foster growth. But does this energy dilemma hold in the medium and long term? Will we ultimately face a choice between protecting the climate and growth?

A successful carbon transition implies the harmonious unfolding of two processes related in complex ways at the material, economic and financial levels. First, a process of disbandment must take place.

---

6 'Les autorités chinoises demandent à 72 mines de charbon d'augmenter leur production',*Connaisance des Energies*, 8 October 2021.
7 'Rice Set to Climb as Fertilizer Rally Drives Up Farm Costs', *Bangkok Post*, 20 October 2021.

Sources of carbon emissions must be drastically reduced: above all hydrocarbon extraction, electricity production by coal and gas, fuel-based transport systems, the construction sector (due to the high level of emissions involved in cement and steel production) and the meat industry. What is at stake here is degrowth in the most straightforward sense: equipment must be scrapped, fossil-fuel reserves must stay in the soil, intensive cattle-breeding must be abandoned and an array of related professional skills must be made redundant.

All things being equal, the elimination of production capacities implies a contraction of supply which would lead to generalized inflationary pressure. This is even more likely because the sectors most affected are located at the commanding heights of modern economies. Cascading through the other sectors, pressure on costs will dent firms' mark-up, global profits and/or consumer purchasing power, unleashing wild recessionary forces. In addition, degrowth of the carbon economy is a net loss from the point of view of the valorization of financial capital: huge amounts of stranded assets must be wiped out since underlying expected profits will be foregone, paving the way for fire sales and ricocheting onto the mass of fictitious capital.[8] These interrelated dynamics will exacerbate each other, as recessionary forces increase debt defaults while a financial crisis would freeze access to credit.

The other side of the transition is a major investment push of the kind proposed by Robert Pollin to accommodate the supply shock caused by the degrowth of the carbon sector. While changing consumption habits could play a role, especially in affluent countries, the creation of new carbon-free production capacities, improvements in efficiency, electrification of transport, industrial and heating systems (along with the deployment of carbon capture in some instances) are also necessary to compensate for the phasing out of greenhouse gas emissions. From a capitalist perspective, these could represent new profit opportunities, so long as the costs of production are not prohibitive relative to available demand. Attracted by this valorization, green finance could step in and accelerate the transition, propelling a new wave of accumulation capable of sustaining employment and living standards.

Yet it is important to bear in mind that timing is everything: making such adjustments in fifty years is completely different to having to disengage drastically in a decade. And from where we are

8 S. Battison et al., 'A Climate Stress-Test of the Financial System', *Nature Climate Change*, vol. 7, March 2017.

now, the prospects for a smooth and adequate switch to green energy are slim, to say the least. The scaling back of the carbon sector remains uncertain due to the inherent contingency of political processes and the persistent lack of engagement from state authorities. It is illustrative that a single Senator, Joe Manchin of West Virginia, could scuttle the US Democrats' programme to facilitate the replacement of coal- and gas-fired power plants.

As illustrated by the current disruptions, the lack of readily available alternatives could also hamper the phasing out of fossil fuels. According to the International Energy Agency: 'Transition-related spending . . . remains far short of what is required to meet rising demand for energy services in a sustainable way. The deficit is visible across all sectors and regions.'[9] In its latest Energy Report, Bloomberg estimates that a growing global economy will require a level of investment in energy supply and infrastructure between $92 trillion and $173 trillion over the next thirty years.[10] Annual investment will need to more than double, rising from around $1.7 trillion per year today, to somewhere between $3.1 trillion and $5.8 trillion per year on average. The magnitude of such a macroeconomic adjustment would be unprecedented.

From the perspective of mainstream economics, this adjustment is still a matter of getting the prices right. In a recent report commissioned by French president Emmanuel Macron, two leading economists in the field, Christian Gollier and Mar Reguant, argue: 'The value of carbon should be used as a yardstick for all dimensions of public policymaking.' Although standards and regulations should not be ruled out, 'well-designed carbon pricing' via a carbon tax or cap-and-trade mechanism must play the leading role. Market mechanisms are expected to internalize the 'negative externalities' of greenhouse gas emissions, allowing for an orderly transition on both the supply and demand sides. 'Carbon pricing has the advantage of focusing on efficiency in terms of cost per ton of CO_2, without the need to identify in advance which measures will work.' Reflecting the plasticity of market adjustment, a carbon price – 'unlike more prescriptive measures' – opens up a space for 'innovative solutions'.[11]

This free-market, techno-optimistic perspective assures us that capitalist growth and climate stabilization are reconcilable. However,

9 'World Energy Outlook 2021', IEA, December 2021.
10 'New Energy Outlook 2021', BloombergNEF, July 2021.
11 Olivier Blanchard and Jean Tirole, 'Les grands défis économiques', International Commission Report, June 2021.

it suffers from two main shortcomings. The first is the blindness of the carbon-pricing approach to the macroeconomic dynamics involved in the transition effort. A recent report by Jean Pisani-Ferry, written for the Peterson Institute for International Economics, plays down the possibility of any smooth adjustment driven by market prices, while also dashing the hopes of a Green New Deal that could lift all boats.

Observing that 'procrastination has reduced the chances of engineering an orderly transition', the report notes that there is 'no guarantee that the transition to carbon neutrality will be good for growth'.[12] The process is quite simple: 1) since decarbonization implies an accelerated obsolescence of some part of existing capital stock, supply will be reduced; 2) in the meantime, more investment will be necessary. The burning question then becomes: are there sufficient resources in the economy to allow for more investment alongside weakened supply? The answer depends on the amount of slack in the economy – that is, idle productive capacity and unemployment. But considering the size of the adjustment and the compressed timeframe, this cannot be taken for granted. In Pisani-Ferry's view, 'Impact on growth will be ambiguous, impact on consumption should be negative. Climate action is like a military build-up when facing a threat: good for welfare in the long run, but bad for consumer satisfaction.' Shifting the resources from consumption to investment means that consumers will inevitably bear the cost of the effort.

In spite of his neo-Keynesian perspective, Pisani-Ferry opens up an insightful discussion on the political conditions that might lead to a reduction in living standards and a green class war fought along income lines. Yet, in its attachment to the price mechanism, his argument shares with the market-adjustment approach an irrational emphasis on the efficiency of CO_2 emission reduction. The second shortcoming of Gollier and Reguant's contribution becomes apparent when they call for 'a combination of climate actions with the lowest possible cost per ton of CO_2 equivalent not emitted'. Indeed, as the authors themselves recognize, the setting of carbon prices is highly uncertain. Evaluations can range from $45 to $14,300 per ton, depending on the time horizon and the reduction targeted. With such variability, there is no point in trying to optimize the cost of carbon reduction. What is important is not the cost of the adjustment, but rather the certainty that the stabilization of the climate will occur.

---

12   Jean Pisani-Ferry, 'Climate Policy Is Macroeconomic Policy, and the Implications Will Be Significant', PIIE, August 2021.

Delineating the specificities of the Japanese developmental state, the political scientist Chalmers Johnson made a distinction that could also be applied to the transition debate:

> A regulatory, or market rational, state concerns itself with the form and procedures – the rules, if you will – of economic competition, but it doesn't concern itself with substantive matters . . . The developmental state, or plan-rational state, by contrast, has as its dominant feature precisely the setting of such substantive social and economic goals.[13]

In other words, while the first aims at efficiency – making the most economical use of resources – the second is concerned with effectiveness: that is, the ability to achieve a given goal, be it war or industrialization. Given the existential threat posed by climate change and the fact that there exists a simple and stable metric to limit our exposure, our concern should be with the effectiveness of reducing greenhouse gases rather than the efficiency of the effort. Instead of using the price mechanism to let the market decide where the effort should lie, it is infinitely more straightforward to add up targets at the sectoral and regional levels, and provide a consistent reduction plan to ensure that the overall goal will be achieved in time.

Morgan Stanley's Ruchir Sharma, writing on this question in the *Financial Times*, raises a point which indirectly makes the case for ecological planning. He notes that the investment push necessary to transition beyond carbon presents us with a trivially material problem: on the one hand, dirty activities – particularly in the sectors of mining or metal production – are rendered unprofitable due to increased regulation or higher carbon prices; on the other hand, investment for the greening of the infrastructure requires such resources to expand capacities. Decreasing supply plus rising demand is therefore a recipe for what he calls 'greenflation'. Sharma therefore argues that 'blocking new mines and oil rigs will not always be the environmentally and socially responsible move'.[14]

As the spokesperson of an institution with a vested interest in polluting commodities, Sharma is hardly a neutral commentator. But the problem he articulates – how to supply enough dirty material to build a clean-energy economy – is a real one, and relates to another

---

13   Chalmers Johnson, *MITI and the Japanese Miracle: The Growth of Industrial Policy, 1925–1975*, Stanford, 1982.

14   Ruchir Sharma, ' "Greenflation" Threatens to Derail Climate Change Action', *Financial Times*, 2 August 2021.

issue with the putative market-driven transition: carbon pricing does not allow society to discriminate between spurious uses of carbon – such as sending billionaires into space – and vital uses such as building the infrastructure for a non-carbon economy. In a successful transition, the first would be made impossible, the second as cheap as possible. As such, a unique carbon price becomes a pathway to failure.

This brings us back to an old but still decisive argument: rebuilding an economy – in this case one which phases out fossil fuels – requires restructuring the chain of relations between its diverse segments, which suggests that the fate of the economy as a whole depends on its point of least resistance. As Alexander Bogdanov noted in the context of building the young Soviet state, 'Because of these interdependent relationships, the process of enlargement of the economy is subject in its entirety to the law of the weakest point.'[15] This line of thought was later developed by Wassily Leontief in his contributions to input–output analysis. It holds that market adjustments are simply not up to structural transformation. In such situations, what's required is a careful and adaptive planning mechanism able to identify and deal with a moving landscape of bottlenecks.

When one considers the economic challenges of restructuring economies to keep carbon emissions in line with the stabilization of the climate, the discussion acquires a new framing. Effectiveness must take precedence over efficiency in reducing emissions. That means abandoning the fetish of the price mechanism in order to plan how the remaining dirty resources will be used in the service of clean infrastructure. Such planning must have international reach, since the greatest opportunities for energy-supply decarbonization are located in the Global South.[16] Moreover, as transformation on the supply side will not be enough, demand-side transformations will also be essential to stay within planetary boundaries. Energy requirements for providing decent living standards to the global population can be drastically reduced, but in addition to the use of the most efficient technologies, this implies a radical transformation of consumption patterns, including political procedures to adjudicate between competing consumption claims.[17]

15 'Organizational Science and Economic Planning', *Proceedings of the First All-Russian Conference for the Scientific Organization of Labour*, Moscow, 20–27 January 1921, no. 1, pp. 8–12 [in Russian].

16 G. Semieniuk, L. Taylor, A. Rezai and D. Foley, 'Plausible Energy Demand Patterns in a Growing Global Economy with Climate Policy', *Nature Climate Change*, vol. 11, April 2021.

17 J. Millward-Hopkins et al., 'Providing Decent Living with Minimum Energy: A Global Scenario', *Global Environmental Change*, vol. 65, November 2020.

A smooth transition beyond carbon is no longer an option. There is no Pareto-efficient way of eradicating fossil-fuel use in a timeframe compatible with the prevention of climate disorders. A zero-sum or even negative-sum game is in play, which means that some parts of the population will bear the cost of the adjustment more than others.

This looming distributive conflict puts drastic constraints on class compromises. At this stage, I do not see what should prevent a large progressive front from rallying in favour of restrictions on the avoidable emissions related to the consumption patterns of the ultra-rich. A class-based punitive ecology could become an effective means to stop ecologically perverse expenditure from rebounding onto the poorest. It could also be a stepping stone to broader social mobilizations. Crucially, the primary implication of the crisis tendency is not the inability of humanity to handle the challenges of the energy transition, but the additional barriers to collective agency erected by the imperative of capital valorization. Subordinating profit-making to rapid decarbonization is, in my view, a price worth paying for the cause of climate justice.

With its longstanding concern for planning and socialized consumption, international socialism is an obvious candidate to take on such a historic task. Though the poor state of socialist politics doesn't conjure much optimism, the catastrophic conjuncture we are entering – along with price volatility and the ongoing spasms of capitalist crises – could increase the fluidity of the situation. In such circumstances, the left must be flexible enough to seize any political opportunity that will advance the cause of a democratic ecological transition.

13

Picking Winners

ALYSSA BATTISTONI

2021

The annual UNFCCC Conference of the Parties, which convenes the 197 states and territories which have signed on to the UN Framework Convention on Climate Change, is one of the anchoring events of climate politics discourse, alongside the release of IPCC reports and increasingly regular occurrence of climate-fuelled natural disasters. Since the first was held in Berlin in 1995, when atmospheric carbon levels were around 358 parts per million (today they hover around 414), a steady procession of COPs has produced a great deal of geo-political drama, but has not yet managed to reduce carbon emissions.

In 1997 there was the fight over the Kyoto Protocol, widely criti-cized for concessions to the US insistence on market mechanisms; followed in 2001 by George W. Bush's announcement that he would not implement it anyway. In 2009, many expected that Barack Obama's election would clear the way for a legally binding agreement at COP15 in Copenhagen – officially branded 'Hopenhagen' by the UN. Instead, negotiations nearly collapsed over bitter disagreement between developed and developing countries, and eventually culmi-nated in a weak deal brokered behind closed doors by Obama and Wen Jiabao. Six years later, the Paris agreement was hailed as a world-historic triumph, even though the voluntary commitments made by individual member states failed to add up to the agreement's stated goals. As climate activists pointed out, and even the text of the agreement acknowledged, although the accords set a goal of limiting global warming to 'well below 2°C', the aggregated commitments would result in an estimated 3°C of warming. Nor were the Paris accords complete: they dictated that signatories update their pledges five years later. This was the key task set for COP26 in Glasgow.

Although more people are paying attention to the COP process than ever before, there has also been a striking decline in public con-fidence. The years since 2015 have seen serious challenges to international action of many kinds. Trump's withdrawal from the Paris agreement prompted subsequent acts of defiance from the likes of Bolsonaro, Modi and Putin, while the *gilets jaunes* protests against Emmanuel Macron's fuel tax prompted new anxieties about the backlash to climate policy. At the same time, rising tensions between the US and China have contributed to pessimism about the prospects for global agreement. The 'Climate Behemoth' – a reactionary alliance between right-wing populism and national fossil capital, schematized by Geoff Mann and Joel Wainwright – has gained momentum, countering the bid for planetary sovereignty Mann and Wainwright see represented in the COP process.[1] Pledges aside, carbon emissions continue more or less unabated.

In many ways the circumstances of Glasgow recall those of the disastrous proceedings in Copenhagen: taking place in the aftermath of a world-shaking economic crisis, marked by protest and dissatisfaction, undercut by the failure of a US president to secure domestic climate policy. Even Greta Thunberg's memorable description of COP26 as a place of talk and no action – 'blah, blah, blah' – was less novel than it initially appeared: 'Blah, Blah, Blah, Act Now!' had already adorned signs at the Copenhagen protests in 2009. On the uselessness of the talks, Thunberg and the world leaders she indicts likely agree: Xi and Putin did not even bother to attend.

By the conclusion of the conference, a few new agreements had materialized, although most came with caveats. Twenty nations agreed to stop financing global oil and gas projects abroad, although most continue to subsidize oil projects at home – echoing the G20's commitment to stop financing coal plants internationally, even as member countries continue to use coal domestically. A hundred countries, led by the US and EU – but excluding China, India and Russia – pledged a 30 per cent methane reduction by 2030. A hundred and forty-one countries agreed to stop and reverse deforestation by 2030 – although Indonesia, where primary forest has decreased by approximately 50 per cent since the 1960s, immediately backtracked, calling the terms 'inappropriate and unfair'. The US, France, Germany, EU and UK struck an $8.5 billion agreement to help South Africa transition away from coal use – important in its own right, but perhaps even more so as a potential demonstration of the feasibility of a 'just transition'. Most incredibly, the text for the first time in the history of the COPs includes the words 'fossil fuels'.

---

1 Geoff Mann and Joel Wainwright, *Climate Leviathan: A Political Theory of our Planetary Future*, London, 2018.

But even most boosters have been forced to admit that Glasgow was a disappointment. By now the problems with the COP process are well-canvassed, ranging from the features of its institutional design to the nature of national sovereignty. The consensus model tends to result in a lowest common denominator approach to agreement. Countries set their own decarbonization goals, but also report their own progress towards them; unsurprisingly, a *Washington Post* report recently found that progress towards decarbonization is seriously overstated.[2] Absent a global sovereign, there is no way to compel action, even when agreements are reached.

So be it, many would say: too much time has been wasted on global diplomacy when real progress is being made elsewhere. The conventional wisdom on climate politics is shifting away from the need for grand global agreements focused on climate specifically, and instead emphasizing the potential for addressing climate change with economic mechanisms: industrial policy, trade agreements, global finance. This is, in many respects, long overdue. In spite of the massive fossil-fuel delegation and distasteful corporate pavilions, COP26 is not really where important investment decisions are made. The UN's array of environmental agencies has always been a shadow to the fora where global capital makes its rules.

Advocates of green industrial policy in particular challenge the 'collective action' framework, suggesting that climate action is no longer a cost to be shouldered, and that free-riding is no longer the central problem to be solved. Rather, the 'energy transition' offers benefits in the form of industrial renewal and jobs: instead of shirking their commitments to decarbonize, states will compete for green market share.

The promise that a brighter green future is just around the corner is another familiar refrain of climate politics: back in 2011, for example, Obama promised to 'win the future' with investments in 'innovation'. But what is genuinely different about this COP is that the private sector is lurching into gear. The recent rash of corporate net-zero pledges and surge of ESG ('Environmental, Social, Governance') funds should not be taken at face value, of course. But Chinese state investment in low-carbon technologies, and solar panels in particular, has catalysed the renewable-energy industry and set a challenge to Western governments.

---

2   Chris Mooney, Juliet Eilperin, Desmond Butler, John Muyskens, Anu Narayanswamy and Naema Ahmed, 'Countries' Climate Pledges Built on Flawed Data, *Post* Investigation Finds', *Washington Post*, 7 November 2021.

The hope of industrial policy advocates is that the US, EU, and China will compete for the green tech market – at least, the sectors which China does not already dominate – setting off a virtuous circle of competition among green capitalists. Politically, state support for fledgling green tech industries is expected to generate constituencies for decarbonization which can serve as a counterweight to the entrenched power of fossil capital. Green industrial policy advocates tend to flatten the differences between labour and capital, suggesting that the central axis of conflict is between carbon-intensive and decarbonizing coalitions, even as clean-energy darlings like Tesla union bust. It is a view which puts most stock in the power of one fraction of capital to counter another; popular mobilization and labour strife feature primarily as threats to stability to be warded off. Joe Biden's pair of infrastructure bills, for example, takes cues not from the public investment-driven Green New Deal proposed by Robert Pollin and popularized in 2019 by Alexandria Ocasio-Cortez and Ed Markey, but from the innovation-oriented Green New Deal of the late 2000s, as outlined by Thomas Friedman and Edward Barbier. The model, which targets subsidies at strategic sectors like clean hydrogen production and carbon capture and storage, is more Silicon Valley than the Tennessee Valley Authority.

Focused on production in one country, industrial policy frequently relies on a methodological nationalism which neglects the global interdependence of contemporary production, while often threatening to tip into a more overtly political nationalism where convenient: this is a vision of climate policy that can coexist with, and perhaps even benefit from, increasing antagonism between the US and China. The key elements of its international policy are not grand global agreements but trade deals like the recent US–EU agreement to reduce steel tariffs and incentivize the production of 'green steel'.

Industrial policy oriented towards boosting 'green tech', however, has limits as climate policy. It does little to directly reduce fossil-fuel use, prevent the construction of new fossil-fuel infrastructure, or even directly reduce carbon emissions. It also faces political obstacles of its own. The tariffs and subsidies necessary to nurture emergent domestic industries are likely to garner objections from the WTO. A state which takes a more active role in 'picking winners' will face familiar challenges of domestic distributive politics. At the same time, as Cédric Durand has argued, by failing to undertake more substantial planning, states risk a slower and more disruptive transition away from fossil fuels. Meanwhile the still-powerful fossil-fuel industry will seek to turn any stumbles to its advantage, as Adam Tooze has warned.

From the perspective of many of those gathered at COP26, however, what is perhaps most concerning about the shift to green industrial policy is that it bypasses the many parts of the world which have little hope of competing with the big industrial powers on green tech. There will be ripple effects down the supply chain, of course. Some countries will garner new interest in minerals like lithium and cobalt. Those with relatively intact forests may be able to sell carbon offsets to help multinationals meet their net-zero promises – nearly all of which are currently premised on carbon removal in some form. But many other parts of the world will be surplus to the 'green economy', except as consumers of the products it generates. It has long been hoped that developing countries would be able to 'leapfrog' fossil fuels altogether and move straight to renewable-powered electricity. The countries most in need of electrification, however, typically face high borrowing costs – a problem which bears directly on the energy transition, since renewable-energy infrastructure is often more capital-intensive than coal-fired power plants. The problem of access to finance is made still worse by the fact that, as Kate Mackenzie observes, countries deemed to have a high 'climate risk' must pay more to borrow.[3]

There was much talk about climate finance at COP26. But for economist Daniela Gabor, what it revealed was simply 'status-quo financial capitalism entering its green age' rather than any more transformative project.[4] The response to Covid-19 spurred talk of the 'end of neoliberalism' and the return of the interventionist state. But the response to climate change thus far suggests a less dramatic reorientation: as Gabor observes, the role marked out for the state in climate finance is not to undertake public investment but to 'derisk' private investments in green sectors.

A different response to the dead end of the COP process, then, would be to make a lateral move, taking climate justice to the global financial institutions. The political scientist Jessica Green argues that international trade and finance ought to replace the UN framework as the 'locus of climate policy', while also calling for major reform to global financial institutions.[5] The problem is figuring out how such long-sought reforms might come about. Labour and environmental

---

3   Kate Mackenzie, 'Uneven Channels', *Phenomenal World*, 30 October 2021.

4   Daniela Gabor, 'The Wall Street Consensus at COP26', *Phenomenal World*, 18 November 2021.

5   Jessica Green, 'Follow the Money: How Reforming Tax and Trade Rules Can Fight Climate Change', *Foreign Affairs*, 12 November 2021.

movements in countries with valuable minerals or powerful industrial sectors may be able to exert some influence over trade deals, as United Steelworkers did in the US–EU steel agreement. The global reach of green supply chains offers the possibility for more internationalist organizing, as Thea Riofrancos has argued.[6] But the prospects for reform of global trade and financial institutions are hazier.

The global climate justice movement has undoubtedly spurred a change in the conversation. But at present, it simply does not have the power to realize its goals. At COP26, climate justice activists criticized the failure of developed nations to make good on their commitment to spend $100 billion annually on climate finance – a sum agreed on in 2009 in an attempt to salvage the Copenhagen talks. Yet the more ambitious demand, both then and now, is for a framework for loss and damage, which would require open-ended funding for harms incurred as a result of climate change – something which might come close to climate reparations. The argument in favour of it is morally unimpeachable. But it is hard to see what could force the US or EU to agree to a programme that would expose them to liability claims long into the future.

Lacking leverage, the movement has resorted to the tools it has available: spectacle, and, most notably, shame. This year, the foreign minister of Tuvalu, Simon Kofe, gave his COP26 speech knee-deep in ocean waves to symbolize the threat that rising seas pose to his island nation's existence. This, too, recalled a previous moment of COP politics, in 2009, when President Mohamed Nasheed of the Maldives held an underwater cabinet meeting prior to the ill-fated meeting in Copenhagen. But if the power players at COP26 have learned to speak the language of climate justice, they have so far remained shameless. Andreas Malm has called for a reevaluation of tactics, arguing that the climate movement must become more combative. Different tactics may help disrupt business as usual – but they are unlikely to solve the fundamental problem of power.

As climate policy is finally incorporated into economic policy, whither the COP process? The COP cycle will continue. But it seems increasingly likely to be an afterthought: a forum where countries with no chance of competing on green tech or being invited to G20-like summits do what they can – which is to say, not very much – to extract concessions from the rich and powerful countries which have built their wealth on ecological destruction, and which are now using that wealth to escape its consequences. In other words, not so much an emergent global sovereign as a charity fundraiser.

---

6   Thea Riofrancos, 'Seize and Resist', *The Baffler*, no. 54, November 2020.

14

Fortunes of the Green New Deal

THOMAS MEANEY

2022

Considered as a piece of rhetoric, the demand for a 'Green New Deal' has been an unalloyed success, embraced across the left side of public opinion. Broadly understood as fiscal stimulus designed to accelerate the transition to a renewable economy with a social-egalitarian component, the Green New Deal has gained its remarkably wide currency over the past decade and a half by promising to dispel the perceived contradiction between economic and environmental priorities that had bedevilled leftward forces during the 1990s and into the new millennium. Unlike degrowth, with which the Green New Deal is frequently contrasted, and which proposes curtailing economic activity and material throughput to ease pressure on the ecosphere, the GND promises a win–win dynamic: far from entailing trade-offs or sacrifice, the effort to stabilize the climate can ignite a manufacturing boom in clean energy, overhauling infrastructure, creating jobs, spurring innovation in green technologies and bolstering 'energy security'.

With the passage of the Inflation Reduction Act in August in the United States – default national context for much GND discussion in the Anglosphere, homeland of the original New Deal and source of by far the highest carbon emissions per capita of any large-population country – inspiring rhetoric for the first time became ambivalent reality. Although a far cry from the $16.3 trillion Green New Deal proposed by would-be presidential candidate Bernie Sanders in 2019, the original Build Back Better legislation devised by the Biden Administration in 2021 nevertheless envisioned spending $3.5 trillion over ten years on an array of social programmes, including tax credits and grants for municipalities and corporations switching to renewable energy, and entailed a gradual phasing-out of fossil fuels in electricity generation. What remained of this bill by the summer of 2022, when it acquired the wishful name of the Inflation Reduction Act (IRA) after last-ditch negotiations between Senate Majority leader Chuck Schumer and recalcitrant West Virginia Democrat Joe Manchin – and reportedly an eleventh-hour phone call from Obama's former Treasury Secretary Lawrence Summers – was less than one seventh as much authorized spending (around $490 billion), with the money earmarked for climate-change mitigation (roughly $390 billion) mostly in the form of tax credits, with the rest using federal subsidies to reduce the cost of healthcare insurance and prescription drugs.[1] Projected to cut US greenhouse gas emissions to 40 per cent below 2005 levels by 2030 – a 10 per cent improvement on the US's pre-IRA trajectory (about 30 per cent below 2005 by 2030) – this was hardly the 50 per cent target the US committed to in the Paris climate accords, let alone the 70 per cent reduction by 2030 proposed by Sanders, to have been achieved through completely decarbonizing the transport and electricity sectors (the two largest contributors to emissions in the US).[2] Indeed, given the IRA's much-diminished scale and the near-total exfoliation of any social-egalitarian component in the legislative wrangling, it is an open question whether the IRA qualifies as a Green New Deal at all, even if the bill is clearly the legislative descendant of Sanders's climate platform.

All the same, though Biden's IRA represents only a modest down payment towards the purchase of a habitable and prospering planet, it amounts, as widely noted, to the most significant climate-change legislation yet undertaken by the US. The current conjuncture – in which the rhetorical dominance of the GND has eventuated, for now, in the pinched reality of the IRA – therefore invites a reconsideration, first, of the Green New Deal as an amorphous body of thought and discursive crusade – the origins and evolution of the idea, its rise as a rhetorical phenomenon and popular slogan; second, a comparative appraisal of the assorted GND-affiliated policy proposals and works of political strategy that have emerged from the English-speaking left over the past few years; third, some reflection on the substance and political import of the dwarf GND that is the IRA, as well as on the contextual factors paving the way to its passage; and lastly, and most

---

1 The Inflation Reduction Act is seemingly a deliberate misnomer: the Congressional Budget Office concluded that the measures would have a 'negligible' effect on inflation. Its advocates claim the bill will curb inflation by reducing the deficit, mostly by closing tax loopholes, and by lowering the price of energy (as well as prescription drugs) and strengthening energy 'resilience' – helping to protect US households against oil price spikes in future.

2 Umair Irfan and Tara Golshan, 'Bernie Sanders's Green New Deal, Explained', *Vox*, 22 August 2019.

pressing, some reflection on how Green New Deal–oriented eco-political strategy might need to reconfigure itself in light of the IRA, and the changed political-economic landscape it portends. Will the Act extinguish the GND momentum, or renew it?

Genealogy of the Green New Deal

Although there were earlier iterations in Germany (see the afterword, on p. 246), the Green New Deal surfaced in the Anglo-American liberal thought-world of the late Blair–Bush years, when its spokesmen viewed the reports from the Intergovernmental Panel on Climate Change as an incentive for American industry and the environmental movement to create a new engine of growth that would correct some of the deindustrializing excesses of the 1990s. The term 'Green New Deal' was widely popularized in early 2007 when it appeared in a *New York Times* column by Thomas Friedman, though it was touted earlier in a discussion between Larry Elliot, the *Guardian* economics editor, and Colin Hines, the former head of Greenpeace's International Economics unit.[3] Explicit in early visions of the GND was the notion – still strongly present in Biden's IRA – that it would 'renew America' and 'get our groove back with the world' in the face of a rising China.[4]

A few years later, the Green New Deal was recognized as a potential 'wedge' issue or 'terrain of struggle' by eco-socialist writers who hoped that a broadly supported reformist legislative agenda might prepare the ground – or at least buy time – for a much more

---

3   Thomas Friedman, 'A Warning from the Garden', *New York Times*, 19 January 2007. The following year the Obama-era impresario and long-time environmental advocate Van Jones published *The Green-Collar Economy*, a deftly marketed epitaph for the period when the cap-and-trade Waxman–Markey Bill (the American Clean Energy and Security Act of 2009) was the preferred Democratic climate fix. In 2009, with little connection to Anglo developments, the first GND book appeared in Germany, authored by the SPD politician Michael Müller and academic Kai Niebert. The term 'Green New Deal' originated in their discussions with the German Green capital guru and former CDU minister Klaus Töpfer.

4   Thomas Friedman, interview with Earthjustice President Trip Van Noppen, 2 July 2012. For enhancing US hegemony as a declared goal of the GND, compare Thomas Friedman's *Hot, Flat, Crowded* (2008) – a book refreshingly honest about great-power competition and forthright in its advocacy for the greening of the US military – to the unremitting wonkery of Bill Gates's *How to Avoid a Climate Disaster* (2021), with its much softer domestic focus, taking inspiration, for instance, from Nixon's founding of the EPA, the later Montreal Protocol, etc.

far-reaching process of decarbonization and public provision.[5] By the later 2010s, American democratic-socialist agendas included the GND in part of a wider left embrace of electoral politics when the prospect of a Sanders candidacy, and a modicum of left representation in the US Congress, suggested that significant green policies might before long be implemented. In 2017, the youth activist group the Sunrise Movement was launched, and the next year – when a landmark report issued by the IPCC suggested that climate change necessitated transforming the global economy at a speed and scale with 'no documented historical precedent' – Sunrise activists rallied behind midterms candidates who supported renewable energy and worked to oust those who did not.[6]

The youth group then embraced the Green New Deal, staging a sit-in outside Nancy Pelosi's office to demand climate action. Recently elected Representative Alexandria Ocasio-Cortez joined the Sunrise protesters, and in February 2019 introduced a non-binding congressional resolution with Senator Ed Markey, asserting that 'it is the duty of the Federal Government to create a Green New Deal', in order to achieve net-zero global emissions by 2050 through 'a fair and just transition for all communities and workers'. Later that year, Bernie Sanders unveiled his $16.3 trillion climate proposal, and ahead of the 2020 election, the Green New Deal was embraced by most Democratic presidential hopefuls, one of whom – Washington's governor Jay Inslee – made the ecological crisis his signature campaign issue.[7]

Meanwhile, in the UK, the Labour Party under Corbyn – couching its programme in a different national idiom of past social transformation – had proposed its own ambitious 'Green Industrial Revolution', which would fund a rapid green transition through direct taxes on capital.[8] By 2020, Green New Deals of one sort or another had proliferated across the world. The European Union announced a 'European Green Deal' (the absence of the modifier 'New' appearing to signify a technocratic project with no particular need to rally the

---

5   For early identification of the GND as a 'wedge' issue, see David Schwartzman, 'Green New Deal: An Ecosocialist Perspective', *Capitalism Nature Socialism*, vol. 22, no. 3, 2011. For 'terrain of struggle', see Thea Riofrancos, 'Plan, Mood, Battlefield: Reflections on the Green New Deal', *Viewpoint*, 16 May 2019.

6   'Summary for Policymakers', IPCC report, *Global Warming of 1.5°C*, 2018.

7   Before it was part of the Sanders platform the Green New Deal had featured in the platform of the US Green Party.

8   The Green New Deal was embraced by left-wing politicians elsewhere in Europe too. In France, for example, Jean-Luc Mélenchon's La France Insoumise included a GND-style ecological transition in its 2017 manifesto, *L'avenir en commun*.

public), defined by the goal of neutral emissions in the bloc by 2050. Seoul promised a 'Korean New Deal', including an allocation of $62 billion to create 659,000 green jobs by 2025, and transform South Korea into a clean-hydrogen-based, green-infrastructure-exporting economy by 2050. Tiny Bhutan, publicizing itself as the world's 'first carbon-negative country' thanks to its thickly forested terrain, pledged its adherence to a green deal for lower-income countries. At the COP26 climate summit in November 2021, Modi unveiled his 'pan-chamrit' – five 'nectars' or climate commitments – which aimed to reduce Indian emissions to net zero by 2070. In the Anglosphere, the sudden rhetorical falling into line by world governments was typically explained as a response to the new tone in Washington. The more decisive factor was likely Xi's declaration in September 2020 that China would be carbon neutral by 2060. However unintentionally, the Chinese bellwether rebuked the focus on the US always latent in talk of a GND – a reminder that a new deal in one country is little better than no deal without a changed international scene.

The rise of Green New Deal-ology

The explosion of GND discourse has been equally global, but in the Anglosphere, the first wave of visions that appeared under the GND rubric formed part of the surge of enthusiasm around the prospect of social-democratic candidates coming to power in the US and in Britain, when left eco-theorists were thrust into the unusual position of crafting maximalist climate plans with which to engage established policymakers. These proposals were distinguished by being explicit policy interventions. Variations included Robert Pollin and Noam Chomsky's *Climate Crisis and the Global Green New Deal* (2020); Naomi Klein's *On Fire: The Burning Case for the Green New Deal* (2019); Kate Aronoff, Alyssa Battistoni, Daniel Aldana Cohen and Thea Riofrancos's *A Planet to Win* (2019); and Ann Pettifor's *The Case for the Green New Deal* (2019). The Green New Deal canon continued to expand in the aftermath of the closure of this electoral window for the left, with the appearance of books like Matthew Huber's *Climate Change as Class War* (2022), as well as lamentations about how GND talk had displaced earlier, more indigenous-centred eco-radicalism, such as Max Ajl's *A People's Green New Deal* (2021) and the indigenous authorial collective Red Nation's *Red Deal* (2021).

The veteran socialist economist Robert Pollin's intervention was a call for governments around the world – led by the US – to conduct massive stimuluses for a transition to decarbonized energy and technology that would conjointly create the conditions for full employment and rising living standards. Since co-founding the Political Economy Research Institute in 1996 at the University of Massachusetts, Amherst, Pollin has made it into one of the leading policy think tanks for 'egalitarian green growth' programmes around the globe, also producing several detailed state-level plans within the US.[9] As Pollin explained in these pages in 2018, cutting fossil-fuel consumption (responsible, he noted, for about 70 per cent of greenhouse gas emissions) 'dramatically and without delay' is 'the single most critical project' in addressing the climate crisis. He proposed dedicating 1.5 to 2 per cent of global GDP per year to building the infrastructure for a green economy.[10]

Although the cost of renewables has plummeted, the private sector has so far failed to scale up clean energy supply rapidly enough.[11] Only a Keynesian model of government spending, Pollin suggests, can accelerate the transition to renewables at an acceptable pace. The point for Pollin is to make this transition as rapidly as possible. In the US, where nearly 90 per cent of all road miles are travelled in private vehicles, this means subsidizing electric vehicles at roughly the same rate as mass transit, the expansion of which involves time-consuming political work. As for the rest of the world? Pollin envisions green financing – in the form of green bonds floated by central banks, transfers away from military spending, and subsidy restructuring – for developing countries to build their own infrastructure. The linchpin of Pollin's vision is the rise of a powerful enough bloc of green-Keynesian politicians in the capitalist core to enact it. In his ideal scenario, the US state would simply buy a controlling interest in Exxon, Conoco, and other oil majors, and phase out fossil production entirely, with income support and retraining provided to workers and communities dependent on defunct industries. Pollin's vision is admirably global in reach: he and his fellow researchers at PERI have produced myriad plans for how to integrate vast swaths of the globe into a US-led climate transition, fulfilling commissions from Korean Greenpeace to the AFL-CIO leadership in various US states. But, whether out of sheer modesty or an overestimation of the efficacy of data-driven road maps, Pollin skirts

---

9 PERI researchers have published Green New Deal blueprints for California, West Virginia, Pennsylvania, Ohio, Maine, Colorado, Washington and New York.

10 See pp. 69–70 in this collection.

11 In the electricity sector, for example – the cornerstone of a low-carbon energy system – roughly half of last year's 5 per cent increase in global demand (the largest year-on-year increase ever) was met by coal, which still accounts for around 36 per cent of total electricity generation (renewables make up roughly 39 per cent): International Energy Agency, *Electricity Sector*, September 2022.

a critical question: how to accumulate the necessary political power to achieve them?

The other early planning for a GND took place across the Atlantic, in a working group called the Green New Deal group founded in 2007 by British economists Larry Elliot, Colin Hines and Ann Pettifor, among other environmental thinkers and activists, whose first report, 'A Green New Deal', published by the New Economics Foundation in 2008, outlined policies to address the 'triple crunch' of 'the credit crisis, climate change and high oil prices'.[12] Pettifor's *The Case for The Green New Deal* appeared a decade later at the height of left-liberal enthusiasm for the AOC–Markey plan back in Washington and the short-lived Labour Party interest in such planning, which peaked in the 2019 manifesto calling for a 'Green Industrial Revolution'. Pettifor, an economist best known for her work on international debt systems, was a leading advocate of the Jubilee 2000 campaign, which called for the abolition of Third World debt ($90 billion) at the end of the millennium, in a movement inspired by the Book of Leviticus. What sets Pettifor's approach apart from the GND programme proposed by Pollin is its stress on the need for international banking reform and a transformation of the financial system to allow nations greater autonomy over monetary and fiscal policy, as a precondition for a green makeover of the economy through climate stimuluses and industrial policy: 'The UK GND makes clear that one of the first tasks will be for society to regain *public authority* over the national and international monetary system.'[13] For all its financial intelligence, Pettifor's plan, like Pollin's, lacked a strategy for mustering the political clout to actualize it.

The leading mainstreamer of the GND in popular discourse across the West is, by some distance, Naomi Klein, whose *On Fire* thoroughly appropriated the liberal slogan of the GND for the socialist left. Her 2014 book *This Changes Everything* became a focal text for the new green left, managing to capture the imagination of both centrist bureaucrats and activists blocking pipelines. Unlike Pollin and Pettifor – whose policy proposals implicitly hinge on galvanizing government officials and enlightened technocrats – Klein has long been preoccupied with popular political mobilizations, and argued that the precondition for the GND's realization would be a diverse and well-coordinated mass movement. 'The single largest determining factor in whether a Green New Deal mobilization pulls us back from

---

12   The Green New Deal Group, 'A Green New Deal', New Economics Foundation, 2008.

13   Ann Pettifor, *The Case for a Green New Deal*, p. 15.

the climate cliff', she wrote in 2019, 'will be the actions taken by social movements in the coming year.'[14]

A striking recapitulation – and elaboration – of the Kleinian line appeared on the cusp of Sander's electoral surge, in the form of the book *A Planet to Win: Why We Need a Green New Deal*, authored by Kate Aronoff, Alyssa Battistoni, Daniel Aldana Cohen and Thea Riofrancos, with a preface by Klein and brandished by AOC in her campaign for the GND.[15] Each author brought their own expertise to bear: Aronoff on green jobs; Battistoni on the politics of care; Cohen on green housing and the idea of a 'last stimulus' to deliver the global economy into a sustainable orbit; and Riofrancos on the delicate questions of resource extraction and 'green-resource colonialism'. The book was of its moment in its effort not to alienate a broader coalition with a laundry list of left demands, notably for climate reparations. As Pollin did, *A Planet to Win* concentrates on the North Atlantic, and envisions a full-employment green economy in the US along Keynesian lines. The authors stress that the climate left must target select sectors of the economy, including housing as well as energy and transportation. And although they are in agreement with degrowth thinkers in stressing the ecological limits ultimately governing the planet, their method of reaching sustainability would be to grow in order to not grow anymore. Far from prescribing anything that could be described as 'eco-austerity', they offer a positive, popular vision of the material gains to come from a green transition, rather than a litany of coming deprivations (as some degrowthers have been accused of furnishing). The overarching argument of *A Planet to Win* is that the oft-invoked mismatch between creaking democratic procedures and the urgency of the climate transition is a false one: only democratic mobilization and legitimation can accelerate the popular acceptance of the transition at the speed required.

Questions of agency

A second batch of GND books appeared after the electoral hopes of the Anglophone left had waned in late 2019–early 2020. These titles had the advantage of being able to speak with more candour than their predecessors about the prospects of a radical climate agenda that seemed

---

14   Naomi Klein, *On Fire: The Burning Case for A Green New Deal*, London, 2019, p. 261.

15   Kate Aronoff, Alyssa Battistoni, Daniel Aldana Cohen and Thea Riofrancos, *A Planet to Win: Why We Need a Green New Deal*, London, 2019.

bereft of mass-movement support and as far as ever from the levers of
state power, and yet still animated by the example of increased state
intervention in response to the Covid-19 pandemic. The most original
solution to the resulting dilemma came from the left geographer
Matthew Huber, whose refreshingly blunt *Climate Change as Class
War* eschewed both electoral illusions and *deus ex machina* popular
mobilizations. Instead, Huber took a sectoral approach to the economy,
concentrating on the possible threat to US capital posed by energy
unions. The book's main intervention was to focus on production –
specifically what Marx called Department 1, 'the production of the
means of production' – rather than consumption. Written against
climate politics based around voluntarism, moralism, local movements,
and anything that smacks of austerity, Narodnism, or neo-Malthusianism, *Climate Change as Class War* is a product of frustration with the
deluge of 'smart policy' proposals for 'fixing' the climate.

In Huber's account, the main culprit in the climate crisis is the
northern ruling class and their fossil capital, but not far behind are
three deluded segments of the liberal professional class. The first
are the 'science communicators', who, for a generation, have treated
the climate crisis as an epistemological conundrum rather than a
problem of power. 'These types of people believe', Huber writes, 'that
the primary problem in environmental politics is a lack of awareness
or an outright denials of scientific knowledge . . . That if the masses
truly *understood* the science, action would follow.' The second type
are 'policy technocrats' who believe the climate crisis can be solved
through 'logic and rational policy design to sway politicians and the
public toward these policies'.[16] Last, Huber identifies 'anti-system

---

16 Matthew Huber, *Climate Change as Class War: Building Socialism on a
Warming Planet*, London, 2022. In fact, environmentalist policy advocates have
mounted a serious intellectual campaign for green reforms, armed with their own
quiver of historical analogies. For Charles Sabel and David Victor, two leading proponents of 'smart governance', clues can be found in the Montreal Protocol of 1987
which set conditions for business-government brokered industry standards to phase
out pollutants to the Ozone layer. This analogy with the challenge of fossil fuel was
ably swatted back by Alyssa Battistoni, who noted that CFCs were a replaceable input
in a niche industry rather than, as with greenhouse gas emissions, the product of the
global economy writ large. More valuable in Sabel and Victor's account is how Beijing
became a party to these agreements, after extensive infighting between its environmental and economic ministries, because the PRC wanted to keep a hand in shaping
international regulations and trade protocols that might bar them from markets. Sabel
and Victor think today's climate crisis can be solved through open-ended agreements
and committees in which states help firms jump from one material base to another
without losing profits: *Fixing the Climate: Strategies for an Uncertain World*, Oxford,

radicals'. With degrowthers in mind, he describes them as 'more likely to understand that the cause of environmental problems is systemically rooted in capitalism, but their political response is to look inwards through moralistic invocations to consume less, reject industrial society, and advocate micro-alternatives at the local scale'.

Huber's alternative is a sectoral campaign to rally a working-class coalition behind a Green New Deal programme of decarbonization and decommodification, anchored in one of the last well-organized bastions of the US working class: electricity unions. The electricity sector in the United States is dominated by investor-owned utilities, though in many states these are still subject to public oversight and price controls. Taking his inspiration from Tony Mazzocchi, the co-founder of the US Labor Party and a former vice president of the Oil, Chemical, and Atomic Workers International Union, Huber advocates a rank-and-file infiltration of energy unions to force energy companies to make a faster green transition. Rather than being motivated by abstract ecological concerns, Huber argues, union members can be mobilized by appeals to more immediate and traditional preoccupations in labour disputes, such as wages, worker safety and adequate staffing of the overly strained electrical grid. 'The working-class strategy would link direct material improvements in people's lives to climate action,' he writes. 'People would intuitively understand jobs, free electricity, or public housing as beneficial, but it would be up to political organizers to *name* those improvements as measures taken to address the climate crisis.' Like Mazzocchi, Huber is focused not on the consumption end of the climate crisis but on its source in industry – 'a small minority of capitalists who own and control the means of production *produce* climate change', in his memorable formulation – and he argues persuasively that no other sector of the US economy is responsible for more pollution and brown-energy usage than the electrical grids. Here he finds a unique chink in the armour of US fossil capital. Even if electricity unions are among those most aligned with business in the US, it is precisely this which makes them attractive sites for radicalization. 'Most climate politics bemoans the ways in which existing union leadership and power structures align against climate action,' Huber writes, 'but rarely raise the question of organizing unions from within to promote strategies that are both pro-worker and pro-climate.'[17]

2022. For the more specific plan, see Dani Rodrik and Charles Sabel, 'Building a Good Jobs Economy', in Danielle Allen, Yochai Benkler, Lelah Downey, Rebecca Henderson and Josh Simons, eds, *A Political Economy of Justice*, Chicago, 2022.

17   Huber, *Climate Change as Class War*, pp. 235, 198, 23, 237.

Unlike many other recent proposals put forward in the GND genre, Huber, like Pollin, is prepared to concede from the outset that the green transition may well begin *without* a mass labour movement. Huber maintains nevertheless that if such a transition is not to be injurious to working-class interests it will need at least one unionized sector to catalyse gains for workers across the economy. In Huber's ideal scenario, nurses, teachers and other workers would swell the movement of electricity-union employees, and begin to form a unified bloc demanding a simultaneously better and more sustainable way of life. Nor does Huber shy away from the problem of scale: 'Only publicly owned electricity can invest and plan with long-term infrastructure – and planetary – goals in mind.'[18] In terms of the global scene, Huber envisions green energy becoming cheap enough in the capitalist core that it becomes possible to supply the rest of the energy-deprived South with much-needed resources, somewhat, one assumes, on the model of the global spread of cellular technology. All the same, possibility is not likelihood, and Huber's vision of 'socialism on a warming planet' appears to leave geopolitical income stratification intact even as substantial decarbonization of the US economy is achieved and replicated elsewhere.

Compared to those of his degrowth critics, Huber's strategy aims to be more attuned to the actual balance of political forces in the US. Even so, at least three objections can be raised. The first relates to time. 'We have so little time to act on the climate crisis', Huber repeatedly stresses, but his scheme for the rank-and-file infiltration of American electricity unions portends a drawn-out process that would take years to show any political results. As he himself readily acknowledges, energy unions such as the International Brotherhood of Electrical Workers (IBEW) are among the most conservative in the US. In 2014, IBEW workers occupied a federal building in protest against Obama's Clean Power plan to decarbonize electrical plants, while union lawyers sued the Administration. It is difficult to envisage any near horizon for a strategy that hinges on a concentrated surge of presumably young well-educated socialist activists radicalizing middle-aged MAGA electricity workers. Second, Huber's spirited antagonism towards the so-called professional-managerial class (PMC) appears oddly out of focus. The portion of American professionals who fall into the categories of 'science-communicators', 'policy technocrats' and especially 'anti-system radicals' is vanishingly small and powerless compared to those who have been captured by the mantras

18   Huber, *Climate Change as Class War*, p. 231.

of green capital and a market-led transition, even if there is some overlap between these groups.

For Huber, any effective climate movement – whether liberal-bourgeois or radical-socialist – needs to make the case that a 'green' economy can provide cheaper energy and more abundant services to enlist working-class support. Like US historians who insist on interpreting the Civil War as a radical revolution, Huber is – quite understandably – not willing to countenance a green transition without a significant class rupture. But as was the case with the American passage out of slavery, the green transition may be achievable through a bourgeois revolution that merely consolidates the dominance of finance capital. This leads to a third objection to Huber's argument: that investor-owned utilities, which make up 72 per cent of the US industry, are already reverse marching towards renewable energy in order to gorge themselves on the unprecedented subsidy bonanza of the IRA – $220 billion in tax breaks, many of which their recipients are in the position to sell to the highest bidder, as well as an overhaul of the federal tax code. The IRA, passed after the publication of Huber's book, may have made union agency towards a green transition in the energy sector all but redundant.[19] In his guide to mobilizing against fossil capital, whose power he never underestimates, Huber barely articulates a mid-term strategy for how to handle the growing momentum of green capital, the full power of which he passes over. The green-friendly portions of Biden's IRA are a case in point: in its vision for a new workforce to build renewable architecture and transportation, the bill is as adamant about onshoring of industrial production as it is mum about whether such production be unionized.

Green colonialism

In passing, Huber envies the strength of French energy unions (and presumably admires the country's national consensus on nuclear power, a more cornerable sector for labour because of the high level of skill required); he acknowledges the weight of China in the climate fight; and he even idly wonders whether electrical-union ecologism

---

19   Eric Lipton, 'With Federal Aid on the Table, Utilities Shift to Embrace Climate Goals', *New York Times*, 29 November 2022. Union attempts to secure their own gains from the windfall of the subsidies is another story, but the question of the industry's turn to renewables does not seem to come into it.

could find traction in countries like Nigeria.[20] For the most part, however, the world beyond US borders is conspicuously absent from Huber's scheme. This is by no means the case for Max Ajl's *A People's Green New Deal*, which explicitly takes up a Global South perspective. The book represents a direct attack on the popularization of the Green New Deal among US democratic socialists, with Ajl claiming that nationalistic GND variants, explicitly aiming to revitalize domestic manufacturing, have displaced earlier, more radical and internationalist environmentalist movements. Lest one charge Ajl – who calls for the disbandment of the US military – with facile utopianism, he refuses, to his credit, to simply hand over the mantle of realism. 'What is "realistic" in a US/EU political context reflects the values of the evaluators more than any kind of objective assessment of what is reasonable', he writes. There are several facets to Ajl's brief against standard Green Dealism. The first is that the northern left has become far too addicted to electoralism, even after the defeats of Sanders and Corbyn. Ajl argues that the left should abandon the self-flattering illusion that it will have any meaningful influence over state power or policy creation in the North. He also flatly rejects the productivist proposals of Pollin, Chomsky and Huber in favour of what he calls 'a principled programme for worldwide energy democracy'.

Taking up the line of the People's Agreement of Cochabamba from 2010, Ajl's programme would entail not only a radical reduction of energy consumption in the North – a demand familiar from degrowth proposals – but also historically calculated climate debts to be paid to the peoples of the South by those of the North. Poorer nations will use these funds not for industrial development, but rather to escape the global commodity trade through the expansion of traditional farming techniques. Like Huber, Ajl emphasizes that in the North the strategic focus should be on the site of energy production, and on a transition from fossil fuels to renewables that can be accomplished through 'very high and rising redistributive carbon taxes, paid at the point of production.' He is concerned, however, that while a renewable make-over of the energy sector of the North might be good for northern workers, it would further immiserate expanses of the South, which would only see more of its natural resources extracted for the sake of electric vehicles and solar arrays. In nearly all the GND literature outside the Degrowth camp, Ajl therefore spies a 'dirty secret:

---

20   Assessing alternative energy sources not in terms of 'costs or its environmental safety' but according to which 'contain bases of *working-class power*', Huber writes: 'on this front, nuclear is clearly a winner': *Climate Change as Class War*, p. 251.

the claim that some nations deserve more energy than others'.[21] Ajl is acutely sensitive to the threat of extractivism, and argues that even a 'last stimulus' of the kind the authors of A Planet to Win call for would inevitably mean climate colonialism, as Northern states subject Southern ones to exploitation for lithium, copper, cobalt and other minerals critical for a renewable economy.

If Ajl's claim to political realism may be questioned – he too often confuses it with the value of 'reasonableness' – his dystopian picture of 'green colonialism' is less easy to dismiss.[22] As the Salvage Collective recently put it, colonialism has always been, in some sense, 'green': extracting resources for verdant northern regions, and leaving unwanted waste behind in the tropics.[23] Without a coordinated international effort to ensure fair labour practices and equal exchange in commodity deals, Global South states endowed with the mineral resources necessary for a green transition that is overwhelmingly concentrated in the Global North will be more vulnerable to despoliation than ever before. And yet Ajl shows little willingness to reckon with the actual balance of political power around the globe. He makes no suggestions for how states of the South could pool their resources in order to set the terms of trade for the transition. The thwarting of the 1970s New Economic International Order barely merits mention in his pages, nor do mooted schemes for resource cartelization, whether for nickel reserves, led by Indonesia; a 'Rainforest Opec' joining Congo, Indonesia and Brazil; or a lithium cartel made up of Chile, Bolivia and Argentina. Nor is there any geopolitical strategy for commodity-ransoming, or for how to counter the push of the US and China to onshore critical mineral mining.

The reason for this silence appears to be that even a successful bid by Southern states to bend the terms of the transition would not be

21   Max Ajl, A People's Green New Deal, London, 2021, pp. 73, 70.
22   Meat consumption is a point of contention in several GND accounts. In their new book Half-Earth Socialism, Troy Vettese and Drew Pendergrass argue for the benefits of global veganism, while Ajl, who reads this as yet another type of Western colonialism, points to the sustainability of indigenous meat consumption compared to factory farming, and the deceptively high carbon costs of producing synthetic meat. Huber, who scoffs at how mandatory veganism would go down with workers, in fact broadly adheres to a logic that could theoretically accommodate global veganism – i.e., if laboratory meat becomes cheap and sustainable and delicious enough, there would be little impediment beyond identitarian ones to a shift away from meat-eating: Half-Earth Socialism: A Plan to Save the Future from Extinction, Climate Change and Pandemics, London, 2022.
23   The Salvage Collective, The Tragedy of the Worker: Towards the Proletarocene, London, 2021, p. 57.

acceptable to Ajl. The primary way to mitigate the ecological crisis, he argues, is for the North to abandon the idea of decarbonizing its energy supply, and instead re-ruralize itself in a kind of self-administered Morgenthau Plan. It is not remotely clear, however, that a 'partial re-localization of agriculture and urban farming' could meet the needs of a planet of 8 billion, even as Ajl insists that a revolution in agriculture would 'sew metabolic rifts', while allowing extraction and supply chains to focus narrowly on digital equipment and medical supplies. If persuading North Americans to eat locusts for breakfast seems a less than palatable political platform, Ajl also ignores the elite political dynamics in actually existing regimes in the bulk of the South, which are no longer run by Jacobin-agronomists like Amílcar Cabral. India under Modi is positioning itself for its own bout of green colonialism as Tata gears up to be a leading solar and EV producer; Gabon is developing plans to monetize the conservation of its forests; Malaysia is laying waste to its flora to complete a palm oil monoculture; Ghana hosts a vast electronic trash economy where cows have learned to digest plastic. That this chain of developments originates in the Western capitalist core is beyond question; the point is that Ajl identifies no plausible counter-formation. He invokes the example of Evo Morales in Bolivia, but the rate of mining extraction and Amazon destruction in Bolivia expanded under Morales's administration, as the country became ever more dependent on a boom in primary commodities.[24]

Characterizing the Inflation Reduction Act

How, then, to characterize and assess the Inflation Reduction Act against the backdrop of this variegated Green New Deal output – visions, blueprints, polemics, political strategies – of which, in the US, the Act represents at least the temporary culmination? Despite the fanfare in the liberal press after its passage through the Senate in August – 'Did Democrats Just Save Civilization?', asked the *New York Times*'s Paul Krugman – across the spectrum of the climate left, from degrowthers and half earthers to left Keynesians and eco-Leninists, the IRA has broadly been recognized for what it is: a local, formal expression of a passive revolution underway in the Western capitalist core, whose elites aim to lay a more durable foundation – both ideological and

---

24   See Jonas Wolff, 'The Political Economy of Bolivia's Post-Neoliberalism: Policies, Elites and the mas Government', *European Review of Latin American and Caribbean Studies*, no. 108, 2019; Bret Gustafson, *Bolivia in the Age of Gas*, Durham, NC, 2020.

ecological – for the public subsidization of private capital's returns.[25] It is tempting to view the bill, though it received not a single Republican vote in either chamber of Congress, as a fragile truce – a Missouri Compromise for our time – between two fractions of US capital: fossil/brown and finance/green. (As Tim Sahay has pointed out, the IRA was a case of the Republican Party [unsuccessfully] lobbying fossil industry officials, not the other way around, to block legislation that could potentially hand the Democrats a win that could become a valuable, untouchable legacy, on the model of Social Security.)

Both brown and green capital have in large part supported the Biden's Administration's signature piece of legislation, and appear prepared to confine their feud to the softer terrain of a culture war. But the face-off is not entirely symbolic. The state treasuries of Texas, West Virginia, and other red states in the US have recently withdrawn billions of dollars from asset-manager firms that they regard as having too strongly signalled ESG agendas, despite these firms' heavy and enduring investment in fossil-fuel companies.[26] The distinction between 'green' and 'brown' capital cannot yet be neatly drawn, and in future is likely to be the retroactive product of political and bureaucratic bloc formation.[27] Firms increasingly compliant with green mandates may nevertheless continue to identify as 'brown' for cultural and political reasons. Likewise, carbon financiers have incentives to pass themselves off as 'green'.[28] In this sense, the IRA is a snapshot of an ongoing process of delineation – green from brown – in motion, with its extended prerogatives for fossil industries posed alongside its ground-work for a warmer investment environment for renewable energy.[29]

---

25   The question was the title of Krugman's NYT column of 8 August 2022.

26   Texas, for instance, barred the big municipal debt issuers (Citi, BofA, Goldman Sachs) due to ESG policies regarding firearms. The result is a projected minimum $300 million increase in the cost of municipal borrowing. Daniel Garrett and Ivan Ivanov, 'Gas, Guns, and Governments: Financial Costs of Anti-ESG Policies', 11 July 2022, available at SSRN.

27   The flagship newspaper of green capital is the *Financial Times*, while the *Wall Street Journal* consistently takes the side of fossil capital, declaring that any state that adopts a GND will implode like the Rajapaksa regime in Sri Lanka.

28   For an illuminating recent discussion of the identitarian dimension in brown–green capital disputes in West Virginia and beyond, see Adam Tooze's substack, 'Chartbook #46: West Virginia – the Historic Roadblock to US Climate Policy', *Chartbook*, 17 October 2021.

29   When appropriate periodization is determined, it should be possible to produce a capital-fraction analysis of the class composition of the Green New Deal in the Biden era, along the lines of Thomas Ferguson's pioneering studies of the original New Deal, 'From Normalcy to New Deal: Industrial Structure, Party Competition and American

While these interests found ample room to negotiate about a 'Green' agenda (read as decarbonization), much less leeway was afforded to the 'Deal' (read as union jobs with rising wages) component of progressive proposals. The IRA may be studded with 'buy American' commitments, but, outside of special provisions for nuclear power, the green boom it envisions will largely be supplied at the lower rungs by non- or under-unionized labour, a political approach that has been aptly described as 'industrial policy without industrial unions'.[30]

The IRA represents a one-step forward, one-step back approach to the climate crisis. It combines expansion of wind farms across politically amenable swaths of the US mainland with the escalation of oil extraction in the Gulf of Mexico and Arctic Alaska; and carbon off-set profiteering with companies reaping tax advantages from leaving unthreatened forests alone, poised to proceed alongside a boom of subsidized retrofitting and solar-panelling for home-owners. National rail networks seem set to stagnate – not a single provision of the IRA invests in public transportation (although the $1.2 trillion Bipartisan Infrastructure Deal, passed in November 2021, committed nearly $90 billion in funding for public transit over the next five years) – alongside the near-total conversion of the US car market to EVs. The binding of populations to environmentally destructive developments such as the Mountain Valley Pipeline across Virginia and West Virginia – one of several projects dear to the fossil industry, and greenlighted by the IRA – will entrench local connections to and identification with fossil fuel, with the result that some of the regions most conducive to alternative energy infrastructure may be the most likely to oppose it.

Among its other features, the IRA also represents the latest and most sophisticated in a series of fiscal stimuli shaped by the asset-holding class in the United States to mobilize the state on its behalf. It remains to be seen whether green investment can be groomed for the same role that military spending has had in heating and cooling the job market and the US economy more widely. During the financial crisis of 2008, when US unemployment reached 18 per cent, federal bailouts were largely restricted to the finance and auto industries,

---

Public Policy in the Great Depression', *International Organization*, vol. 38, no. 1, winter 1984, pp. 41–94; 'Industrial Structure and Party Competition in the New Deal: A Reply to Webber', *Sociological Perspectives,* vol. 34, no. 4, winter 1991, pp. 493–526.

30   Lee Harris, 'Industrial Policy Without Industrial Unions,' *The American Prospect*, 28 September 2022. Around 4 per cent of the solar industry is unionized, and about 6 per cent of the wind industry. Non-unionized labour has long been the norm in both industries, with even Democratic Party stalwarts like Van Jones sounding the alarm about 'solar plantations' back in 2008.

laying the tripwire for a popular backlash exploitable by any politician willing to question the basic tenets of neoliberal orthodoxy. Twelve years later, in response to the Covid-19 pandemic, the Trump Administration authorized more than $3 trillion in stimulus, and Biden added another $1.9 trillion with the American Rescue Plan. The peculiar nature of the pandemic – the sudden, acute lack of material supplies, but also the fact that, unlike during the financial crisis, the state payments would need to include all citizens because coronavirus supposedly did not distinguish between tax brackets – made talk of industrial policy and government-directed production more utterable in government offices than at any time in a generation.[31] Yet after the outlay of stopgap provisions, the asset-holding imperatives of impeding wage growth and loosening the labour market came back to the fore as soon as the virus, which now had to compete for headlines with the Ukraine war, appeared to have become a manageable disruption.

If the 2008 financial crisis showed that large-scale national stimuli were still possible, and the response to the Covid-19 pandemic renewed interest in industrial policy, the IRA has at least proven that either undertaking can include climate-related mandates and provisions. But even as American Democrats tout their 'breakthrough', and the Biden Administration congratulates itself for having deflected and absorbed the radicalism of a rising generation of activists, the amorphous campaign for a Green New Deal has sputtered towards something more closely resembling what the political economist Daniela Gabor has called the 'BlackRock Deal'. Until recently it had been imagined by proponents of a new industrial policy that any Green New Deal in the US would see the state directly investing tax monies into renewable technologies and infrastructure, and exercising a degree of control over their prices (with the finance industry playing an auxiliary role by establishing a market for green sovereign bonds). The IRA, by contrast, is mostly a programme, enacted through elaborate webs of tax credits, which concedes that the climate transition will be managed by the private sector rather than the state. Its greatest accomplishment has been to evacuate older Democratic Party preoccupations such as carbon pricing and emissions trading from the

---

31   At the height of the Covid-19 pandemic in 2020, many argued that a state-led investment programme to construct a post-carbon energy system to kickstart 'a green job-filled recovery' was the obvious solution to the economic crisis. See, for example: 'The pandemic is an opportunity to tackle the climate emergency by creating productive green jobs for those made redundant by the crisis', editorial, 'The *Guardian* View on a Green New Deal: Save Jobs and the Planet', *Guardian*, 9 June 2020.

political horizon. Already in the offing is a future in which the US state subordinates public finance to private finance for green projects at home and abroad by guaranteeing private revenue streams ('derisk-ing' investment) in any number of ways: preferential loans, completion grants, protections against political and market risk, high fixed prices, an equity stake for the state, etc. Alongside a few sops to domestic 'disadvantaged communities', the bulk of the IRA's popular pro-visions are directed at high-income Americans, with nary a word about the prospective increase in resource extraction from 'disadvan-taged communities' in the so-called Global South.[32]

Strategic upshots

The shortcomings of the GND genre, and its critics like Ajl on the margins, become plain when the offerings are taken together as a body of thought. On the one hand, the proposals of Pollin, and Pettifor, and the *Planet to Win* co-authors demonstrate the abstract feasibility of large-scale planning, but neglect the question of political agency. Implicitly, the premise of such work was the potential triumph at the polls of a left populism capable of realizing these writers' visions: a scenario that no longer seems as likely as it did a few short years ago. On the other hand, Huber and Ajl – who do focus on the question of political agency and clearly specify their preferred histor-ical actors for the role of prime mover – present implausible agents. For Huber, as we have seen, this is a double struggle: first Huberites must persuade eco-socialists to become power-industry workers, then these incomers must convert their fellow-workers into Huberites. For Ajl, the task is much larger: the peasant and labourer majorities who now vote for Modi in India, Jokowi in Indonesia or the Sharif dynasty in Pakistan, to name just the three largest Southern states, must be converted from their present allegiances to Ajlist parties; or, alter-natively, the Modis, Jokowis and Sharifs themselves must be won to revolutionary eco-socialism.

The proliferation of Green New Deal discourse has, however, done a great deal to clarify the demands and opportunities of the present historical moment. One of the signal paradoxes of the age is that while the climate crisis and its attendant zoological upheaval represent the gravest threat to capitalism since its infancy in the industrial revolu-tion, the promise of socialism has at the same time rarely been farther from realization. We do not have world enough and time to suppose

---

32 The IRA provisions are rife with cruel ironies, such as a rebate for electric vehicles which only kicks in for lower tax brackets that cannot easily afford them.

that capitalism will enter a severe enough crisis so early as for a flourishing socialism to be mounted on its ruins. The most pressing question
to ask of any green proposal is therefore not how likely is it to achieve
a socialist alternative, but rather how plausibly it contributes to
keeping portions of the planet sufficiently habitable for any ecologically viable socialism to have a chance of taking shape in the twenty-first
century.[33] With this overarching objective in mind, among the key
issues to reckon with are: what is the appropriate position of the
climate left vis-à-vis the rise of green capital? Is the mass labour
movement traditionally stipulated by the left for the achievement of its
ends really required for ecological stabilization? How can green colonialism and extraction – especially of crucial minerals – in the South
states be avoided or at least minimized? What is the role of the Chinese
behemoth in the climate fight? What opportunities are opened and
foreclosed by geopolitical and planetary crises – from wars in Europe
and Asia to new outbreaks of global pandemics?

The major strategic question runs along the axis of time: what
concessions to capital are worth making and where, on the other
hand, is implacable opposition in order? Even this question could
rapidly become obsolete. No one who has read Klein's indelible
description in *This Changes Everything* of greenwashing by the multinationals ('the disastrous merger of big business and Big Green') can
be under any illusions about green capital's record to date; it was this
that provided the grounds for eco-socialism's post-2008 resurgence,
after all. If technocratic elites and capitalist firms continue to fail to
mitigate the climate crisis in any meaningful way – as the planet
becomes hotter, more routinely catastrophic, and subject to more
globally comprehensive human displacement – the result is likely to
push citizens to more political extremes: towards the forces of
already-emerging eco-fascisms and nationalisms, guarding territory
against climate migrants, as well as perhaps towards more radical
eco-socialist regimes, guiding refugees from catastrophe to their new
temporary shelters. In such a scenario, the more utopian socialists
who were most mocked for having the least realizable immediate
plans may leapfrog in 'realism' those who entertained a tactical alliance with green capital in the decisive decade of the 2020s.

The likeness between the Green New Deal and Roosevelt's New

---

33   Pierre Charbonnier has argued that the political playing field shaped by decarbonization will be beneficial to the left – steadily allowing it to 'repoliticize needs' – but
that this zone of engagement may well be created without much direct socialist
confrontation: 'Ouvrir la brèche: politique du monde post-carbone', *Le Grand Conti-
nent*, 14 June 2021.

Deal has more often been taken for granted than interrogated – indeed the GND has in some respects functioned more as tactical propaganda than strategic programme.[34] For the ordinary Democratic politicians and voters who supply the GND's main constituency, the appeal of the magic formula is obvious: the nostalgic patriotism and mere welfarism conjured up by the words 'New Deal' indicated, accurately, that they harboured none of the socialist designs of which the GOP was bound to accuse them. For eco-socialists and other anti-capitalists, on the other hand, the Green New Deal has functioned as an attractive euphemism: unlike calls for a revolutionary overhaul of society that might well be required to avert climate disaster, the rhetoric of a GND could finesse conflicts between radicals and moderates.

After all, the historical New Deal could hardly be invoked strategically, since Roosevelt's policies had stabilized rather than sapped the depressed capitalist system of the 1930s. However much radical Green New Dealers may have taken inspiration from isolated Roosevelt Administration policies – whether the public takeover of failed banks, the agronomic and electrification initiatives of the Tennessee Valley Authority, or jobs-and-infrastructure programme of the Works Progress Administration – the more apposite analogy was always that of the US war economy of the 1940s, which finally brought about full employment and ended the Depression by way of the thoroughgoing mobilization of society in service of a single-minded and desperate purpose. Here the stabilization of the climate would correspond to the defeat of fascism.

But this analogy, too, would have been a stretch: even were the twenty-first-century US to build up a giant green renewables market, there is no destroyed Europe or undeveloped Asia to receive its exports. In an analogy to the war economy of the 1940s, a host of powerful companies headquartered in apparently 'Allied' nations – ExxonMobil, Shell, BP, Monsanto, Sinoma, Gazprom, Freeport McMoRan, Rio Tinto, Lafarge-Holcim – would stand in for so many divisions of the Wehrmacht. As for the force that principally defeated fascism, the role of the Soviet Union – if the analogy is to hold – would appear to have passed to the

---

34   Other historical analogies for ecological mobilization have been proposed. Ted Fertik, the leading strategist for the Working Families Party, has wondered whether the more immediate imaginary of the Civil Rights Movement would not be more appropriate, especially for a generation no longer in deep contact with the heroism of the New Deal. Quinn Slobodian points to the even more proximate example of the Alter-Globalization movement of the 1990s. Andreas Malm prefers the analogy of the Bolshevik war economy of the 1920s. The liberal television commentator Chris Hayes has popularized the analogy of nineteenth-century abolitionism, which was criticized and refined by Matt Karp, 'A Second Civil War', *Jacobin*, 1 May 2014.

Communist Party of China. In World War II, only the Soviet state was able to summon the will, mass production and manpower to defeat German fascism. China is likewise uniquely situated in the age of climate catastrophe: capable of giant economic stimuli and sophisticated manufacture at unmatchable scale, as well as of directing sharp waves of mass ideological indoctrination towards any number of ends.[35]

In the near future, the most plausible agency of an adequate decarbonization – sufficient to keep the planet cool enough for other purposes later on – is the coordination of three global forces: Wall Street, the European Union and Communist China, each with their immense financial, regulatory and productive capacities. In the short term the Russo-Ukraine war and heightened tensions over Taiwan may be a boon to fossil capital – with German Greens stooping to cut ribbons at coal plants, while China and India feast on Russian oil and gas – but the longer-term prospects may play towards the hand of green capital.[36] Beijing has long grown wary of its reliance on Western-delivered food and fossil fuel, and no US national security briefing is complete without a deferential passage about renewable energy; among the chief explicit aims of the 'historic investments in American clean-energy manufacturing' secured by the IRA was to 'lessen our reliance on China'.[37] The modern science of climate change, which originated with atmospheric tests for satellites and nuclear weapons, was itself was a product of Cold War geopolitics; it is reasonable to expect that renewed great power competition will have a green dimension. The rest of the world may then find itself in the tight spot of an Indian revolutionary in the 1940s, caught between the British Empire and Japanese fascism: choose your imperialism. Green capital or brown? Put this way, the choice is bleak but clear. Mere survival is not victory; yet the former is surely the condition of the latter.

---

35   Geoff Mann and Joel Wainwright refer to the Chinese leading the war on climate change as 'Climate Mao' – one of the four principal scenarios in their *Climate Leviathan: A Political Theory of Our Planetary Future*, London, 2018.

36   For a sure-footed tour of the geopolitical pressures on the energy transition in the wake of the Russian invasion of Ukraine, in particular how US economic coercion has jeopardized the supply chains for renewables, see Nicholas Mulder, 'Building Big Green States in a Tumultuous World', *Noema*, 1 September 2022.

37   See 'Summary of the Energy and Climate Change Investments in the Inflation Reduction Act of 2022', available online at democrats.senate.gov.; Robinson Meyer described the IRA as 'a law that passed in part because American legislators did not want to cede the clean-tech industry to China': 'The World Could Be Entering a New Era of Climate War', *Atlantic*, 23 November 2022. Also notable in this regard is that semi-conductor technology – whose export to China Biden restricted with the CHIPS and Science Act, passed in October 2022 – is used in electric cars (among other consumer electrical goods).

A GERMAN LEFT-GREEN PRECURSOR

In an earlier iteration, the idea of a Green New Deal (sometimes referred to as a 'Grüner New Deal' or 'Ökologischer New Deal') percolated in discussions among the German Greens in the mid-1980s, when the notion of 'Ökologischer Keynesianismus' or an 'alternative Keynesianism to Keynesianism' circulated among academics and economists associated with the new party.[38] The Linke Forum, led by Ludger Volmer, developed the idea of ecological socialism, with a focus on shorter working hours and on nationalizing and greening industry (in foreign policy it took a hard anti-NATO, but pro-Perestroika, position). The key thinker in this constellation was the political economist Elmar Altvater, co-founder of *PROKLA*, and coiner of the term 'Capitalocene'.

The vision of an ecological make-over of German industry within a socialist framework gained further momentum in the 'Crossover' initiative of the early 1990s, which sought to bring together the left wing of the Greens, the left wing of the SPD, and the PDS (the successor party to the SED). Each of these parties developed eco-socialist publications, with the Greens publishing *Andere Zeiten*, the PDS producing *Utopie kreativ*, and the SPD updating their older publication *SPW—Zeitschrift für sozialistische Politik und Wirtschaft*. This faction of the party held considerable sway in the early 1990s, with Volmer, a moderate member of the party's left flank, becoming Green Party Chairman, and successfully integrating the fledgling East German Green Party. Yet this left bloc within the Greens would be rebuffed by both the 'Realo' camp led by Joschka Fischer, which criticized it for its willingness to enter into coalitions with former East German communists and socialists, and by the 'Fundi' wing, which regarded the left faction as too focused on traditional economic growth (as well as too open to working with communists and socialists). The neoliberalizing 'Realo' Greens triumphed in the 1990s, absorbing the rhetoric of the Green New Deal, which soon faded out of German discussions. Ironically, when German neoliberals picked up the term again around 2009 they did so in mimicry of their American Third Way counterparts, for whom 'Green New Deal' was synonymous with green capitalism.

38　See, for instance, Projektgruppe Grüner Morgentau (Hg.), *Perspektiven ökologischer Wirtschaftspolitik: Ansätze zur Kultivierung von ökonomischem Neuland*, Frankfurt, 1986.

Afterword

LOLA SEATON

2022

In her reflections on COP26, the UN climate talks held in Glasgow in November 2021 ('Picking Winners'), Alyssa Battistoni reported a dispiriting sense of déjà vu. The summit recalled not only the circumstances of COP15, the 2009 Copenhagen conference – both followed global economic crises, were compromised by the US's failure to pass major domestic climate legislation and ended in some disappointment (coal, for example, would be 'phased out' rather than 'phased down'). The 2021 talks, Battistoni observed, even elicited the same gestures of critique. Greta Thunberg's 'blah, blah, blah' – rebuking governments' lack of action – recapitulated signs at COP15 ('Blah, Blah, Blah, Act Now!'), while a foreign minister's speech delivered knee-deep in ocean waves echoed a stunt in the build-up to the Denmark negotiations – an underwater cabinet meeting. Such presumably unwitting pastiche is a sure indication of stall.

Not that one was needed. Except for the blip in the depths of the Covid-19 lockdowns in 2020, the years since Copenhagen concluded, or rather virtually collapsed, have seen global carbon emissions continue their relentless rise (from 30.5 gigatonnes in 2009 to 36.3 gigatonnes in 2021, when emissions from coal also reached an all-time high of 15.3 gigatonnes).[1] Each of the essays in this book, originally published in NLR in the series 'Debating Green Strategies', can be dated by their empirical coordinates – the atmospheric concentration of carbon dioxide, for example, which hovered around 280 parts per million before the onset of industrialization, had reached 385 ppm when the late Mike Davis was writing in 2010, and had surged to 411 ppm by the time Troy Vettese was preparing his contribution in 2018; at the time of writing, in late 2022, it is 420 ppm. The striking,

---

1 These emissions figures are for energy combustion and industry: 'Global Energy Review: CO_2 Emissions in 2021', *International Energy Agency*, March 2022.

demoralizing fact is that even the earliest text in the series, Davis's landmark essay 'Who Will Build the Ark?', which precedes the others by nearly a decade, has not, for the most part, been gainsaid by events. The planet has now warmed by 1.1 to 1.3°C above pre-industrial levels, and the chance of limiting warming to 1.5°C and 'well below' 2°C – the contentious thresholds enshrined in the 2015 Paris accords – is now, most admit, extremely slim. 'Say goodbye to 1.5°C', ran a cover of the *Economist* in late 2022; according to the World Meteorological Organization, there is a 50:50 chance that the annual average global temperature will temporarily surpass 1.5°C in at least one of the next five years.[2] The political dilemma Davis so memorably diagnosed with 'analytic despair' appears, in its broad features, intact: 'coordinated global action' on behalf of 'the poor and the unborn' (the two groups most threatened by global warming) 'presupposes either their revolutionary empowerment' or 'the transmutation of the self-interest of rich countries and classes into an enlightened "solidarity" with little precedent in history'.

Delay, during which the ecological situation has continued to deteriorate, has only sharpened the political dilemma. The increased concentration of carbon dioxide in the atmosphere means that halting its further accumulation through a transition to clean energy must be accomplished at a speed that may prove traumatically disruptive – and more expensive than if it had been attempted earlier.[3] Decarbonization, argues Cédric Durand ('Zero-Sum Game'), writing in the throes of a global energy crisis, is unlikely to consist of an orderly supersession of fossil fuels by green alternatives. Deferred by several decades, the energy transition is now liable to be studded with crises, the brunt of the costs to be borne by consumers, even as the oil supermajors report record-busting profits thanks to elevated prices

---

2   'Say Goodbye to 1.5°C: Why Climate Policy Is Off Target', *Economist*, 5 November 2022; 'Three Degrees of Global Warming Is Quite Plausible and Truly Disastrous', *Economist*, 24 July 2021; 'WMO Update: 50:50 Chance of Global Temperature Temporarily Reaching 1.5°C Threshold in Next Five Years', WMO, 9 May 2022. According to the sixth IPCC report, released in April 2022, to have a half-chance of avoiding breaching the 2°C threshold, emissions of all greenhouse gases would have to peak by 2025 and fall to net zero by the early 2070s: 'A new IPCC report says the window to meet UN climate targets is vanishing', *Economist*, 4 April 2022.

3   Robert Pollin suggested in 2018 that global investment in clean energy would need to increase by between '1–1.5 per cent of global GDP – about $1 trillion at the current global GDP of $80 trillion, then rising in step with global growth thereafter.' The *Economist* now reckons that 'global investment in clean energy needs to triple from today's $1trn a year', to $3 trillion a year: 'The World Is Missing Its Lofty Climate Targets. Time for Some Realism', *Economist*, 3 November 2022.

and plough what they don't dole out to shareholders into expanding production.[4]

But though the overall picture of unabated carbon emissions remains bleakly consistent, elements within the frame have evolved. Writing in the recessionary wake of the 2008 crisis, Davis feared that the slumping eco-energy stocks and drying up of investment capital following the financial crash would leave 'some of the most celebrated clean-energy start-ups, like Tesla Motors' – now the most valuable car company in the world – 'in danger of sudden crib death'. The cost of renewables has continued to plummet, especially solar, and decarbonization of the world's energy supply has progressed: low-emissions technologies now account for nearly 40 per cent of worldwide electricity generation, the centrepiece of a low-carbon energy system. But coal still supplies roughly 36 per cent of global electricity demand; the market, in other words, as the *Financial Times*' Martin Wolf concedes, cannot deliver the transition fast enough 'to be transformative within the relevant timescale'.[5]

The broader political atmosphere has shifted in encouraging directions, too. Although the most recent UN climate summit, COP27, held in Egypt in November 2022, ended with a failure to commit to 'phase down' fossil fuels – the talks concluded with a promise to wind down 'inefficient fossil-fuel subsidies' – net-zero pledges have abounded, including from the US, EU (by 2050), China (by 2060) and India (by 2070). There has also been some legislative progress – most recently, the passage, in August 2022, of the Inflation Reduction Act (IRA) in the US. Hailed as 'the most ambitious climate package ever passed in the US', the IRA is worth about $390 billion in subsidies for the transition to renewables – a fraction, as Thomas Meaney points out in his analysis ('Fortunes of the Green New Deal'), of the $16.3 trillion Bernie Sanders had earmarked for his climate plan, but nonetheless delivering a momentous boost to the clean energy industries of the world's largest economy.[6]

---

4 Justin Jacobs, 'ExxonMobil and Chevron Shatter Profit Records after Global Oil Price Surge', *Financial Times*, 29 July 2022. Saudi Aramco, the world's largest oil exporter, had planned to raise capital expenditure to $40–50 billion in 2022, allowing it to increase output by one million barrels a day by 2027: 'Why Saudi Aramco Could Be Eclipsed by Its Qatari Nemesis', *Economist*, 26 March 2022.

5 International Energy Agency, *Electricity Sector*, September 2022; Martin Wolf, 'The Market Can Deliver the Green Transition – Just Not Fast Enough', *Financial Times*, 22 November 2022.

6 Bill McKibben, 'Congress Looks Set to Finally Pass Historic Climate Legislation', *New Yorker*, 8 August 2022. The total climate spending in the IRA is less than Sanders's plan had committed to electrify school and transit buses ($407 billion).

Building on the spells of civil disobedience and protest during the Obama presidency, most prominently against the construction of the Keystone XL and Dakota Access pipelines, the climate movement witnessed a spirited renaissance following the heatwaves of 2018, with school children across the world striking each week – a million and a half in March 2019, in what Andreas Malm speculates might have been 'the largest coordinated youth protest in history' – and Extinction Rebellion staging shutdowns in central London, subsequently emulated in cities around the globe. 'For the first time', Malm wrote in his short polemic *How to Blow Up a Pipeline* (2020), 'the climate movement had become the single most dynamic social movement in the global North.'[7] As Thomas Meaney observes, recent years have also seen a proliferation of rich ecopolitical theorizing and analysis, from visions of degrowth and 'half-earth' utopias to strategies for building a political coalition behind a Green New Deal (GND).

Yet despite the efflorescence of activism and theory, the global climate justice movement, as Alyssa Battistoni notes, 'simply does not have the power to realize its goals'. And the uptick in practical engagement, social concern and state intervention must also be seen as in part a reaction to the sheer frequency and severity of weather events that have made the danger humanity faces increasingly glaring: the extraordinary wildfire season in Australia in 2019–20 and California in 2020; deadly flooding in China and Germany in 2021; the lethally hot spring in India in 2022; a couple of months later, the blistering heatwaves and drought that withered Europe and swathes of China, the US and the Middle East; the monsoon flooding in Pakistan, submerging a third of the country and displacing 8 million – to name, of course, just a few among countless disasters.

Lines of convergence

The most energetically contested line of inquiry in the series concerned economic growth: its definition, relationship to capital accumulation, ecological consequences, compatibility with decarbonization, general desirability and systemic causes (an *idée fixe* among governing elites or a collateral effect of the compulsive pursuit of profit?). The issue acquired different emphases in the course of the series. Among the most salient could be distilled as the question of which macroeconomic environment – a growing, a steady-state, or a

---

7   Andreas Malm, *How to Blow Up a Pipeline: Learning to Fight in a World on Fire*, London, 2020, pp. 16, 18.

shrinking economy – would be most conducive to rapidly effecting the transition to alternative energy. Those in the degrowth camp made the intuitive case that the continuing expansion of economic activity, since this entails increased energy consumption – at present carbon-intensive – makes the *technical* task of retiring fossil fuels harder: 'maintaining aggregate expansion of the economy', Mark Burton and Peter Somerville suggest ('Degrowth: A Defence'), 'will add to the hill that has to be climbed'.

Advocates of green growth such as Robert Pollin ('Degrowth vs a Green New Deal') countered that curbing economic activity would not on its own lower emissions sufficiently. And since a rapid transition to clean energy would still be the principal route to decarboniz-ation, attempting to freeze or shrink the economy would be counter-productive, reducing the resources available for this colossal task.[8] Pollin added that imposing degrowth would render the transition 'utterly unrealistic' in *political* terms too. Mass joblessness and tumbling living standards – 'the immediate effect of any global GDP contraction' – would not be propitious circumstances in which to rally robust popular support for decarbonization.

Yet, as leading participants in the Green New Deal–degrowth dispute have themselves elsewhere observed, the fixation with growth has sometimes occluded substantive convergence between the two putatively incompatible positions. There appears a consensus, in par-ticular, on the core need to virtually shutter ('degrow') the fossil-fuel industry and simultaneously massively expand ('grow') clean-energy production and distribution. Arguing over whether growth is desir-able, both on its own terms, and as a congenial context in which to forge a post-carbon economy, may be beside the point, with a global recession looming if not already underway in some quarters, and tepid growth rates increasingly the norm. Is growth any longer a plausible long-term objective for societies battered by climate-related shocks, and forced to decarbonize their energy supply at speed? While Robert Pollin argues that large-scale public investment in green energy will stimulate the economy – creating jobs and supporting living

---

8   Alessio Terzi, an enthusiastically pro-market economist at the European Commission, argues that a government's ability to finance investment programmes of the kind necessary to accelerate the energy transition, including funding the social provisions to support and retrain workers in moribund industries, would be radically diminished in a steady-state or contracting economy, both by the shrunken tax base and the government's reduced capacity to borrow: Alessio Terzi, *Growth for Good: Reshaping Capitalism to Save Humanity from Climate Catastrophe*, Cambridge, MA, 2022.

standards – Cédric Durand foresees 'an energy mismatch that could derail the transition altogether', as fossil fuel dwindles faster than other energy sources can be scaled up to meet demand. In this sense, Durand does not so much advocate degrowth as consider some version of it probable, expecting 'wild recessionary forces' and distributional conflicts to be unleashed by the now-unavoidable abruptness of the energy transition.

For Durand, the 'burning question' is: 'Are there sufficient resources in the economy to allow for more investment alongside weakened supply? The answer depends on the amount of slack in the economy – that is, idle productive capacity and unemployment. But considering the size of the adjustment and the compressed timeframe, this cannot be taken for granted.' Neo-Keynesian advocates of Green New Deals are inclined, by contrast, to be more optimistic about the degree of 'slack' in the economy. The US economist J. W. Mason has argued that 'in tackling climate change, we should not start from the idea of an economy that is operating at full capacity': 'Contrary to orthodox theory, the US economy is not operating at its maximum productive potential; there is a great deal of unused capacity that a major public investment programme could mobilize.' In an economy where output is constrained by demand – 'the willingness of people to spend money' – rather than by technology, 'structural' constraints or finite resources having to be allocated among competing ends, the 'fundamental economic problem', according to Mason, 'is not scarcity but coordination'. Rather than the 'zero-sum or even negative-sum' scenario envisaged by Durand, in which 'parts of the population will bear the cost' of the rocky transition to clean energy 'more than others', Mason maintains that 'action to deal with climate change doesn't require sacrifice' – an important theme running through the series. The transition to clean energy not only does not subtract from 'the resources available to meet other needs', but 'can come from an expansion of society's productive capabilities, thanks to the demand created by clean-energy investment itself'. 'We do not need to choose between a robust response to climate change and meeting people's material needs today.'[9]

Although left commentators differ in their optimism about the amount of spare capacity in the economy, and so about whether dealing with climate change could enhance living standards or is likely

---

9 J. W. Mason, 'Decarbonization: A Keynesian View', The Slack Wire blog, 7 July 2018; J. W. Mason, Mark Paul and Anders Fremstad, *Decarbonizing the US Economy: Pathways Toward a Green New Deal*, Roosevelt Institute, June 2019.

to erode them, it is worth noting an implicit point of overlap about the need, from an ecological perspective, for some kind of economy-wide planning or coordination: to dislodge the profit imperative as the linchpin of the economy, and instead to organize productive activity around meeting 'human needs', within the limits of the biosphere.

The question is whether capitalism is capable of any such thing. Durand appears to accept at least the possibility of an ecologically rational capitalism, deploying the political scientist Chalmers Johnsons's contrast between a 'regulatory, or market rational, state' which concerns itself with the rules of economic competition, and a 'developmental state, or plan-rational state' which sets 'substantive social and economic goals':

> Given the existential threat posed by climate change . . . our concern should be with the effectiveness of reducing greenhouse gases rather than the efficiency of the effort. Instead of using the price mechanism to let the market decide where the effort should lie, it is infinitely more straightforward to add up targets at the sectoral and geographical levels and provide a consistent reduction plan to ensure that the overall goal will be achieved in time.

In his contribution ('Naive Questions on Degrowth'), Kenta Tsuda argues that normative assessment of growth in abstraction is 'meaningless' in any case; growth can only be evaluated 'as applied', in specific, historical circumstances, its alleged redistributive effects dependent on the prevailing distribution of power. It is perhaps, then, worth bracketing the contested abstract question about whether there is a trade-off between the requirements of growth and those of stabilizing the climate in order to attend to the concrete question of how to sustain living standards while curtailing fossil-fuel use. If the first question is to some degree empirical – dependent on the amount of 'slack' in the economy – the second question is thoroughly political, and will be determined chiefly by the balance of power.

The problem of power

The theoretical emphasis on growth as an all-important fault line not only meant the differences between the GND and degrowth approaches could be overstated (though noting commonalities, Pollin called them 'dramatically divergent'). The centrality of growth to the debate in NLR also contributed to its insistently speculative character and macro-focus. 'Strategy', an equivocal concept in this context, was typically interpreted by the contributors in a technical or technocratic sense (examining the relative merits of low-carbon solutions or weighing policies for driving down emissions), rather than as an invitation to elaborate properly political agendas for building mass support for such policies, and for consolidating a countervailing social force with the political power to overcome the interests intent on obstructing them. That the contributors for the most part didn't directly engage with such political problems – of power, agency, ideology, hegemony – is in part a reflection of the provenance and original audience of their approaches: degrowth began as, and to some degree remains, an academic movement, while the Green New Deal, despite having become the rallying cry of social mobilizations, is also a capacious rubric, not only embraced by left ecologists but affixed to technocratic proposals enumerating a series of green policies and spending commitments which, however impressive, mostly do not add up to a truly comprehensive picture of an alternative future.

But the programmatic (or ends-focused) rather than strategic (or means-focused) character of the series can also be interpreted as a reflection of persistently unpromising practical circumstances, and in particular of the real-world intractability of the problem of state power. The NLR contributors occasionally allude to this issue – the 'powerful vested interests' in the fossil-fuel industry, Pollin remarks in passing, 'will have to be defeated' – or to its omission: Nancy Fraser ('Climates of Capital') observes that 'orientations associated with degrowth' such as 'prefigurative experiments in commoning . . . tend to avoid the necessity of confronting capitalist power'. But power does not become a sustained or explicit focus of the series, and virtually all of the texts omit to outline in any detail a historical dynamic or mechanism of transformation that would catalyze the recalibration of the balance of forces that their climate-stabilizing proposals imply – a shortcoming of eco-politics highlighted as early as the second piece in the series, Benjamin Kunkel's interview with the late Herman Daly.

In this sense, the prospectuses could be characterized less as furnishing strategies than adumbrating the ends or apogees of strategy – partial or incipient visions. The realization of these visions, especially those of a strongly redistributive cast – featuring, for example, Herman Daly's maximum income – would itself depend upon immense prior political successes. Visions can of course themselves be not only clarifying but motivating, even transformative – and so a crucial part of strategy: revolutionizing popular expectations, informing the articulation of intermediary reforms, and altering the terrain on which political advance can be imagined, demanded and achieved. As Erik Olin Wright wrote in *Envisioning Real Utopias*: 'What is pragmatically possible is not fixed independently of our imaginations, but is itself shaped by our visions . . . A vital belief in a utopian ideal may be necessary to motivate people to set off on the journey from the status quo in the first place, even though the likely actual destination may fall short of the utopian ideal.'[10] But visions of this kind are not their own self-causing means of transformation.

Notable too in this regard are the gestural conclusions of some of the texts – Burton and Somerville end with the admission that 'How degrowth might happen we don't know', except for some 'fortuitous combination of popular struggle and collapse of the capitalist system'; Durand finishes by conceding that 'the poor state of socialist politics doesn't conjure much optimism', though hopes 'the catastrophic conjuncture we are entering' could 'increase the fluidity of the situation'. Olin Wright's warning in the conclusion to *Envisioning Real Utopias* is salient here: 'Suffering and irrationality are never enough to generate fundamental social transformations . . . so long as a viable alternative to capitalism is not actively on the historical agenda – and with broad support linked to a political movement able to translate that support into political power – capitalism will remain the dominant structure of economic organization.'[11]

Agents of change

This lack of attention to strategy in a strong political sense must arise in part from the deficit of obvious candidates with the social power to, for example, suppress the fossil-fuel industry – the shortage of what Richard Seymour terms 'politically efficacious' means of aggregating individuals in an era of weakened labour.[12] Thomas Meaney predicts that in the immediate term the 'three global forces' likely to determine the course of the climate transition are 'Wall Street, the European Union and Communist China', but the constituencies more often invoked in left eco-political discussion are the working class and

---

10   Erik Olin Wright, *Envisioning Real Utopias*, London and New York 2010, p. 6.
11   Ibid., p. 366.
12   Richard Seymour, *The Disenchanted Earth: Reflections on Ecosocialism and Barbarism*, London, 2022. Most contributors do not only omit to identify an agent of change capable of effecting the transformations they envisage, but are reticent about specifying an institutional administrator of them too – though the state, perhaps dragooned or reinforced by an improbably empowered global authority, remains the de facto agent, and the national economy, the de facto field of action.

the climate movement. In his book *Climate Change as Class War* (2022), Matthew Huber argues that an ecologically conscious coalition of workers would be the most effective promoter of a Green New Deal: it is workers' strategic leverage – their ability to disrupt profit-making, especially in critical industries (Huber identifies the US's heavily unionized and ecologically salient utilities sector as a good starting-point) – that would give the movement real power.[13] Cédric Durand, too, concludes his analysis of the 'energy dilemma' with a call for an explicitly antagonistic 'class-based punitive ecology' against 'ecologically perverse expenditure', although the class antagonism he has in mind, perhaps more feasible in the near term, seems closer to Occupy's 1 per cent and 99 per cent than capital and labour – a revolt against the space excursions of Bezos and co: 'I do not see what should prevent a large progressive front from rallying in favour of restrictions on the avoidable emissions related to the consumption patterns of the ultra-rich.'

In *The Future Is Degrowth* (2022), by contrast, co-authors Aaron Vansintjan, Andrea Vetter and Matthias Schmelzer are committed to a pluralism of local initiatives and small-scale experiments, and to a heterogenous coalition that spans regions – the kind of 'movement of movements' that Naomi Klein hoped for in *This Changes Everything* (2014) – rather than the class-based, state-administered, US-led green industrial revolution envisaged by Huber.[14] Huber convincingly argues that truly fervent popular support for a Green New Deal can only be built if climate initiatives are successfully linked to material improvements in everyday lives, arguing that vital sectors like food, transport, electricity and housing must be not only decarbonized but decommodified and their products supplied to the public by right. Not dissimilarly, Nancy Fraser insists that the fight against climate change must be embedded in a wider social revolt engaged on multiple fronts. Noting that capitalism is 'deeply implicated in seemingly non-ecological forms of social injustice – from class exploitation to racial-imperial oppression and gender and sexual domination' and 'figures centrally, too, in seemingly non-ecological societal impasses – in crises of care and social reproduction; of finance, supply chains, wages and work; of governance and de-democratization', Fraser argues that 'eco-politics today must transcend the "merely environmental" by

---

13   Matthew Huber, *Climate Change as Class War: Building Socialism on a Warming Planet*, London and New York, 2022.

14   Aaron Vansintjan, Andrea Vetter and Matthias Schmelzer, *The Future Is Degrowth: A Guide to a World Beyond Capitalism*, London and New York 2022.

becoming anti-systemic across the board . . . green movements should turn *trans-environmental*, positioning themselves as participants in an emerging counter-hegemonic bloc, centred on anti-capitalism.'

Beyond a transition

A recent discussion titled 'Debating Eco-Socialist Futures', chaired by Thea Riofrancos, suggestively evoked the differences in political sensibility between the eco-modernist GNDers and the degrowthers. Matthew Huber emphasized that the climate crisis is 'mostly about building. We have to just *build* an entirely new energy infrastructure', so 'channelling this kind of working-class movement to build and produce and create a new world has to be at the core of what we [eco-socialists] do'. 'I disagree', Andrea Vetter (co-author of *The Future Is Degrowth*) responded. 'I think it is really time to let go [of] the fantasies of making big plans, of building everything anew and shiny. It's more a time to think about, What does it mean to live in the ruins of capitalism, to achieve a truly just society?'

Christian Parenti warned a decade ago that 'a more radical approach to the crisis of climate change begins not with a long-term vision of an alternate society but with an honest engagement with the very compressed timeframe that current climate science implies'.[15] Yet Vetter's comment about 'letting go of fantasies' of total regeneration is a useful reminder that however urgent the crisis and compressed the timeframe for mitigating it, ruthless pragmatism must be informed by the recognition that at stake is not a leap away from our current, existentially threatened world into a wholly new world in which catastrophe has been permanently averted – a fact that official climate rhetoric (the 'energy transition', the deadlines, tipping points, emission reduction targets and temperature thresholds) can sometimes obscure. Rather, while it's true that organizational energies and resources are finite and a coordinated climate movement will be stronger than one riven over priorities and tactics, the question of our response to climate change is not binary and discrete – will we act or won't we, will we focus on a modestly 'realistic' Green New Deal or, as Robert Pollin put it, 'waste time on huge global efforts fighting for unattainable goals' like worldwide climate justice. In the absence of a ruptural upending of the social order, the challenge is rather continually to struggle to determine the manner of our ongoing

---

15   Christian Parenti, 'A Radical Approach to the Climate Crisis', *Dissent*, Summer 2013.

response: slow or decisive, equitable or less equitable, humane or less humane, serving capital or the needs of ordinary people. No one can doubt that driving down emissions as fast as possible is the overriding priority, insofar as this is the minimal prerequisite for the flourishing of any kind of society. But vivid, comprehensive visions of a safer, fairer, freer future must still animate and shape our strategies for forging a world that is different from the one we know in more ways than for having foresworn carbon.

About the Contributors

Alyssa Battistoni teaches political theory at Barnard College, New York. She is the co-author of *A Planet to Win: Why We Need a Green New Deal* (Verso 2019) and is currently writing a book titled *Free Gifts: Capitalism and the Politics of Nature.*

Mark Burton is a scholar-activist at Steady State Manchester and lead author of *A Viable Future* (2021).

Herman Daly (1938–2022) was professor emeritus at the School of Public Policy, University of Maryland, and author of *Steady-State Economics* and *Beyond Growth: The Economics of Sustainable Development* (1977).

Mike Davis (1946–2022) was the author of, among other works, *Prisoners of the American Dream* (1986), *City of Quartz* (1990), *Late Victorian Holocausts* (2000) and *Planet of Slums* (2006), and recently co-author of *Set the Night on Fire* (2020).

Cédric Durand is associate professor of economics at the University of Geneva and author of *Techno-féodalisme* (2020) and *Fictitious Capital* (2017).

Nancy Fraser is Henry and Louise A. Loeb Professor of Philosophy and Politics at the New School for Social Research and author of *Cannibal Capitalism* (2022) and *Fortunes of Feminism* (2013).

Sharachchandra Lele is senior fellow and convenor at ATREE, Bangalore, and co-editor of *Rethinking Environmentalism* (2018) and *Democratizing Forest Governance in India* (2014).

Zion Lights is the author of *The Ultimate Guide to Green Parenting* (2015) and was in the media circle of Extinction Rebellion, 2018–20.

Thomas Meaney is a fellow at the Max Planck Society in Göttingen.

Mary Mellor is the author of *The Future of Money* (2010) and *Debt or Democracy* (2015) and was founding chair of Northumbria University's Sustainable Cities Research Institute.

Robert Pollin is a director of the Political Economy Research Institute, University of Massachusetts Amherst and co-author of *Climate Crisis and the Global Green New Deal* (2020).

Peter Somerville is emeritus professor of social policy at the University of Lincoln, England.

Kenta Tsuda is researching the development of federal environmental law in the United States at University College London.

Troy Vettese is a post-doctoral fellow at the European University Institute and co-author of *Half-Earth Socialism* (2022).

Index